MW01106939

REASON, IDEOLOGY and POLITICS

To Ioanna

Shawn W. Rosenberg

REASON, IDEOLOGY
and
POLITICS

Princeton University Press
Princeton, New Jersey

Copyright © 1988 Shawn W. Rosenberg

First published 1988 by Princeton University Press,
41 William Street, Princeton, New Jersey 08540

All rights reserved

Library of Congress Cataloging in Publication Data
Rosenberg, Shawn W.
  Reason, ideology and politics.

  Bibliography: p.
  Includes index.
  1. Ideology.   2. Piaget, Jean, 1896–
3. Social psychology.   I. Title.
HM33.R67   1988   306´.2   88-5985
ISBN 0-691-07785-1

Printed in Great Britain

Contents

Acknowledgements

I would like to thank Ioanna Dimitracopoulou and Jonathan Mendilow. They critically reviewed each step of the argument: Ioanna from her perspective as a developmental psychologist and Jonathan from his perspective as a political theorist. The book is clearly better for their efforts.

I would also like to thank Lawrence Kohlberg, Robert Lane and David Easton. They gave me support at times when I needed it most. I owe them a special debt.

1

Introduction and Overview

The study of political behavior blossomed in the 1950s and 1960s. During those twenty years, a broad consensus over concepts and methods was achieved throughout most of the research community. A paradigm had been established and normal science proceeded apace. Important discoveries regarding people's political thought and behavior, discoveries of interest to the entire political science community, were made. Energy was abundant, optimism pervasive and the mainstream flowed. In the 1970s, the situation began to change. Despite a massive research effort, progress in the field slowed. There was a virtual absence of significant new results and doubt was cast on established findings. Although this did not lead to any serious questioning of the basic orientation and concepts guiding the research, it did yield almost a decade of argument over method and statistical technique. Despite the ensuing methodological refinements, little substantive progress was made. The research seemed to circle in on itself; the mainstream stagnated.

The 1980s has been a period of confusion. A continued lack of progress has led to a questioning of basic concepts and accepted methods, but little new direction has been offered. The situation was well illustrated at the 1982 American Political Science Association Meeting where a featured panel on the 'state of the art' of the public opinion research was convened. Among other things, the panelists concluded that ideology was not a useful concept and the survey questionnaire was not an appropriate method of collecting data on people's political thought. Despite this dismissal of basic elements of current research, little in the way of an alternative was presented. A few new concepts such as 'schema' and 'contextual cueing' were introduced, but these generally offered little more than slight variations on the framework they were intended to replace. No new methods were suggested. Since that time, no further progress has been made.

In my view, the current state of affairs suggests the need for a basic theoretical reorientation, not simply a refinement of techniques or the addition of isolated concepts. What is intractable or anomalous when viewed from one theoretical perspective, may be readily understood from another. In order to advance, research on public opinion and political behavior must adopt a new perspective – one which can both address present difficulties and provide a new basis for future conceptualization and empirical research.

It is in this context that I offer an alternative approach to the study of public opinion and political behavior. This approach draws on the developmental psychology of Jean Piaget. Piaget provides a very different perspective from which to study political behavior – one which offers both interesting insight into the problems encountered in current research and fruitful direction for future investigation. In applying Piaget to the study of politics, I modify aspects of his theoretical approach. Most important, greater emphasis is placed on the interplay between social environments and subjectivity in the development of cognition. This leads to the claim that how people reason is influenced by the structure of the sociopolitical environment to which they are exposed. Oriented by these considerations, the work presented here follows a somewhat different direction from that of classical Piagetian research. Unlike in most Piagetian studies, questions are raised regarding the interdependence of subjective and intersubjective constructions of meaning, the study of political reasoning is considered central to the study of cognition, and empirical research is conducted on adult political thought.

In the present book, this neo-Piagetian approach is applied to the study of how individual political actors understand and judge the political events which envelop them. A theory of political reasoning is developed and supporting empirical research is presented. Despite this focus, the inquiry is not limited to the study of individuals. The reconceptualization of individuals' political thinking naturally leads to a reconsideration of the nature of the polity in which they participate. In this vein, such notions as 'institution', 'culture' and 'legitimacy' are reconsidered. Overall, the aim is not to present a work of applied psychology, but to provide an analysis which explicitly recognizes what I regard to be fundamentally true – that, at all points, political and psychological studies are inextricably intertwined.

To orient the reader, this first chapter is devoted to a general overview of the arguments developed in the book. Initially, the difficulties encountered in the research on political behavior are discussed. Piaget's psychology is then introduced as a solution to these difficulties. In explicating Piaget's position, the emphasis is placed on the basic assumptions which orient his theoretical and empirical efforts. To conclude, the implications of adopting a Piagetian approach to the study of politics are discussed. Throughout, my aim is to provide a brief introductory statement of the issues raised in the book. The requisite elaborations, justifications and supports are provided in the chapters which follow.

THE STATE OF THE RESEARCH ON POLITICAL BEHAVIOR

The research on political socialization and ideology is central to the study of political behavior. These two areas of inquiry combine to provide the basic ideas on how people learn about, and finally understand, politics. While important, other research, such as that on voting behavior or political participation, is derivative. It draws on the results developed in the more fundamental work on thinking and learning. Of current concern, both the research on ideology and that on socialization have stalled. As suggested earlier, the research on political ideology has devolved into a series of technical debates leading some researchers to suggest that it be abandoned altogether. The political socialization research is equally troubled. Once an effort which yielded dozens of articles annually, now only a few articles appear in the major journals each year. The question is: What is the nature of the problem here and how is it to be resolved?

The research on political ideology focuses first on description. For the most part, it has been guided by the concepts and methods developed in the work of Philip Converse (Campbell et al., 1960; Converse, 1964, 1975). Following Converse, the majority of researchers define ideology as a belief system, that is, as a set of related attitudes. Individual attitudes are regarded as the basic units of conceptual and empirical analysis. The relations between attitudes are assumed to be culturally defined. Depending on the quality of their exposure, people learn these more or less well. Given these assumptions, ideology is studied through the use of closed-ended surveys and the data collected are analyzed in the aggregate. In the end, ideology is described in terms of the belief system of the prototypical person of the population studied.

A mass of empirical research followed which adopted this belief systems approach. Three basic results emerged, results which largely confirmed the conclusions Converse drew from his own early research. First, the political beliefs expressed by the average American are not strongly related to one another. Rather than possessing a bona fide belief system, most Americans seem to have a collage of largely unconnected political beliefs. Second, the specific beliefs people express do not appear to be very stable over time. For example, being strongly in favor of a strong defense in one election only weakly suggests that one will be so inclined two years later. Third, there are clear differences between individuals. Some think in abstract terms about issues, while most do not think about issues at all. The important and controversial conclusion drawn from this research was that the vast majority of Americans do not exhibit the political sophistication required of them by a liberal democracy.

Despite their immediate political interest, these findings ultimately raise questions regarding the adequacy of the model guiding the research upon which they are based. Consider first what thirty years' research tells us about how people think about politics. In fact, it tells us very little. The belief systems research reveals what people don't do – they do not think in an ideological, systematic or constrained manner. It does not, however, indicate what they *are* doing. This is lost in the obscurity of low interattitude correlations and oblique designations such as 'nature of the times' or 'no issue content'. The problem here is central. More important, it cannot be resolved within the belief systems perspective. The results of the research suggest that different individuals may think about politics differently – they may differ in the very rationality or logic of their reasoning. However, the research itself is predicated on the assumption of a single standard of rationality (or, at least, of culturally defined meaning). Therefore, it can do no more with evidence of variety than intepret it in negative terms or regard it as instances of degeneration of the single assumed logic. After first illuminating the apparent irrationality and/or incoherence of individuals' political beliefs, the belief systems approach is unable to lead us any further.

Basic questions are also raised when we consider the more specific result, that the attitudes people express are unreliable. This long-standing finding on the ephemeral quality of people's attitudes is supplemented by relatively recent research which indicates that merely changing the order of the questions on an opinion survey may significantly affect the attitudes expressed (e.g., Bishop and Oldendick, 1978). The question then is, if an individual's attitudes are so unreliable, in what sense do they provide a useful way of describing how that individual thinks about politics? Again, the evidence encountered contradicts a basic assumption guiding the research, that an 'attitude' is a basic element of people's thought. Overall, it appears that a political attitude is more an artifact of a researcher's instrument than it is a reflection of what is going on in a citizen's mind.

The political socialization research is based on the same basic assumptions as the research on ideology. Thus, it defines political thought in terms of attitudes and relies on closed-ended surveys and aggregating techniques for data analysis. It differs only in its primary focus. Whereas the work on ideology focuses on description, the research on socialization is more centrally concerned with explanation. Like the research on ideology, it is oriented here by the essentially sociological assumption that individuals' political beliefs are a product of the environment to which they are exposed.

The political socialization research flourished in the sixties and early seventies. Literally hundreds of studies were done to examine the influence exerted by various social entities that mediated the child's contact with the political environment, the so-called agents of socialization. Correlational analyses were done of the relations between the child's political attitudes on the one hand and those expressed by the child's parents (e.g., Jennings and Niemi, 1968; Langton and Karns, 1969), peers (e.g., Langton, 1967; Sebert et al., 1974; Campbell, 1980; Tedin, 1980) or prevalent in his school environment (e.g., Langton and Karns, 1969; Dowse and Hughes, 1971).

Although it yielded a number of interesting findings, this research also produced results which contradicted the conceptual model upon which it was based. Most important, its key premise, that an individual's political thinking is best explained as the simple result of his exposure to social or cultural influences, is called into question. This is the case whether the premise is cast in particular or in general terms. The evidence suggests that particular social influences do not shape thought. In the research on children, little of the variance (usually around 10 to 15 per cent) in their attitudes could be accounted for in terms of the attitudes of agents of socialization to which they were exposed. Similarly, the evidence suggests that the culture at large does not shape people's thought. Like the research on ideology, the political socialization research found that people's attitudes toward politically significant issues are unreliable (e.g., Vaillancourt, 1973). Although the culture may define beliefs in a clear and stable fashion, individuals do not.[1]

In sum, the evidence encountered in the research on political ideology and socialization points to basic problems with the model of thinking and learning on which they are based. These problems are not, in the first instance, methodological. They will not be resolved by more carefully worded survey techniques or more sophisticated data analyses. The problems are theoretical and suggest the need to develop a new approach to the analysis of political thinking. None the less, we can learn from the results of the belief systems research. They highlight conceptual dead ends and suggest directions which a new approach should take. First, any new definition of political thinking must reflect an awareness of the inadequacy of the concepts of political attitude or belief and belief system. An attempt must be made to forge a notion of political thinking which adopts a new conception of the quality and organization of thought. Second, such a definition must also account for very fundamental differences in the ways in which individuals conceive of and respond to political phenomena. To do so, it must be based on a recognition that political logic or rationality may take various forms. Finally, any explanation of political thinking cannot rely on an assumption of the simple or direct influence of the environment on the individual. Some attempt must be made to recognize the individual as the author of his own political understandings.

CURRENT PROBLEMS AND PIAGETIAN SOLUTIONS

Piaget offers an alternative framework – one which can directly address those problems which have impeded the progress of the research on ideology and socialization. Indeed, his theoretical perspective presumes the anomalies and difficulties encountered in the mainstream political behavior research. Consider first the problem of the descriptive inadequacy of the concepts of attitude and attitude system. The problem here is that attitudes seem to bear no strong relationship to each other at any moment or to themselves over time. According to Piagetian theory, this is to be expected. Attitudes are derivative and epiphenomenal, the product of people's judgments and reasoning. The meaning and use of attitudes can only be understood in the context of the reasoning that produces them. Considered out of this subjective context, attitudes are fragments which are not interpretable unto themselves and consequently cannot be considered units for theoretical or empirical analysis. To regard them as such can only yield the lack of reliability or consistent relation generally found in the public opinion literature. Consequently, Piagetian theory abandons such notions such as attitude or attitude system in favor of concepts that pertain to judgment and the structure of reasoning.

The difficulties inherent in any attempt to study attitudes without reference to the terms of their subjective definition are readily illustrated. Take for example three people who express the attitude that the federal government should not provide welfare to the unemployed. The first may hold this belief because he thinks that President Reagan cannot possibly have enough money or time to go around and take care of all the poor people in the country. The second may be against welfare because it is undermining to give money to people who don't earn it. They lose their initiative to work and people only feel good about themselves when they work. The third may be against welfare because he believes in limited government. In this vein, he may regard the provision of welfare as an intrusion of government into a domain which is properly the prerogative of either the individual or the community.

Underlying each of these three welfare attitudes is a very different understanding of the nature of government and politics. In other words, each of these three people's attitude toward welfare has a different subjective meaning. Therefore, to be properly understood, each attitude must be interpreted in light of its subjective definition. Only then will it be possible to comprehend how it is related to other attitudes, how it may affect behavior, and the conditions under which it would change. The first two people used in our example clearly understand politics differently from the typical political scientist. Consequently, the failure to interpret their attitudes in light of their subjective understanding of politics will necessarily produce the apparent irregularities and incoherence so often found in the current political behavior research.

Considered in this context, Piaget's psychology is valuable because it is founded on the premise that attitudes are not comprehensible unto themselves and, therefore, are not proper units of analysis. Piaget redirects our focus from specific political beliefs to the reasoning and understanding which underlie them. In so doing, he provides a theoretical vocabulary for conceptualizing that reasoning, and empirical methods for exploring its nature. [2]

The preceding example also applies to our consideration of the second problem confronting current research, the difficulty of adequately characterizing the ways in which people think about politics which do not conform to conventional logic or rationality. Piaget's work is again immediately relevant. In fact, it was initially motivated by a parallel problem – that of making sense of the mistakes students made in their response to Binet's intelligence test. Dissatisfied with simply describing these students' responses as deviations from the standards of logic, he became interested in the way in which the students reasoned so that they would err as they did. Piaget's entire corpus of work followed from this. Throughout, he accepts the evidence that people solve problems, reason or understand stimuli in a variety of ways. In his research, he creates methods for exploring these differences and concepts for describing them.

The third basic problem impeding current research efforts is the over-reliance on an essentially sociological or cultural conception of the origin and definition of political attitudes. The search for cultural explanations of the content and organization of political thinking has not been successful. Offering a more psychological view of thinking, Piaget offers an alternative direction. He views the individual as a subject – not only in the sense of a purposeful actor seeking to achieve personal ends, but as a subject who defines the quality of the objects of his thought and the general framework in which those objects may be interrelated. In taking this view, Piaget does not suggest that environments or experience do not play an important role either in the general development of an individual's subjective capacities or in the specific content of his beliefs. However, he does suggest that these external effects are mediated by an individual's subjective constructions. In the first instance, the meaning of a person's beliefs and behaviors must be understood in light of the subjective rather than the objective conditions of his or her thought.

In sum, Piaget's theory of reasoning is initially attractive because it offers a conceptual orientation which is capable of directly addressing and resolving precisely those problems which have proven so intractable in the face of current theoretical and empirical research efforts.

EPISTEMOLOGY, PSYCHOLOGY AND COGNITION: THE PIAGETIAN PERSPECTIVE

Piaget is concerned with the nature of reasoning and understanding. In the language of the discipline, he offers a psychological theory of cognition. His psychology is based on a number of interrelated assumptions regarding the nature of thought and theory. The concepts he defines and the methods he employs can only be properly understood with reference to these underlying assumptions. In this regard, his psychology reflects his epistemology. Indeed, a central lesson to be learned from a reading of Piaget is that psychology and epistemology are inextricably interrelated disciplines.

One basic assumption that orients Piaget's psychological investigations is that thought is best conceived as an activity, as an operation on the world. Two points should be noted here. First, thought is not defined in static terms, that is, in terms of its constituent ideas or representations, but in dynamic terms, as the activity of thinking or reasoning. Viewed from this perspective, mental representations and ideas are phenomena of interest, but are of secondary concern. They are understood as derivative, the products of thinking. Second, thought is regarded as continuous with action in the real world. In basic respects, thought and action are two manifestations of the same phenomenon, the individual's purposive attempt to operate on and in the world. In this regard, Piaget's work may be considered, in part, as a continuation of a tradition of focus on praxis which extends from Marx through American pragmatism.

Adopting this view of thought and action, Piaget conceives of the problem of elucidating the nature of knowledge quite differently from most traditional epistemological perspectives. Often, epistemological analysis is predicated on the assumption that mental representations are the basic constituents of thought. These subjective representations are clearly distinguished from objective reality. In this framework, a key analytical problem then is to understand the connection between subjective representations and real objects. In other words, the problem is one of understanding the nature of knowledge and how it is acquired.

A number of strategies have been adopted in the attempt to resolve this problem, each of which engendered a line of psychological research reflecting its assumptions. One approach frequently adopted by seventeenth- and eighteenth-century philosophers involved a radical reduction of one aspect of knowledge, either subjectivity or objectivity, to the other. This reductionism took two basic forms. In the empiricist tradition, it was assumed that the environment impresses itself on individuals. In this view, knowledge is produced through experience and consists of bits of information which are 'given' to the individual as sense data. This epistemological vision underlies much of contemporary associationist or behaviorist psychological research. An opposing reduction of object to subject is offered in the Cartesian tradition. From this perspective, it is subjectivity which is basic. Reality, to the degree to which it may be addressed, must be seen in the light of its compatibility with the nature of human subjectivity. This rationalist tradition is reflected in much of cognitive (especially Gestalt) psychology and cognitive science.

Beginning with the assumption that thought is an operational activity, as Piaget does, leads epistemological investigations in a very different direction. In this dynamic view, the static features of thought, its constituent representations and its relation to reality, are conceived as products and, therefore, as only properly understood with reference to the process whereby they are produced. This process is conceived as follows. In the course of operating on the world, the individual attempts to coordinate his various purposive acts. Through this coordination, reversible relations among actions which occur through time are established. The temporal dimension of purposive activity is thereby suspended and the static features of thought are constructed.

In this context, the central questions which arise from a static conception of thought are rendered relatively uninteresting or misconceived. The problem of the relation between representations and reality, the subject–object problem, dissolves. The *structures* of both subjectivity and reality are intertwined in the individual's operations or purposive action. In this sense, the relationship between subject and object is assumed and constitutes the starting point for analysis. Thus, the focus shifts from the analysis of reference to the analysis of how representations and structures of inference are constructed by the individual through purposive interaction with the environment. Consequently, the central orienting questions do not revolve around the possibility of knowledge, but rather around the nature of the various forms of knowledge which may be subjectively constructed. This epistemological focus is reflected in Piaget's psychological research on the quality of thought which emerges at each stage of intellectual development.

A second basic assumption Piaget adopts is that thought is structured. The view here is that an individual has a basic capacity to think or reason. In the language of operations, an individual has a general way in which he is able to purposively act on the world. In the course of actually acting, this general capacity is realized in a variety of specific and concrete operations. It is substantively differentiated. For example, an individual may have a basic capacity to think in causal linear terms. In the course of experience, this capacity is realized in the specific links the individual forges when he thinks that the Soviet Union's aggressive attitude is an effect for which there must be some cause or that the city council must act if downtown development is to be controlled. While substantively quite distinct, these two understandings are structurally identical outcomes of the same kind of thinking or mode of operation. Thus, in Piaget's view, thinking, and the understanding it yields, are defined in formal terms and, at least in the first instance, are regarded as subjective acts. In this regard, Piaget adopts concerns and strategies similar to those of continental structuralism. Like the structuralists, he assumes that there is a deep structure underlying the manifest content of human thought and that this content can only be properly understood with reference to its relation to that deep structure.[3]

The concept of structure, as used by Piaget, is frequently misunderstood. This is often a result of failing to properly distinguish the concept of structure from the concept of system.[4] As the concepts are used here, the difference between them is that structures are basic and generative and systems are derivative and organizational. Structures constitute or define possible systems of manifest relations and elements. Systems depend on these definitions and are orders of manifest content. The relation between structures and systems is a dynamic one. Systems are produced by structures and are particular manifestations of more general or basic processes.

For the purposes of analysis, the differentiation or equation of structures and systems is critical. When the two terms are equated, as they are in much of systems theory, structures are reduced to systems. In this case, it is generally assumed that the task of describing a system is simple and straightforward. One merely observes the relevant objects (or activities) which are involved over time or across comparable cases and discovers the pattern of their interrelationship. The resulting description details the observed spatial and/or sequential organization. An example of such an analysis is offered by the characterization of political thought in the belief systems research. Political thought is defined in terms of its constituent attitudes and then the connections between these attitudes are empirically explored. Neither the definition of an attitude nor the possible quality of the relations between attitudes is theoretically explicated or justified. The heart of the investigation is empirical, not theoretical.

The assumption that structures are generative and systems a product suggests that a theoretical explication of the elements and relations of a system – that is, an explication of the system in terms of its formal structure – is a precondition of successful analysis. Failure to begin in this manner can only lead to an analysis which does not locate the structural foundation of the phenomena observed (be it in the phenomena themselves or in the mind of the observer) and thereby fails to establish criteria for decoding the nature of those phenomena. The result can only be partial and distorting. In this structuralist view, the possibility of a system depends on the existence of an underlying generative structure. The system must be defined with reference to this structure if the terms of its coherence and the conditions of its transformation are to be understood. Given these assumptions, structural analysis involves a recursive process of interpretation and empirical validation. The focus is on the formal quality of manifest systems. For Piaget, this analysis extends to a consideration of the type of process which could produce the observed system. Because structures are more basic and general than systems, it is possible for analysis of this type to lead to the discovery that a variety of systems as manifestly different as algebra and liberal democratic theory have a common structure and, therefore, are two realizations of the same generative structure.

The third basic assumption which distinguishes Piaget's perspective is that thought develops. This third postulate is best understood in relation to the preceding two and to a metaphysical assumption, largely implicit in Piaget's work, that reality itself is structured. The argument is that thinking is a subjectively structured attempt to operate upon an objectively structured world. Insofar as the structure of an individual's thought is inconsistent with the structure of the environment, his or her attempt to operate will prove unsuccessful. Through a process of 'reflexive abstraction', a process of reflecting on how one thinks rather than simply focusing on the objects of one's thought, the structure of the individual's thought is transformed. As a result of this process, the individual comes to operate in a new way, a new structure of thought emerges. Consequently, thinking develops.

An example may help illustrate this process. Consider the novice's understanding of chess. Initially, he may only understand the game in terms of the pieces used and the movements they make. In structural terms, the objects of understanding are perceptually discriminated pieces and his operation on those objects consists of moving them according to the rules. Armed with this understanding of the game, our novice begins to play, charting his moves and viewing the moves of his opponents in these terms. Of course this understanding is inadequate and our novice will lose continually. The experience of this loss engenders doubt and reflection. There is something wrong, something he clearly cannot comprehend given his understanding of the game. Rather than focusing on his object, the pieces, he begins to consider his operation on them, the way in which he moves them. These moves become his new object of thought and he seeks to interrelate them. His thinking about the game develops. The final result is an understanding which does not consist of moving different pieces, but of relating the different moves which can be made. This new understanding of the game leads to a redefinition of old concerns. Thus, a bishop is no longer a tall piece which can be moved diagonally. A bishop is now a potential to move diagonally which constitutes an attack, a support or a feint depending on the circumstances.

This developmental process generates a universal and invariant sequence of structural transformations or stages. For all individuals, the starting point is the same – the repertoire of reflexes and perceptual abilities that is common to the species. This process ends when the structure of the individual's thought parallels that of the environment. Here, we see the dialectical elements of Piaget's thought. In fact, Piaget's theory of cognition may fruitfully be understood as a realist revision of Hegel's *Phenomenology of Mind*.

In sum, Piaget adopts three basic assumptions: (1) thought is a pragmatically constituted activity; (2) thought is structured; and (3) thought develops. He orients his cognitive psychology accordingly. For Piaget, the descriptive aim is to delineate the various forms which thinking assumes in the course of its development. This involves describing the mode of thinking and the formal qualities of the understanding constructed at each stage of development. Piaget pursued this descriptive goal in two ways. In a series of book-length analyses presented from the late 1920s through the 1940s, he attempted to establish the stages involved in the development of the *a priori* categories of thought defined by Kant such as causality, time, space, etc. In his later work, he forged a more integrated conception of the stages of development. Here, he attempted to describe the general forms of operation which cut across the various Kantian categories. This led to his definition of four general stages of cognitive development. These are sensorimotor, preoperational, concrete operational and formal operational thought.

The explanatory goal of Piaget's psychology is to explicate how it is that development occurs. Piaget explains development in complementary ways in the course of his discussions of equilibration (the dynamic of adaptation of subjective to real structures) and reflexive abstraction. These discussions are, however, much more abstract and less elaborated than his analysis of the particular stages of development. Furthermore, little empirical research has been done to investigate these explanations. While such research has not been conducted, it is not, in principle, impossible.[5]

Piaget's empirical research is designed with these goals in mind. The goal of describing the structural qualities of the various forms of thinking sets two guidelines for the design of descriptively oriented research. First, the investigation must focus on individual subjects. The possibility that different individuals may think in structurally dissimilar ways suggests that the common practice of using aggregate data to characterize typical performances is inappropriate. Second, the investigation must require each subject to perform several specific tasks. In this manner, a content-free assessment of each subject's performance may more readily be made. Although little research has been conducted on the conditions of development, the design requirements are easily inferred. Individual subjects must be observed over time and, using quasi-experimental designs, an attempt must be made to examine the impact of differently structured environments on subjects' current thinking and long term development.

Like his research designs, Piaget's methods reflect the dictates of his concept of cognition. Given his assumption that thinking is structured and may vary across individuals, the methodological problems Piaget faced were quite similar to that of the historian of philosophy. The task confronting the historian of philosophy is to determine how a particular philosopher thinks. Aware that a philosopher may think in a quite distinctive way, the historian approaches the task of interpretation in such a way as to avoid reducing the terms or logic of the philosopher's thought to his or her own. This is accomplished first by examining a number of the philosopher's assertions and arguments and then by building a model that renders these various claims sensible and coherent. Only when these claims and additional ones made by the philosopher are comprehended in this manner, does the historian feel comfortable with the interpretative model.

Viewed from a Piagetian perspective, people are lay philosophers with their own metaphysics and social theory. Consequently, like the historian of philosophy, the psychologist must attempt to build an interpretative model of the logic of people's thought. The psychologist, however, must begin by making subjects think in an observable manner. Recognizing that any single attitude or claim may mean different things to different people and, therefore, may be easily misinterpreted, the psychologist uses empirical methods that give subjects the opportunity to make a set of related judgments or claims about a specific problem or issue. Methods of this kind include open-ended interviews and clinical experiments. Both methods involve the presentation of a problem to subjects and then a continual probing of their responses to allow a clear determination of the nature of the connections they are making. Using these techniques, the psychologist ensures that the data collected are sufficiently rich – that each subject has made a sufficient number of related claims – to allow for the construction and/or testing of an interpretative model of that subject's thought.

To summarize, Piaget offers a distinctive approach to the study of human nature. He focuses on reasoning and the understanding it engenders. He defines reasoning as a structured pragmatic activity and explains the nature and development of structures of thought with reference to the general progress of intellectual development. His clinical experimental methods of psychological research complement this theoretical orientation. The result of his efforts is an extraordinary body of theoretical writings and empirical research on the nature and development of thinking. The significance of his contribution to psychology is widely recognized. Its implications for political science and social theory have only been explored to a very limited degree.

PIAGET AND POLITICS

Piaget's psychology has important implications for the conduct of political science at a number of levels. Most obvious is its relevance to the study of public opinion and political behavior. It suggests an alternative concept of ideology and an accompanying set of guidelines for the study of political behavior. Less clear but equally significant is the relevance of Piaget's ideas to the general study of politics. In his work, Piaget suggests a novel concept of human nature. In so doing, his ideas enter the discourse of macropolitical analysis by raising as problematic the psychological assumptions upon which institutional and social structural analyses are based.

The study of ideology

Most contemporary American research on ideology can be traced to its roots in the enlightenment and liberal philosophy of Bacon, Hobbes and Locke. In this tradition, ideology is defined as a set of prejudicial beliefs. Individual beliefs are identified in terms of their content – that is, with regard to the objective (and later to the intersubjective) phenomena to which they refer. Once formed, these beliefs shape the ideologue's perception and evaluation of events. Ideology is explained as the product of forces beyond the individual's rational control – forces which are both external (cultural traditions, philosophies and discourse) and internal (the passions). According to Bacon, these forces produce the idols of the cave, the tribe, the theatre and the marketplace in which men, in their weakness, believe.

Central to this conception is the differentiation between ideology and reason. Reason is based on clear, unbiased observation and consists of rational deduction. Reason is defined as a process distinguished by its logical form. It is also regarded as a quality of mind, a capacity shared by all human beings at all times. In contrast, ideology exists prior to observation and operates to shape observation according to its own prejudices. It is defined by its content, its constitutive beliefs, and is regarded as a product of learning. In the latter regard, ideology is understood to be culturally relative. Whereas reason is a personal, self-conscious and controlled process, ideology is a product of social and irrational forces. Although all people are capable of reason, individuals frequently fail to make the effort. Instead, they tend to submit passively to cultural direction. The remedy is those positive influences, liberal education and scientific investigation, which foster critical thinking. Shared by all people, reason provides a basis for common discourse. Cultures and ideologies divide people from one another; science and reason transcend those divisions.

This conception of ideology underlies the vast majority of the contemporary research on political ideology. Piaget's work provides the basis for developing an alternative concept of ideology, one which is generally consistent with a post-Hegelian structural and dialectical philosophical tradition (e.g. Marx, 1974; Goldmann, 1964; Lukacs, 1971) quite different from that of the liberal enlightenment. Here, ideology is defined not as a set of attitudes, but as a way of thinking. Thinking is the activity of placing objects in relation to one another and, in so doing, defining the essential nature of the objects themselves. Observation and reason are regarded as two dimensions of a single process, a process involving and bound by the construction of inferential frameworks and the definition of the formal qualities of objects observed.

In this light, a number of distinctions critical to the liberal approach dissolve. First among them is the distinction between ideology and reason. According to the structural dialectical tradition, ideology is the product of reasoning and reasoning is an ideological activity. The divide between ideology and reason evaporates. Both are modes of observation and deduction and both are socially and historically relative. In the latter regard, reason loses its universality and its singularity. In place of a concept of a single rationality, we have instead the idea of different forms of rationality such that reasoning may vary from individual to individual and from culture to culture. Second, the distinction between the form of reasoning, its logic, and the content of reasoning, specific objects and beliefs, is dissolved. Treading the line between materialism and idealism, both the form and content of thought are viewed as products of a common process, at once subjectively directed and objectively determined. Third, the distinction between reason and learning also breaks down. Learning is regarded as a structured phenomenon - a process delimited to the incorporation of objects and relations that are consistent with the structure of the individual's reasoning. At the same time, reasoning is itself learned - the structure of thought is transformed by particular practices and experiences. Learning is, in part, delimited by the qualities of mind, while reasoning is, in part, a product of culture. Guided by these definitions, the studies of reason and ideology are joined in a historical enterprise. The focus is on the development of political reasoning. Explanations are cast with reference to the dialectical interaction between the psychological structure of understandings and purposes on the one hand and the social structure of culture and interaction on the other.

The potential contribution of Piaget's work to the study of ideology is best appreciated in this context. On the one hand, it clearly advances this structural dialectical tradition. First, much of the investigation done in this tradition has focused on the general issue of the relation between reason, ideology and history, but comparatively little has tried to specify the nature of the forms of ideological reason. Piaget contributes here by offering an extraordinarily well elaborated definition of the various forms reasoning may take. His description of the stages of cognitive development is important as a possibly correct description of different structures of thinking and, equally important, as a model for descriptive analysis. Second, structural dialectical theorists have focused primarily on the cultural manifestations of ideological reason. Little attention has been devoted to the study of individuals. Having developed a theory of how individuals reason, Piaget's addition to the tradition here is clear. Third, the emphasis placed by structural dialectical investigation on theory building has been matched by a relative failure to address the methodological problems inherent in the kind of interpretative empirical research which the theory requires. Here, Piaget offers a vast body of careful and systematic empirical research on hundreds of individuals. This research is valuable not only for its specific results, but also as a model of innovative designs and carefully developed methods for empirical research.

The structural dialectical conception of reason and ideology also provides a framework in which the relevance of Piaget's theory of reason, his cognitive developmental psychology, to the study of ideology may be understood. According to this conception, reason and ideology are isomorphic. The analysis of one illuminates the nature of the other. Consequently, Piaget's theory of reason is immediately a theory of political reason, his psychology of cognition, a psychology of political cognition. In this light, I adopt Piaget's perspective and formulate the following concept of ideology. This concept is implicit in my research on political thought and is suggested as a guide for further theory and research on public opinion.

Viewed from a Piagetian perspective, ideology is most fruitfully conceived with reference to the activity of political reasoning. Political reasoning itself is defined as a social psychological phenomenon, a product of both the thinking subject and a determining social environment. These forces combine to determine the nature of reasoning at any moment in time and establish the conditions of its transformation or development. Within this frame of reference, a central theoretical concern is to define types of political reasoning and to identify the structures of ideological thought they engender.

This view of ideology is based on two key assumptions. The first is that ideological thought is structured and, therefore, constitutes a coherent whole. The structure and coherence of ideological thought is understood with reference to the nature of the activity of political reasoning. Like all reasoning, political reasoning consists of the individual's attempt to operate upon the world and then assimilate the results achieved. Thus, political reasoning provides the medium of exchange between the individual and the political environment. In so doing, it determines the structure of the individual's social and political experience. How the individual thinks (his or her capacity to operate and reflect) delimits both the nature of what the individual can experience (the quality of possible objects of thought) and how the individual will organize those experiences (the type of analytical relations between objects established). The activity of reasoning produces the structure of the individual's ideological thought. This structure then defines the terms (both relational and elemental) in which the political environment will be rendered subjectively meaningful.

The second basic assumption underlying this view of ideology is that ideology develops. Like its structure, the development of ideology is understood to be a necessary result of the activity of political reasoning. Political reasoning is a fundamentally pragmatic activity: it is embedded in interaction with the environment and yields a guide to future interaction. Thus, political reasoning provides the individual with a knowledge of how to act and what to expect. The individual directs future action and forms future expectations accordingly. In so doing, the individual relates his or her subjectively constructed ideology or political understanding to the realities of social and political life. Although the individual's action is subjectively structured and directed, it actually occurs in a socially structured environment. Therefore, the individual's action is necessarily regulated by the rules inherent in the sociopolitical environment in which he acts. Given these social constraints on action, the individual's ideology (as the guide to and reflection upon his own and others' action) is necessarily constrained by the structure of the environment.

The claim that political reasoning is socially as well as subjectively structured is critical to the developmental view of ideology. It is the interaction between these two structuring forces, subjective and social, that constitutes the developmental dynamic. To the degree to which the individual's ideological construction of political experience is inconsistent with the real constraints imposed on that experience by the environment, the individual's ideological understanding of the world will prove unworkable. This leads to reflection, a shift in focus from what one knows to how one knows. This in turn leads to the construction of a new structure of ideological thought. With reflection, the terms of the old ideological understanding are objectified and, thereby, transcended. The act of taking one's way of understanding as object prefigures the emergence of a new mode of political reasoning. With the application and consequent elaboration of this new mode of reasoning, the structure of ideology is transformed and political experience is reconstructed.

In sum, ideology is embedded in an ongoing process of subjective construction, denial, reflection and reconstruction. It is the product of a structural developmental process whose dynamic is such that ideological development has the following characteristics: First, because each stage in the process builds on the preceding stage and creates the foundation of the succeeding stage, the order of development will not vary across persons. Second, because each stage emerges as a reflective response to the inadequacies of thought at the preceding stage, development leads both to an ever greater cognitive sophistication and to a more appropriate adaptation to the political environment. Third, because environments stimulate development and the structure of environments may vary, different individuals may achieve different levels of development. These developmental differences will produce structural differences in reasoning and ideology across individuals.

Here, it is important to note that this notion of social environments and their role in conceptual and ideological development goes well beyond Piaget's own thinking. Piaget saw participation in a social environment as essential to development. The requirements of participation in cooperative social interaction were regarded as critical pressures to develop higher order thinking. However, this was conceived in only the broadest and vaguest sense. In Piaget's view, all social environments require some level of cooperative interaction. He did not suggest any cognitively relevant distinctions among forms of cooperative interaction. In this context, it made little sense to investigate the relation between environments and forms of political thought.[6] I believe that the interactional structure of social environments does vary in a way which is relevant to the development of political thought. In Piagetian terms, I suggest that there are different modes of social cooperation which place different cognitive developmental demands on the individuals involved. As we shall see in chapter 4, this leads to a reconceptualization of the dynamic of development and the nature of the understanding achieved at each stage in its progress.

Accompanying this theory of ideology is a general program for empirical research. There are two orienting aims: (1) to characterize the various forms which political reasoning may take, and (2) to explain the conditions of the structural transformation of political reasoning. The first aim directs research to offer an account of the patterns in individuals' political arguments, evaluations and judgments in terms of structures underlying their thought. The key concern here is the formal structure, the quality of the constituent relations and elements, of individuals' political thinking. Two points should be noted regarding this investigation of the quality of individuals' political thought. First, the emphasis on the analysis of the structure underlying the manifest content of individuals' political beliefs is not meant to suggest that particular beliefs are insignificant or impossible to study. They are likely to have important consequences in particular situations and are, therefore, significant. The point here is that the meaning of a particular belief, and by implication its relation to other beliefs and external circumstances, is structurally delimited. Consequently, to study individuals' political beliefs, one must begin by having identified the structure which underlies their constitution and organization. Only in this context can analyses of the relations among beliefs and the conditions of specific attitude change be explored. Second, it should also be noted that this Piagetian program does not limit research to the study of thinking about only those phenomena which the culture defines as political. Central to any ideology is the definition of the boundaries of politics itself. Insofar as ideology is itself a subjective construction, the domain of phenomena which constitute politics or are relevant to political belief are themselves subjectively determined. Thus, research must be guided by individuals' definitions rather than cultural definitions of what is political.

The second aim of Piagetian research on ideology is to provide an account of how structures of ideological thought are transformed. Here, the focus is not simply on the individual but on the relationship between the individual and the polity, between subjective and intersubjective constitutions of politics. According to my neo-Piagetian view, political reason is constructed at different levels by both individuals and by the collectivity. The relationship between these two levels of structuration is dialectical – each is potentially transformed by virtue of its relation to the other. Consequently, changes in the structures of individuals' ideologies must be accounted for in terms of the structure of the sociopolitical environment to which the individuals are exposed.

The study of behavior

It is important to recognize that Piaget's perspective suggests more than just a theory of ideology or public opinion. It extends to a theory of political behavior as well. The key here is the theoretical definition of the relationship between thought and behavior. This relationship may be conceived of in a variety of ways. Following the direction of attitude psychology, the mainstream research on political behavior presumes that thought (attitudes) is quite distinct from specific behavior, but that a close relationship exists between them. In this conception, attitudes direct behavior, they dispose an individual to behave in a particular way. (For a classic definition of attitude, see Allport, 1935.) The problem with this conception, and the implicit view of thought and behavior underlying it, is that it was not supported by empirical research. The problem was first noted in the social psychological research. Put simply, attitudes do not predict behavior at all well.[7]

In the Piagetian view, this social psychology of attitudes and behavior and its analog in political science depend on inappropriate concepts and therefore misconstrue central issues. Thought and behavior are not distinct, they are inextricably united in attempts to operate on the world, either through representation or observable action. Therefore, behavior, like thought, is purposive and subjectively structured on the one hand and is performed on objects and subject to the real conditions of action on the other. The implication here is that behavior must be viewed as subjectively defined action. Through interaction with the environment, the structure of this subjective definition develops. Therefore, to understand the meaning of a behavior, its inherent nature and relation to either attitudes or other behaviors, one must identify the subjective structure of the individual's political reason. Whereas in conventional research the problem is one of explaining behaviors in terms of attitudes or contexts, the key problem for a Piagetian investigation appears at a prior step – that of appropriately describing the behaviors or attitudes themselves in light of the structure that underlies them both. Only in this context can specific behaviors and attitudes be appropriately identified and the relationships between them be properly investigated and understood. Failure to proceed in this manner can result only in a potentially inappropriate and largely unself-conscious translation of an individual's behavior into the analyst's own terms of reference.

Let us consider an example, the analysis of political participation. More specifically, let us consider the impact of community organizers' efforts to increase individuals' political participation. Typically, researchers view the problem in the following terms. An organizer arrives and attaches himself to the community leadership. He then discovers local problems and interests and educates the local population in the various ways in which they can use government and politics to achieve their ends. This will generally include walking people through the steps of going to the ballot box or filling out petitions for a particular public service. In the problematic of the participation research, the organizer has provided a context in which individuals are made aware of how their interests may be successfully pursued through a range of particular forms of political participation. The implicit assumption here is that the members of the local population, the organizer and the analyst all understand the specific behaviors learned in the same way. Armed with this assumption the analyst, like the organizer, presumes that individuals now have the requisite knowledge coupled to the preexisting interest to continue to participate. The problem for both the analyst and the organizer is that this does not generally happen. Typically, the targets of this effort lapse back into the earlier nonparticipation shortly after the organizer departs. Where there are no obvious countervailing factors at work (e.g., negative rewards such as possible jeopardizing of personal safety, status or economic security), such a result is incomprehensible.

For the Piagetian analyst, the foregoing result is readily comprehended. As suggested by our theory of ideology, the subjective definition of the participatory behaviors which the organizer attempted to teach to the target community must be analyzed. Interest here is in both the organizer's and the local community members' understandings of those behaviors. The aim is first to discover the underlying structure of each person's political reasoning. Then, their understandings of politics, political action, government and themselves can be determined. In this context, the behaviors identified as political and participatory by the organizer can be appropriately identified.

In the case in question, it may be that the failure of the organizer to produce the desired result reflects the fact that the structure of the organizer's political reasoning and that of his targets differ fundamentally. For example, it may be that the organizer has a clear understanding of the place of the local community relative to the relevant level of government and, in this context, understands the dependence of that government on the initiatives of the local populace (in a benign case) and the services that government can provide. The members of the target community may not share that understanding. For them, the relevant boundaries of social life may not extend beyond those with whom they have regular face-to-face contact. Consequently, they lack the conceptual framework in which to properly place themselves relative to a remote and faceless institution. Moreover, they also may view their own existence in terms of the day-to-day regularities which they confront. As a result, they may lack a sense both of the possibility of changing the pattern of their lives and of the alternatives that might be introduced. If this were the case (and it would have to be determined by empirical research), one would then expect that these local community members would view the participation they were being taught simply as behaviors which a new person whom they have come to like and trust was asking them to perform. They perform these behaviors because of his request. When he leaves, the direction and rationale for their behavior disappears and so does their ostensible political participation.

The lesson to be drawn from this example is that political action should be theoretically conceived in the same terms as political thought. Both are subjectively structured phenomena. Therefore, any analysis of political action, either theoretical or empirical, must begin with an interpretative definition of the subjective meaning of that action. Only then can that action and the conditions which sustain or deter it be properly understood.

The study of institutions and society

We have considered the implications of Piaget's work for the study of micropolitical concerns, individuals' ideology and behavior. Given Piaget's psychological focus, the connection here has been direct and straightforward. The relationship between Piaget's psychology and macropolitical analysis is less direct. To appreciate the relevance of his work, it is necessary first to consider the role which concepts of human nature play in the study of politics. In contemporary parlance, the question here is one of the general relevance of psychology to political science. Despite the illusion of distinctiveness fostered by the current administrative division of the social sciences, it is my belief that these two disciplines are intimately, indeed inextricably, intertwined.

At its core, political science addresses two related types of questions. One type I shall call analytical. Questions of this type concern the actual organization of political life. Theory and empirical research are used to explore the realities of governance and the distribution of power. The second set of questions are ethical. Their focus is the desirability of possible alternative forms of political organization. Here, debate revolves around questions of rights, obligations and legitimacy. In both analytical and ethical investigations, the nature of the problems posed and the kinds of answers deemed satisfactory reflect essentially psychological assumptions regarding human nature. To illustrate, let us consider the example of two currently dominant forms of political theorizing, liberal and sociological.[8]

Liberal political theory is based on the assumption that individuals are, to a significant degree, the masters of their own destiny. This is true in two respects. On the one hand, there is an assumption that individuals are reasonable or rational. The claim here is that individuals are able: (1) to discern their preferences and the environmental context of their action; (2) to deduce the set of possible alternative courses of action they may follow to realize their preferences; and (3) to determine the course which combines the optimum level of valued outcome and likely success. Although limited by circumstance, individuals can choose among the alternatives available, and evaluate and possibly change the conditions which constrain them. On the other hand, liberal theory assumes that there are certain basic values which all individuals share.[9] The specific sociocultural conditions of life may determine how these values are realized as culturally and historically specific preferences, but the underlying values themselves remain attributes of individuals and are therefore universal.

Here, we have the psychological foundation of the liberal study of politics. Its assumptions regarding cognition and motivation suggest that the individual rationally orients to the realization of preferences which reflect his or her own essential nature. The individual is viewed as a fundamentally self-guiding actor. Following from this, the critical assumption of liberal political thought is made: political activity (its valued ends as well as its dynamic) is a product of individuals. Oriented by this assumption, the liberal study of politics begins with a consideration of the nature of individuals and its effect on their tendencies to act and react in various social settings. The focus then turns to the collective consequences (unintended as well as intended) produced when individuals interact with one another. Thus, the creation, maintenance and transformation of political life is understood as the aggregated result of individual action and intention. This individualist orientation is reflected in both liberal analysis and ethics. Analysis may focus on the institutional or structural organization of power in a community, but this organization is described in terms of the way it regulates the rational purposive behavior of individuals and it is explained as the aggregate result of their actions. Similarly, ethical inquiry may focus on cultural mores or norms, but these are ultimately evaluated in light of the requirements and values of individuals.

Sociological theory emerged in opposition to this liberal formulation. Basic to the dispute were the assumptions made regarding human nature. For the most part, sociological theory is premised on the assumption that individuals are not rational, reasoning, self-guiding actors. On the contrary, they are regarded as merely good learners. According to this view, individuals' cognitive capacity consists of little more than the ability to perceive and associate bits of information present in their social environment. Thus, what individuals know and how they put information together is determined by the particular configurations of information to which they are exposed. Individual motivation consists of an undifferentiated desire to maximize bodily pleasures and minimize its pains. In response to the reward structure present in the social environment, this general motivation becomes differentiated as a set of externally determined wants and needs. Taken together these psychological assumptions suggest that the logic of thought and action and the criteria of evaluation are not individual level phenomena. It may be that it is individuals who know, act and want, but the logic and values orienting their behavior are a social, not an individual, construction. Individuals themselves are merely a collage of the fragments of chains of thoughts or behaviors they have learned in response to the societally determined situations to which they have been exposed.

This sociological psychology leads to a very different understanding of politics. The individual is no longer regarded as self-directing, but as socially directed. Thus, in the sociological tradition, the individual is regarded as derivative and the society as the basic unit of analytical and ethical investigation. Therefore, the focus is on the qualities of society itself. Political life is both described and explained with reference to these qualities. In this context, any attempt to describe or explain politics with reference to the characteristics or intentions of individuals is regarded as superficial, distorting and fundamentally misguided. Ethical investigations also reflect the primacy of the collective. Consequently, the individual is no longer regarded as the standard of value. Traditional liberal concerns over essential human nature, universal values and individual rights are abandoned in favor of a discussion of the nature of community, the cultural and historical relativity of social values, and the obligations of the individual to the collective.[10]

As should be evident by this brief discussion of liberal and socio-logical political theory, political science is at its very core a psychological discipline. The sense and logic of any general frame-work for political analysis depend on an acceptance (or, more rarely, a validation) of basic assumptions regarding cognition and motivation. Given the centrality of psychology to political science, it is clear that Piaget's theory, insofar as it offers a distinctive conception of cognition, may be of fundamental significance to general political inquiry. Insofar as it suggests a model of cognition that differs from that underlying either liberal or sociological conceptions of politics, Piagetian psychology provides a basis for a fundamental and en-compassing critique of those two perspectives. Accepted as a basis for the construction of a new conception of politics, it provides a new and exciting direction for political inquiry.

To illustrate its potential as a basis for critique, let us briefly consider the implications for macropolitical analysis of one aspect of the Piagetian view of cognition, the claim that there are develop-mentally generated differences in reasoning among adults. This claim runs contrary to the cognitive assumptions which underly both liberal and sociological theories of politics. Although these two theories vary in their assessment of individuals' capacities, both assume that all individuals think in fundamentally the same way. Moreover, both types of macropolitical analysis depend on this assumption of common cognitive capacity.

Consider first the liberal view of human nature and politics. According to this view, all individuals share a common capacity to reason rationally. Some people may be quicker or more knowledge-able than others, but all share the same basic capacity for rational thought. The centrality of this assumption is readily apparent when considering the liberal conception of a political institution. As stated earlier, an institution is defined by the ways in which it regulates the interaction among citizens. Examples of institutions include various governmental bodies, the laws they create and the policies they pursue. Key to the conception of any institution is that all individuals appreciate the regulatory imperatives of the institution similarly and respond in a comparable fashion. It is in this context that it is possible to conceive *the* institution in question. The singularity of its identity depends on its common impact and realization in day-to-day activity.

The liberal assumption of a common rationality assures this. The only qualification is that individuals share comparable exposure to the same basic information.

In this regard, the sociological view of politics is not very different. Individuals are regarded as less able, but, as with the liberal view, it is assumed that they all have the same basic cognitive capacity, in this case, the same capacity to perceive environmental stimuli and to associate rewards as they pertain to various responses. Again, this microlevel assumption is critical to macrolevel conceptualization. Central to the sociological view of politics is the assumption that society is a structured coherent entity. It defines an interactive or organizational framework which shapes politics. While an extra-individual or objective phenomenon, this social organization is ultimately manifest in the behavior of individuals. It must define their goals and direct their action. This is achieved through a process of socialization. Critical to this view is the assumption that all individuals share a basic capacity to perceive and learn the role requirements imposed on them by their place in this social organiz-ation. This ensures that all will recognize and respond in the same designated manner. In this context, it is reasonable to refer to the single collective organization of their action.

The Piagetian view of cognition denies the validity of the assump-tion that all individuals think in basically the same way. On the contrary, it suggests that they may perceive, reason and comprehend in fundamentally different ways. By thereby denying the assumption of common cognition, the Piagetian view necessitates a basic recon-ceptualization of both liberal and sociological views of politics. The assumption of individual differences in cognitive processing suggests that the same objective environment will be understood differently and therefore responded to differently by different individuals. In the liberal case, this implies that a given institution's regulatory initiatives will be understood and responded to according to a variety of logics. The intersubjective agreement as to the nature of the institution is lost. Therefore, it does not make sense to refer to *the* institution because in fact there are several, each with its own subjectively mediated definition and behavioral realization. The implications for the sociological view are similar. Insofar as individuals vary in their capacity to perceive stimuli and rewards and to relate them to each other and behavior, it makes no sense to talk about a single organizational framework or culture which determines their interaction. The common perception which assures the singular realization of an objective phenomenon like social structure is denied.

Differences in the subjective mediation of objective phenomena suggest that multiple organizational frameworks may be operative in a single social setting.

In sum, the Piagetian assumption of individual differences in cognition constitutes a fundamental critique of both liberal and sociological theories of politics. At stake is both theories' assumption that the polity or society is a coherent entity and hence an appropriate object of theoretical analysis. The Piagetian claim of structural differences in individuals' reasoning denies the common subjectivity which underlies the liberal assumption of intersubjective agreement and the sociological assumption of a common perception. In so doing, it suggests that the polity or society is not a coherent, single entity, but rather a loose confederation of occasionally overlapping patterns of exchange which are best described and explained at a more local level of analysis. In coming to this conclusion, we see how Piagetian theory, as a psychology, pertains to macropolitical analysis. It offers theory and evidence on individuals from which the nature of interpersonal exchange and possible forms of political organization may be deduced.

Of course, Piagetian theory not only provides a basis for criticism, it also suggests new directions for political theory. With its emphasis on structural developmental analysis, Piagetian theory builds on an epistemology which favors an interpretative analysis of patterns of action and an explanation of those patterns with reference to under-lying structures. In this respect, it is sympathetic to the general theoretical orientation of much of sociological analysis. At the same time, Piaget places the locus of structure in the individual; he regards it as a cognitive phenomenon. In this respect, his theory stands in opposition to sociological analysis. The inherent tension in these twin considerations delineates the direction for political theorizing. It calls for a truly social psychological conception of political life – one which realizes the full ramifications of the claim that politics is at once an individual and collective phenomenon.

PLAN OF THE BOOK

This first chapter has offered a general introduction to the nature and relevance of a Piagetian approach to the study of ideology. An attempt was made to demonstrate that Piaget's work speaks directly to critical problems which have been encountered in current research on political behavior. The general epistemological and psychological orientation Piaget adopts in his work was outlined and its implications for political research were discussed. This included a consideration of the relevance of Piaget's work to the study of both microlevel and macrolevel political phenomena.

In the remainder of the book, we extend the arguments made here. Chapter 2 offers an in-depth analysis of the current study of ideology. The nature of the mainstream research on ideology is described and analyses of its achievements and inherent limitations are offered. Chapter 3 provides a full explication of the Piagetian approach. Both epistemological and psychological dimensions of this approach are discussed here. Chapter 4 presents my extension of Piagetian theory. More expressly sociological considerations are introduced and three stages in the development of political thinking are defined. Chapter 5 presents empirical research which supports the theoretical arguments made in chapter 4. Three studies are presented. The first focuses on the question of the relation between political and nonpolitical thought, the second on people's understanding of domestic politics, and the third on their understanding of international relations. Chapter 6 addresses the question of the place of my research on individuals in the general study of politics. Its relevance both to current behavioral research and to contemporary social theory is discussed. The chapter concludes by sketching the outlines of a social and political theory informed by my structural developmental analysis of political reasoning.

2

The Empirical Study of Ideology: Comprehensiveness, Power and Heuristic Value

---

Do people understand politics? On what basis do they judge the relative merits of political alternatives? These questions are at the heart of all political inquiry. Any theory of how the polity does or should function is built on the answer to these questions. Once, these matters were the sole preserve of the political theorist and were addressed by casual observation and assumption. With the advent of the behavioral revolution and the birth of 'political science' in the forties and fifties, the situation changed dramatically. No longer did the student of politics have to rely on personal experience and in-tuition as a basis for theorizing. Instead, he or she could conduct systematic empirical research and discover what the citizenry under-stood and valued.

This move to empirical research offered great promise. Perhaps the most theoretically interesting of the early research focused on political thought and ideology. Drawing on an examination of the belief systems of mass publics, it depicted the average citizen as insuf-ficiently informed, interested or sophisticated to responsibly fulfill his or her role in a representative democracy (Campbell et al., 1960; Converse, 1964). The implications of this finding for the classical debate between liberal and conservative were clear.

Excited by these initial discoveries, two generations of American political scientists (and increasing numbers of their European counterparts) have conducted research on political thinking and ideology. From the perspective of the eighties, it appears that the promise of this research has not been realized. In the last several years, an increasing number of those political scientists actually involved in the research have begun to express disillusionment. Basic questions regarding the value of the research effort of the last thirty years have been raised (e.g., Lane, 1973; Kinder, 1982).

This is the context in which our review of the research on political ideology is offered. The review is presented in three parts. In the first part, the 'mainstream' of the empirical research is examined. Here, the basic parameters governing the research are accepted and an insider's view of thirty years' product is offered. In this light, basic concepts are explicated, findings are summarized and the overall result of this research effort is evaluated. In the second part of the review, we step outside the mainstream of the research. From this vantage point, the basic premises of the research are questioned and its fruitfulness is reconsidered. Three issues are addressed: (1) the quality of the evidence generated, (2) the power of the concepts employed, and (3) the contribution of the theory to the study of politics. The review concludes with a discussion of what a more adequate approach to the study of political ideology must encompass. An attempt is made to define the standards which must inform the construction of alternative theories of political thought and ideology. The aim here is to specify the criteria which must be met by a theory of ideology if it is to be empirically useful, theoretically powerful and politically interesting. [1]

THE POLITICAL BELIEF SYSTEMS RESEARCH:
THE VIEW FROM WITHIN

Orienting concepts

Both the interest in the empirical study of political thinking and the conceptualization of that thinking in terms of beliefs or attitudes reflect the influence of the American attitude psychology of the thirties and forties. [2] Perhaps the most influential person in bringing this social psychological perspective to the attention of political scientists is Philip Converse (1964, 1970, 1975). Indeed, his work has dictated the direction of the 'mainstream' theory and research for the last two decades. While other researchers are divided on the appropriateness of the specific methods Converse has used, critics as well as supporters have adopted the conceptual framework he has defined.

Converse conceives of people's political understanding and evaluation in terms of the belief systems of individuals. These belief systems are defined with reference to their constituent elements, beliefs, and the relations which exist among these elements. In Converse's conception, a belief (or 'idea-element') consists of a knowledge of a specific object and a preference with respect to that object. Beliefs have two qualities: (1) they are interpretable unto themselves – that is, each belief has its own core meaning apart from whatever additional meaning it derives from the belief system of which it is a part; and (2) beliefs may be related to each other and thereby be articulated into a larger network of beliefs. In his discussion of the nature of the relations which exist among beliefs, Converse draws on the language of systems theory. Thus, he speaks in terms of systems of beliefs and the constraint which exists among them. In dynamic terms, this constraint suggests that the relationships among beliefs are regulated so that when one belief is changed, other related beliefs also change. In more static terms, this suggests that the relationships between beliefs are structured by categories which define specific associative (implicative) and dissociative (contradictory) relations among beliefs.

Characterizing political reasoning in these terms, Converse then discusses the basis of the systemic quality of beliefs – in his terms, the sources of constraint. He identifies three sources of constraint: logical, psychological and social. The first, logical constraint, refers to the regulation of beliefs imposed by deductive logic (itself undefined). Converse does not regard logical constraint to be a particularly significant force in the organization of belief systems. The second source of constraint is psychological. This constraint is the result of the individual's experience of what beliefs seems to go with what other beliefs and how. Despite his ostensibly psychological point of view, Converse does not consider this experience to be, in any important sense, a personal or idiosyncratic product. Instead, he emphasizes how it is dependent on the nature of the sociopolitical environment to which the individual is exposed. Thus, it is the third source of constraint, social constraint, that is seen to be the most critical factor in the organization of belief systems. The individual's social environment provides information on which aspects of political life are deserving of attention, how these are to be evaluated, and how they stand in relation to each other. Through exposure to this information, the individual learns about politics and organizes his or her beliefs accordingly.

Method

Converse also offers a model of research which has been adopted in most of the empirical studies which have followed. To gather data, he administers a survey. Typically, this includes a number of closed-ended questions which enable respondents to express their preferences about a number of issues and candidates. In addition, a few questions which allow short answers are included. These give respondents the opportunity to explain briefly their preference for particular presidential candidates and the major political parties. Most research on belief systems centers on the consideration of the closed-ended survey items; comparatively little focuses on the more unwieldly short-answer items. For the most part, these data are gathered through national sample surveys conducted by one or two survey research centers.

While there is broad agreement, there is some debate over this method of data collection. This debate focuses on two points. First, some researchers have argued that the early surveys included items which were poorly constructed, thereby biasing subsequent analyses and conclusions (for an example of some of the issues raised, see Nie et al., 1976; Sullivan et al., 1978; Wray, 1979; Kinder, 1982). Most of the concerns voiced by these critics are accepted by the Converse school and research instruments are now designed with greater attention to issues of questionnaire comparability and bias. Second, there is some debate over the appropriateness of the issues covered by the survey items. Critics have suggested that different issues be included or that the issues be chosen by subjects rather than by researchers (for example, Lane, 1962, 1973; Brown, 1970; Nelson, 1977; Neumann, 1981). Some have made it clear that whatever the basis of the choice, the nature of the items included will affect the kinds of results achieved (Judd and Milburn, 1980). Again it should be noted that this debate falls largely within the parameters of the method Converse has adopted although its resolution is more difficult. Pretesting allows for a degree of sensitivity to the concerns shared by the group surveyed, but the survey format does not allow for the consideration of the idiosyncratic concerns of particular members of that group.[3]

In addition to a method of data collection, Converse also suggests three complementary strategies for data analysis. The first entails the statistical analysis of the interrelationships among responses to survey items. This consists of the examination of the average correlation of pairs of items coded along a liberal–conservative continuum. Here again there has been some debate. A number of researchers have argued that the dimensions around which belief systems are organized should not be presumed by the researcher. Therefore, rather than imposing a liberal–conservative dimension on the data as Converse does, his critics have relied on various factor analytic techniques to allow the appropriate dimensions to emerge from an analysis of the data (Luttbeg, 1968; Jackson and Marcus, 1975; Stimson, 1975; Judd and Milburn, 1980; Himmelweit et al., 1981; Conover and Feldman, 1984).[4]

A second strategy suggested by Converse focuses on the stability of individuals' attitudes. The rationale behind this focus is that insofar as the individual does have a belief system, the attitudes which constitute the belief system should remain relatively stable over time. The test of attitude stability involves an examination of the test-retest correlations of specific survey items. Both this focus on attitude stability and the way it has been measured have been subject to criticism. Himmelweit has raised the problem that the salience and meaning of specific issues change over time and, therefore, one should not expect attitudes toward them to remain stable (Himmelweit et al., 1981). Others have criticized the data analysis for failing to account for such factors as measurement error (Achen, 1975) and the variety of possible sources of attitude change (Judd and Milburn, 1980).[5]

The third strategy involves the content analysis of the short answers to questions asking subjects to explain their evaluations of political parties and presidential candidates. This is done in an attempt to complement the analysis of inter-item correlations with a direct investigation of the principles governing the individual's belief system. Based on the content analysis of their responses, subjects are divided into five groups: ideologues (those who correctly employ the terminology of liberalism and conservatism), near-ideologues (inappropriate use of the terminology), group interested (group loyalty mediates preferences), nature of the times (some issue content but no apparent organizing principle) and no issue content (Converse, 1964). Slightly different categories have been developed in subsequent research (e.g., Field and Anderson, 1969; Nie et al., 1976). Debate here has centered around the issue of whether the analysis successfully captures how the people think or only measures the political rhetoric people use (Wray, 1979; Smith, 1980).

In reviewing the research on political belief systems, I have noted that aspects of Converse's methods of data collection and his procedures for analyzing the data have been subject to debate. *In this context, it is important to remember that these debates have been conducted largely within the conceptual parameters defined by Converse. Researchers have not questioned Converse's basic theory or the logic of research which follows from it. Instead, they have questioned the adequacy with which this has been operationalized in specific instances.* For example, one popular line of attack has been to begin by reiterating Converse's theoretical claim that political reasoning is an externally mediated process and then to argue that certain aspects of his survey items or analytical procedure fail to account adequately for the immediate or remote externalities influencing subjects' responses (e.g., bias in question wording, inappropriate characterization of the culturally defined dimensions around which beliefs are organized, or environmental change in the assessment of attitude stability). Another line of attack involves an explicit acceptance of Converse's research goals and general analytical strategy while offering a technical critique of his statistical analyses.

In sum, despite some methodological controversy, the broad outlines of Converse's research strategy are still accepted. Virtually all the research, including that currently being conducted, relies on surveys for data and analyses these data through examinations of inter-item relationships, response stability over time and the content of short answers.

Evidence

What then has been the result of this apparently rather cohesive research effort? Relying on the aforementioned concepts and methods, researchers have produced a considerable body of evidence on political belief systems. Needless to say, the methodological debates have produced controversy over some results. None the less, a certain pattern, one suggested by Converse, does emerge. The evidence indicates that: (1) the political beliefs expressed by the average American are not meaningfully related to one another nor are they stable over time; (2) there are significant differences among individuals: some express beliefs which appear more coherent and principled, while most do not; and (3) these differences may only be partly explained in terms of demographic variables such as class or race. Pointing to issues of question construction and analytical technique, Converse's critics have raised questions about the appropriateness of all three conclusions. In the main, however, it appears that the overall impact of their criticism has been to add a note of caution rather than to reverse the conclusions drawn by Converse and his supporters.

To conclude, the main thrust of Converse's position on the political thinking of mass publics remains intact after almost thirty years of research. His conception of political thinking in terms of systems of beliefs is accepted by even his most extreme critics (e.g., Lane, 1973; Nelson, 1977). His methods, with some technical improvement, continue to be employed in current research. Even his initial conclusions remain accepted by most scholars in the field. This result speaks well not only for Converse's analyses, but for the field itself. The fact that researchers do share a common conceptual framework and have produced some reasonably durable results suggests a healthy and productive research effort. In sum, it appears that the belief systems research has achieved considerable success.

A REASSESSMENT: THE VIEW FROM WITHOUT

In the preceding account of the belief systems research, we adopted an 'insider's' perspective, accepting its theoretical definitions and terms of analysis. Here, this insider's account is supplemented with an outsider's review. As a result, new issues are raised. Instead of examining the consistency of the research results and the agreement on orienting concepts, we consider the insight offered by the results so consistently achieved, the power of the concepts so generally used and the contribution of the research to the general study of politics.

The quality of the evidence

Earlier, we concluded that the evidence on belief systems is reliable; thirty years of research yielded a reasonably consistent set of results. Here, we ask how good that evidence is. Even if it is reliable, how much does it really tell us? A close consideration of the evidence leads me to conclude that the belief systems research tells us very little about how the mass of people think about politics; furthermore, what little it does tell us stands on very uncertain ground.

The first conclusion, that we know very little about how people reason about politics, is based on a consideration of how much of the mass public's beliefs is captured by the research. A brief review of the research on levels of conceptualization and inter-item correlations indicates that very little is accounted for by the results. In the case of levels of conceptualization, only 2½ per cent (Converse, 1964) (6 per cent for Klingemann (1973)) of the population seem to think about politics along ideological lines which are readily interpretable.[6] Very little can be said about the remainder. About 30–40 per cent appear to be oriented by the concerns of one group or other and the remaining half either use ideological terms in an inappropriate or uninterpretable fashion or exhibit no apparent organization to their beliefs whatsoever. Averaging results across studies, it appears that we can make clear sense of the understandings of approximately 10 per cent of the population and less certain sense of an additional 30 to 40 per cent. All we can say about the remaining half is they do *not* think along lines defined by our concepts. We can make little claim to knowing how they *do* think.

A similar problem emerges when we examine the research on inter-item correlations. Here the problem is that the model accounts for little of the variation in responses. Looking only at the most favorable case, inter-item correlations among assessments of domestic issues, the amount of variance explained varies from a mere 4 per cent in the worst of times (late fifties, Converse, 1964) to 25 per cent in the best case (late sixties, Nie et al., 1976). In other words, somewhere between 75 and 96 per cent of the variance in beliefs remains unexplained. This suggests that the conception of political thinking underlying the correlational analysis allows us to make sense of only a small proportion of the political beliefs of mass publics.

In this context, we should note the work of those researchers who, in recognition of the shortcomings of the analysis of inter-item correlations, have argued that the use of the liberal–conservative dimension to structure the data analysis is inappropriate and necessarily leads to an underestimation of the coherence of people's beliefs. These researchers have suggested that the dimensional structure of belief systems should be a matter of empirical discovery, not theoretical definition. Using various kinds of factor analytical techniques, they have discovered a number of factors – anywhere from one (Judd and Milburn, 1980) to five (Luttbeg, 1968; Himmelweit et al., 1981) or seven (Jackson and Marcus, 1975). In so doing, they have been able to account for about half the variance in responses. Given that these dimensions are generated from the data rather than being theoretically identified, it is surprising how little of the variance is explained. These *a posteriori* accounts fail to explain half the variance in the case of the very data from which those accounts were derived.

Based on evidence of low inter-item correlations and the small proportion of people who score high on the levels of conceptualization measure, researchers adopting the belief systems approach have concluded that mass publics tend not to have constrained belief systems or think in ideological terms. In my opinion, this conclusion tells only half, and perhaps the less significant half, of the story. The other conclusion to be drawn from the evidence is that the research on political belief systems tells us very little about how most people think about politics.

Having criticized the beliefs system research for telling us little, let us now examine the little it does tell us. Consider first the evidence on inter-attitude correlations. While the lack of correlation gives us no insight into how attitudes might be organized, at least the presence of strong correlation should. Upon closer examination, however, it is not at all clear that evidence of correlation among attitudes tells us very much. Let us consider the example of a subject who responds favorably to survey items A and B. What does this tell us about the relationship between A and B? The answer is that the information offered is ambiguous because the subjective meaning of the relationship is uncertain. It may be that the subject has a general view X which defines his or her orientation to the specific attitudes A and B. In this case, the subject understands A and B as specific cases of a general rule. The evidence of correlation is often interpreted in these terms. Alternatively, it may be that the subject adopted attitude A under one set of circumstances or for one set of reasons and adopted attitude B for different and subjectively unrelated reasons. In this case, the subject may express attitude A and attitude B, but not forge any subjective link between them. Finally, it may be that the subject holds attitude C and associates both attitudes A and B with it. In this instance, A and B are not related to each other or to a general principle, but to a third attitude. The key problem here is that the evidence of inter-item correlation does not allow us to determine which of these three alternatives truly characterizes the connection underlying the observed correlation.

As a result of this ambiguity, we cannot be sure of the subjective meaning of the relationship between the beliefs correlated. Evidence of attitude correlation (or the lack of such correlation) cannot provide an adequate basis for drawing inferences regarding how people are thinking. Moreover, whatever conclusions we do draw will not give us any conceptual leverage. Because the evidence does not allow us to determine *how* subjects relate their beliefs, we cannot determine *why* they are linked. In Converse's terms, we cannot determine the source of constraint. Therefore, we cannot go beyond the specific data in hand to predict what other attitudes the subject may hold or the conditions under which the subject's attitudes may change.[7]

The problem of interpretation of the data also arises in the research on levels of conceptualization. While it is true that the open-ended question format gives the subject greater opportunity to reveal his sense of the issues, the problem of interpreting the meaning of the concerns voiced and the nature of their interrelation remains. The difficulties here are: (1) that subjects generally do not offer sufficient elaboration of their claims and justifications to allow for confident interpretation and, (2) that interviewers are not sufficiently sensitive to the requirements of interpretation to probe subjects' responses effectively. Thus, even in the most favorable circumstances, where the data appear quite comprehensible and are being directly examined by a coder, interpretation remains uncertain. Consider, for example, the case where the coder is confronted with a response such as the following. 'I like Ted Kennedy.' 'Why?' 'Well, I tend to be pretty liberal and so is he. I mean who wants a President who isn't concerned with the poor and just wants to protect the rich from taxation.' Such a response is readily coded as ideological according to the Converse scheme. While it appears that the respondent is an ideologue, can we be sure? Is there sufficient evidence to conclude that his thought is mediated by some abstract liberal principle regarding the role of government in society? Why not assume that the respondent views liberals as a group, identifies himself with this group and has learned the set of views that liberals hold? In fact, we lack sufficient data to choose between the two interpretations and must conclude that no confident interpretation can be made. Remember that this is a result of an apparently clear case. Interpretations of responses which provide less, or contradictory, information must be considered even more suspect.

Like the inter-item correlations, the content analyses of short answers do not yield data which can be interpreted with confidence. Failing to probe deeply enough the subject's sense of his own claims, the research does not afford certain insight into what the subject is thinking. It cannot be determined whether the subject's responses are rhetorical or reasoned and, if the latter, what the nature of the reasoning is. So limited, these content analyses cannot offer an adequate basis for determining the conditions under which those responses will be maintained or altered. Suggestions that a subject's level of conceptualizing political phenomena should be reliable over time have proven incorrect (e.g., Smith, 1980).

In sum, the evidence generated by the belief systems research is not very good. Little is said about how most people think about politics and what is said stands on uncertain ground. Conclusions based on the use of these data must be regarded with caution.

Power of the concepts

Most of the attention in the belief systems research is focused on the operationalization of accepted concepts and the analysis of empirical results. These are appropriate concerns for scholars working within an accepted theoretical framework. When approaching a framework from the outside, however, prior concerns must be addressed. To start with, it is necessary to judge how powerful the concepts are. In the case of the belief systems approach, it is necessary to determine how far concepts such as attitude, belief system and socialization enable us to go beyond the formation given.

These questions may be answered either empirically or theoretically. To answer on empirical grounds, it is necessary to consider the demonstrated ability of the theory to enable investigators to predict the emergence of new attitudes or the conditions under which old ones will be sustained or modified. Investigators who have adopted the belief systems approach have not been able to make these predictions. Not only have they been unable to predict new attitudes, they even have difficulty in predicting responses to different measures of the same attitude (for example, see Sullivan et al., 1978; Bishop and Oldendick, 1978). Investigators have also been unable to predict the conditions of change and continuity in people's political thinking. Specific beliefs which are expected to vary with political climate do change, but the determinants of the change are largely unclear. Conversely, the level of conceptualization underlying a person's beliefs is expected to remain unchanged, but research demonstrates the contrary (Smith, 1980). In short, the evidence suggests that the concepts which guide the belief systems research do not provide much theoretical power or leverage.

While this empirically grounded response is informative and may be persuasive, it cannot be considered definitive. The fact that the research has not yet managed to demonstrate its predictive capacity does not necessarily imply that it will be unable to do so in the future. The shortcomings of current efforts may be due to methodological rather than conceptual difficulties. Allowing for this possibility, it is clear that the assessment of the power of a set of concepts must be answered analytically; that is with respect to the inherent qualities of the concepts themselves and the theory which underlies them.

Let us consider the theoretical framework structuring the belief systems research with respect to the power of the concepts it offers. According to the theory, political thinking is an environmentally determined rather than a subjectively directed activity. It is important to note that the theory goes no further than this. It offers no conception of how this determining environment is structured. Thus, on the one hand, the theory denies or ignores the possibility that there is any subjective logic that governs political thinking and attitude formation. On the other hand, the theory does not offer any explication of the objective or social logic that may structure these processes. So constituted, the belief systems theory lacks an organizational foundation upon which to build a concept of political thought. The limits or logic of the kinds of associations an individual will make or of the configurations of stimuli to which he may be exposed remain theoretically undetermined. Consequently, political thinking can only be analyzed on the basis of its discovered content, not on the basis of any theoretical definition of its formal organization.

What conceptual power can such a theory provide? Its power will necessarily be very limited. Lacking a concept of a logic or rule governing either what an individual will be exposed to or how the individual integrates the information presented, the theory provides no basis for going beyond the immediate evidence. Therefore, researchers guided by this theory are bound to the specific beliefs observed and to the conditions of the observation (the sociohistorical moment, the particular survey or interview, etc.). In this context, one can more readily understand the inability of researchers to define beliefs or levels of conceptualization such that reliable (across time or measurement instrument) description is possible.

The value of the theory

Finally, we evaluate the theory guiding the belief systems research with regard to the requirements of political inquiry. In so doing, we go beyond a consideration of the extent to which the belief systems research provides an empirically valid or conceptually powerful depiction of political thinking and ask whether the approach characterizes political thinking in a manner which contributes to the pursuit of the analytical and normative aims of political inquiry. What then are these aims by which the analysis of political thinking must be judged? They are, of course, relative to the theory of politics one adopts. For present purposes, we will consider two broad classes of political theory: one which offers an institutional conception of politics and one which conceives of politics with regard to social structural considerations. In each case, we will briefly discuss the analytical and normative standards the theory establishes and then judge the political belief systems research accordingly.

Institutional theories define political reality as the set of governmental arrangements created to regulate the interaction between people. These arrangements are understood to be the result of the purposive actions of individual political actors. Viewed from this perspective, a key concern of political analysis is to determine both how individuals understand their political environment and on what basis they value various courses of political action. These issues are critical to two of the central foci of the institutional analysis of politics: determining the impact of governmental arrangements on behavior and creating institutions which will best serve the interests of the people. In both cases, individuals' perceptions, understandings and values play a critical mediating role.

How relevant is the belief systems conception of political thinking to this concern with political understanding and judgment? Despite its explicit regard for the concerns of institutional analysis, the belief systems perspective fails to address key issues. The institutional analyst is interested in the reciprocal determination of institutions and individuals' political action – the regulative impact of institutions on individuals' political action and the creative impact of individuals' political action on the development of institutions. Central to this reciprocal determination are individuals' responses to events. Thus, rather than being interested in attitudes *per se*, the institutional analyst is interested in the reasoning process whereby attitudes are engaged, integrated and then contribute to the formation of responses to particular political events. For the most part, the institutional analyst makes assumptions regarding this reasoning process and focuses on macrolevel concerns. To contribute, the student of ideology and public opinion must explore these assumptions and empirically investigate the process of political reasoning.

Seen in this light, the belief systems approach is problematic because it does not address directly the process of political reasoning. Its focus is more narrow. It addresses only the product of that process, the attitudes finally expressed. There is no direct examination either of how attitudes are initially engaged or how they are integrated for the purpose of facilitating a judgment of, and response to, a particular political event. Therefore, when called upon to explicate the nature of political reasoning, the belief systems researcher has no direct evidence upon which to draw. The position he is left in is unsatisfactory in two respects. On the one hand, he is forced to infer the nature of people's political reasoning from observation of its result, their expressed attitudes, and, at the same time, to interpret the meaning of that result by presupposing the very reasoning processes to be inferred. On the other hand, the data collected leave the researcher with a basis for analyzing political understanding, reason and judgment which is really no different from that already available to the institutional analyst. In short, the belief systems researcher's attempt to explicate the nature of people's political reasoning must be considered a suspect and largely redundant enterprise.

The other perspective to be considered is the social structural perspective. Here, politics is regarded as one aspect of a structured social totality. It is not seen to be the product of individuals, but of social phenomena which structure both the polity and individuals themselves. Thus, political facts are defined and explained with reference to qualities of society itself, its culture or its economy. Within this general approach, two important analytical threads may be distinguished, one which maintains an orthodox sociological focus and another which has moved to more social psychological considerations.

The more orthodox sociological conception views political phenomena in strictly macrolevel terms. Thus, there are collective forces (either cultural or material) which shape political realities in particular and the forms of interpersonal exchange in general. In this context, individuals are regarded as determined rather than determining and are not, therefore, an appropriate focus of analytical attention. Insofar as one does consider the individual, it is likely one will find him to be a rather incoherent amalgam of determined activities and learned beliefs and orientations. (For examples of this general position, see Marx, 1973; Durkheim, 1938).

Given such an orthodox sociological conception, it is clear that the belief systems research can only be of very limited utility. First, the methodological individualism which underlies the research must be regarded as illegitimate. Collectivities are causal and coherent, not individuals, and these collectivities are, therefore, the only appropriate analytical focus. While the findings of the belief systems research, that belief systems are an incoherent amalgam of learned attitudes, may be regarded with some satisfaction, the exercise must be considered a largely uninteresting one. From the sociologist's perspective, the final conclusion to be drawn from the belief systems research, that we must look to social environmental factors to explain beliefs, only brings one to the very place where sociology dictates one should start. Moreover, not only does the research effort bring one to the understanding from which the sociologist already has started, it offers a corrupted vision of the starting point. This corruption is evidenced in two ways: (1) in the failure to conceive of environmental influences as social structurally defined and determined, and (2) in the misguided consideration of those environmental influences with respect to their effect on persons rather than with respect to their influence on each other.

The second analytical thread to be found among social structural analysts has evolved more recently. It represents a shift in focus from the orthodox concern with collective phenomena to a more social psychological consideration of the relationship between the collective and individual bases of social action. In this respect, it reflects an accommodation to the liberal concerns of institutional analysis. From this perspective, individuals as well as collectivities are understood to have qualities which contribute to the determination of thought and action. Forms of social exchange are regarded as the products of the relation between psychological and social determinations. A central concern of this social psychological theorizing has been the development of politics and society. (For varying examples of this perspective, see Mead, 1934; Fromm, 1960; Vygotsky, 1962, 1978; Unger, 1975;

Habermas, 1979, 1984; Giddens, 1979.)

Theorists of this persuasion turn to psychology in general, and psychological studies of ideology in particular, to elucidate the nature of personality structures and the subjective bases of meaning. They require a vision of individual activity which (at least to some degree) presents the person as an independent cause, a self-determining influence on social and political realities. Such a psychological vision has two benefits: (1) it defines a psychological causality whose dialectical relation to social causality may be explored in an attempt to understand the dynamics of social transformation, and (2) it defines a concept of humanity and possibly a direction to human development which is independent of culture and history.

The belief systems research offers very little to theorists with these interests. While the view of political beliefs as internally incoherent and externally determined is at least sympathetic with the assumptions of an orthodox sociological perspective, it offers nothing to a perspective which seeks to understand the integrated and self-determining properties of human social reasoning. Moreover, even the normative conception of reasoning which guides the belief systems research, that of rational processing, is of no value. This is true for two reasons. First, the structural qualities of 'rationality' have never been articulated by those conducting the research. Rather than specifying the relations and objects of rational thought, researchers have relied on some loose, commonsense notions of what it means to be rational. Second, even if such a theoretical elaboration of the concept of rationality were offered, it would be of little use to theorists who presume a dialectical or mutually constructive interrelationship between the psychological and social construction of meaning. Such a presumption necessitates a recognition that thought does not have a singular existence, but rather that it may take several forms (there may be various rationalities) which are sociohistorically relative.

Epistemological considerations and conclusions

It is essential to note that the target of our criticism is not any particular piece of research, but the general approach taken by all the belief systems research. Underlying this approach is a certain shared epistemological understanding based on the Lockean tradition. Two assumptions are central: (1) that reasoning consists of an awareness of particular phenomena and the determination of the relations which exist among them – thus, it is a subjective process which is mediated by objective circumstance; and (2) that all individuals reason in fundamentally the same way – some individuals may be quicker or some more educated, but they all perceive and process information similarly. Only if these assumptions are accepted do the concepts and methods adopted in the belief systems approach make sense. In an important sense, the belief systems research may be considered an application of a Lockean epistemology to the empirical study of political ideology and public opinion.

That these two assumptions do in fact provide the epistemological foundation for the belief systems research is best illustrated by considering each assumption and the specific orienting presuppositions it suggests. For brevity's sake, the two assumptions and their associated conceptual and methodological presuppositions are simply listed below.

First Assumption   Reasoning involves an awareness of phenomena and the establishment of the relations which exist among them.

A   Consequences for concept definition

   1 Reasoning begins with the awareness of particular phenomena which are represented as ideas. These ideas have meaning by virtue of the relationship to the objective phenomena they represent. In this sense, ideas have significance independent of their subjectively defined relationship to one another. Consequently, political thought may be conceived to consist of specific elements (e.g., idea-elements or beliefs) which have meaning independent of the relationship they have to one another in any given person's mind.

   2 Because reasoning involves the establishing of relations among the elemental beliefs being considered, it results in a weave of interrelated beliefs. Therefore, an individual's political thought may be defined to be a system of beliefs.

   3 Because reasoning requires an awareness of phenomena and is guided by the observation of how these phenomena are objectively interrelated, the nature of any particular belief system may be explained with reference to the information to which the individual holding those beliefs has been exposed.

B   Consequences for research design

   1 Because the relationships among beliefs are externally mediated and insofar as the culture defines politics to be a discrete area of concern, political thinking can be studied by examining the associations forged among only those beliefs which the culture defines as political. In this context, the

domain of beliefs examined may be expanded if empirical investigation demonstrates strong association between these political beliefs and other nonpolitical beliefs. Such an association would not, however, be expected to exist.

2 Because beliefs have an objective (or intersubjective) definition, they may be investigated without regard for any subjective variation in their essential meaning. Thus, political belief systems may be explored using non-interpretative methods such as short-answer surveys.

3 Because beliefs are systematically interrelated and independently meaningful, belief systems may be described both in terms of their relational structure (i.e., their constraint, their range and the dimensions around which that constraint is organized) and in terms of the specific beliefs related. Consequently, the empirical study of political belief systems should include the examination of the correlation among beliefs (dimensions may be defined or discovered through factor analytical techniques) and through the analysis of the content of beliefs.

Second Assumption All individuals reason in fundamentally the same way.

A Consequences for concept definition

1 The quality of the associations made or the understanding of the core meaning of specific idea-elements may be assumed to be the same for all. Hence little concern need be shown for issues of basic comprehension or reasoning capacity.

2 All belief systems have the same essential relational qualities – the same form of connection, necessity and non-contradiction. Therefore, a single set of definitions may be used to characterize the formal quality of all belief systems. They all may be characterized in terms of their inter-attitude constraint.

3 Considered in the light of the first assumption (that reasoning involves awareness and relation), this second assumption allows that individual differences in political belief will exist. These are, however, understood to involve differences in the particular associations forged among idea-elements and/or in the specific content of the idea-elements themselves. These differences are explained in terms of the variation in the environments to which individuals are exposed and in terms of the variation in the nature of their exposure to those environments.

B Consequences for the design of empirical research.

1 If the researcher is familiar with the subjects' political environment, understanding of the meaning of subjects' responses may be assumed. Hence, correlations among items may be interpreted with confidence. Similarly, the surface or apparent content of responses to short-answer questions may be regarded as direct indications of their meaning.

2 Belief systems of individuals who share a common political environment may be studied by aggregating responses across individuals. The results may be used to depict how the typical member of that community thinks.

3 Within a given political environment, differences in belief systems may be examined with respect to demographic factors (e.g., class, education and race) which affect the nature of the individuals' exposure to and involvement in politics. These differences will be substantive. To the degree to which some individuals' thought appears to be qualitatively different, their thought will be viewed as degenerate or incomplete.

In sum, our critique of the belief system research applies quite generally. In so doing, it extends to the epistemological foundation of that research. As questions are raised regarding the adequacy of the approach, so they are raised regarding the appropriateness of the underlying epistemology upon which that approach depends.

DIRECTIONS FOR FUTURE RESEARCH

Our review suggests that the belief systems approach is not a satisfactory one. It fails in three critical respects: (1) it does not generate appropriate and unambiguous evidence; (2) it does not offer concepts which are sufficiently powerful to allow for theoretically informed generalization and prediction; and (3) it does not offer a theory of political thinking which is of heuristic value to political science. Throughout, it has been suggested that these shortcomings do not stem from the inappropriate or inadequate application of the belief systems approach. Rather, they reflect basic conceptual and methodological limitations of the approach itself.

The question then is what alternative theory of political thinking would provide more fruitful direction for empirical research. A general answer is offered here. It does not include the formulation of a particular theoretical position or a specific method for conducting research. Rather, a set of requirements are specified which *any* theory of political thinking must meet if it is to yield a more satisfactory basis for the study of ideology. An attempt is made to build on the lessons of the belief systems research and delineate what a theory of political thinking must be like if it is to: (1) lead to the gathering of more adequate empirical evidence, (2) provide concepts which have greater theoretical power, and (3) contribute to the general study of politics.

Quality of the evidence

In the review of the evidence generated by the belief systems research, two key problems are identified: one of interpretation and one of coverage. Any alternative theory of ideology must orient the design of future empirical research so as to ensure these problems are properly addressed. To do so, it must provide a framework in which the significance of the two problems is readily understood.

Consider first the problem of interpretation. The difficulty here is the inherent ambiguity of the data collected. Subjects' ideological statements or survey responses are susceptible to multiple plausible interpretations. Earlier, I concluded that this is the result of a characteristic lack of attention to methodological issues related to possible problems in interpreting people's responses. Going one step further, I suggest this lack of attention reflects a theoretical position in which the subjective dimension of the construction of meaning is denied or ignored and the potential problems associated with the intersubjective communication of that meaning are regarded as inconsequential. This theoretical position is itself based on the epistemological assumption that personal statements are meaningful by virtue of their relation to their objective (or intersubjectively defined) referents. The claim here is that because meaning is objectively (or intersubjectively) determined, each individual's meanings are pieced together by building on a ground common to all. Given this common ground, the basic sense of one person's meaning may be readily comprehended by another person.

The foregoing analysis suggests that in order to generate less ambiguous data, the design of future research must reflect an appreciation of the problem of interpreting what people say and do. This requires the adoption of an epistemology which stipulates that the construction of meaning is, at least in part, a subjective act. Only on such a foundation would it be possible to build a theory of political thinking which clarifies how objective or intersubjectively defined realities are appropriated by individuals and then redefined according to the terms of their own personal ways of understanding. This, in turn, would provide a basis for determining how, in the course of empirical research, these understandings could be evoked and then decoded. The requirements of interpretation could be delineated, an appropriate unit of empirical analysis could be defined and an effective method for gathering the relevant data could be designed.

In addition to the problem of interpretation, the belief systems research is also faced with the related problem of coverage. The difficulty here is not the ambiguity of the data, but rather their inadequacy as a basis for generating a full and coherent description of how most people think about politics. In my view, this problem stems from the application of a mistaken epistemological assumption – that the 'sense' of all individuals is 'common' or, in other words, that everyone thinks in fundamentally the same way.

To offer a more complete account of the variety of people's political thinking, research on ideology must begin with the awareness that the structure of thinking, its form or logic, may vary from person to person. Oriented by this epistemological assumption, a theory of ideology may be constructed which focuses on individuals and the possibly different ways in which they may think about and understand politics. In this context, it is important to remember that the 'commonsense' perspective of the belief systems research does not deny the fact that individuals have different political points of view. Rather, it emphasizes that these differences are substantive (differences in preference and information) and are a product of socio-cultural influences. This line of thinking must be supplemented by an understanding that differences in political thinking may be qualitative and reflect basic differences in how people reason. This understanding can then serve as a basis for designing empirical research so that these differences may be fully observed and properly interpreted.

Considered together, the problems of interpretation and coverage encountered in the belief systems research suggest that future research must be guided by a theory in which political thinking is defined as a meaning-making activity whose parameters or logic are subjectively determined and may vary from individual to individual. The methodological implications of adopting such a theoretical position are clear. First, rather than focusing on individuals' specific preferences or bits of information, the researcher must collect data on how individuals define, integrate and use information when making sense of their political environment. Second, rather than inferring how the 'prototypical' individual thinks on the basis of the analysis of aggregate data, the researcher must examine individuals singly and infer how each thinks on the basis of his or her performance across a variety of tasks. Adoption of the first guideline ensures that future research will yield data which are less ambiguous. Adoption of the second ensures that future research will provide a basis for description which more fully captures the various ways in which people think about politics.

Conceptual power

A second limitation of the belief systems approach is that it does not provide concepts which are powerful. Researchers have been unable to go beyond their data and predict people's beliefs even when circumstances are varied in the most trivial manner (e.g., the order in which questions are asked). This inability was linked to the fact that the belief systems approach does not provide any theoretical definition of the structure or logic of political belief. The question we must address here is why such a theoretical definition has not been forthcoming and what is required for one to be developed.

Like its view of political thinking, the belief system approach to theorizing is dictated by its underlying epistemology. It is oriented by the assumption that the basic elements of a phenomenon (in this case, political thinking) may be readily apprehended and that the relationships among these elements can be discovered through systematic observation. In this context, description is regarded as primarily an empirical activity, not a theoretical one. The initial definition of the elements and boundaries of the phenomenon is a matter of common sense. Concepts and definitions are then constructed by building on observations of these elements. In the end, descriptive concepts reflect how elements are observed to be associated with (or dissociated from) one another and explanatory concepts reflect the conditions under which these associations are observed to change over time. Composed of a loose aggregation of concepts which are themselves derived from specific observation, belief systems theory is fundamentally empirical.

What then is the potential power of concepts and theory generated in this manner? The key point is that theoretical claims regarding the links among beliefs (either at any moment or across time) are based solely on observation and, therefore, necessarily reflect particular situations observed at specific moments in time. As a result, these claims can be securely applied only to the empirical ground from which they sprung. There is no theoretical basis for determining whether they apply to any other situation or even whether they apply to the observed situation at another time. Lacking such a theoretical base, empirical strategies have been developed to facilitate general-ization. Thus, sampling procedures are utilized in an attempt to ensure that the observed characteristics of the sample can be used to describe the larger target population. Such a strategy cannot, however, yield a basis for generalizing from the population sampled to any other. More basic, it cannot solve the critical problem of determining whether the characteristic or dynamic properties of the target population (or the sample observed) will change or remain the same even over the shortest period of time. Empirical strategies fail here because it is not possible to sample time. Therefore, there can be no strictly empirical basis for extrapolating from the past to the future. In sum, given its epistemological base and the consequent manner in which theory is built, the belief systems concepts will necessarily lack generality or power.

The foregoing analysis of the power of belief systems theory draws on classical sources. It is a brief and partial reiteration of Hume's critique of Locke's epistemology (the epistemology which I have already claimed to underlie the belief systems research). My solution also follows classical direction, in this case, the direction set by Kant's response to Hume's skepticism. Thus, I reject the epistemology upon which both Locke's position and Hume's critique rely and assume that knowledge is not a mere reflection of an objective reality, but is a result of subjective definition. Adopting this perspective, I suggest that theory building has two essential characteristics. First, it is a creative activity. Theory is not derived from empirical observation. Rather, it is subjectively constructed and then imposed on the object to be observed. Second, theory building is essentially a formal activity. A theory defines the quality of both the elements of any objective phenomenon and the relations which may exist among them. In so doing, a theory structures the phenomena it seeks to explain. This is not to suggest that theories determine the content of empirical phenomena. Definition at this point is purely formal. It is only later, through a recursive process of empirical observation and theoretical elaboration, that descriptive and explanatory concepts are generated and claims regarding content are made.

Adopting this view, it is clear that any theory of ideology must begin with a general and formal definition of the structure and dynamic of political thinking. The constituent elements of political thinking must be defined and the kind of relationships which may exist among those elements must be specified. In this manner, abstract categories of description and explanation are elaborated. Empirical observation is then oriented accordingly. Both the object to be observed and the appropriate methods of observation are theoretically determined. In this context, observation is regarded as an inherently theory-driven and necessarily interpretative enterprise.

Two good examples of such theorizing about individuals' thinking are offered by psychoanalytic and Piagetian developmental theory.[8] Piagetian theory will be discussed in the following chapter. Here, we will focus on psychoanalytic theory. It begins with an abstract definition of the nature of psychological functioning. At times the focus is on the resolution of libidinal drives. At other times the focus is on the relation between Eros and Thanatos. In either case, the general theory then informs the formation of descriptive and explanatory concepts. Thus, concept formation focuses on the suggested consequences of this underlying functioning, the cognitive-emotional complexes which emerge during the course of development. In this light, the theory delineates the kind of phenomena to be observed and the terms in which they are to be interpreted. In the course of empirical observation, the abstract and general understanding offered by the theory is elaborated as a set of specific claims (e.g., the relationship between certain neurotic behaviors and the pathological resolution of developmental crises). It is important to note that even at this level of content-specific claims, the definition and observation of content are theory-driven.

The question remains whether or not theory built in this alternative way will be powerful. To answer, it is important to remember that this kind of theory is, in the first instance, developed without reference to any specific observation. Formally specified rather than empirically derived, the theory yields a definitional structure which applies to the totality of possibly relevant situations. It applies equally well both to phenomena currently observed and to phenomena yet to be observed. In this sense, theory of this kind will necessarily be powerful. This is not to suggest that observation does not guide inference. Insofar as a theory provides a differentiated definition of phenomena, it will be necessary to establish empirically the theoretical category to which a specific case belongs. For example, a theory may suggest that there are different ways to think about politics. To draw conclusions about a particular person, it will first be necessary to determine empirically what type of thinker the person is. Once this is done, however, it will be possible to deduce from the theory how that person may think about a variety of topics and under a variety of conditions. Because it is formal and deductive rather than empirical and inductive, theorizing of this kind can be powerful and self-legitimating in a way that empirical theorizing about belief systems cannot.

Heuristic value

Our final concern is to outline the form which a theory of political thinking must take if it is to contribute to the pursuit of the general aims of political inquiry. We begin with the recognition that political thinking can be depicted in a variety of ways. Each of these depictions may, in some sense, reflect the reality of political thinking. Some, however, will be more useful than others. As suggested earlier, the relative utility of any particular one depends on the political theoretical perspective from which it is evaluated. In the critique of the belief systems research, two such perspectives, the institutional and the social structural, were discussed. Here, we will consider the kind of theory of ideology which would be of interest to each.

Viewed from the institutional perspective, politics consists of the governmental or quasi-governmental regulation of individuals and the efforts of those individuals to influence the manner in which they are regulated. Mediating both the regulatory impact of law and public policy on the one hand and the initiatives of the citizenry on the other, is reason. To contribute to such an analysis, a theory of ideology must focus directly on the nature of the reasoning inherent in political understanding and judgment. Adopting such a focus is not, however, itself enough. Institutional analysts assume that political reasoning is rational and conduct their research accordingly. Therefore, only if a theory of ideology challenges this assumption and illuminates the limited and irrational qualities of people's political reasoning, can it make a significant and novel contribution. If the research can go further and shed light on the nature of this limited or irrational reasoning, that is if it can specify the structure of people's irrationality, then its contribution will be immense. All theoretical and empirical analyses of governmental regulation, political behavior and institutional development would have to be recrafted in light of this new understanding.

In this context, it is worth remembering the lesson of the belief systems research. In the early years, the research offered evidence (albeit of an indirect and ambiguous kind) which did undermine the legitimacy of the institutional analyst's assumption of political rationality. As a result, it received the attention of the entire political science community. Unfortunately, having raised doubts regarding the assumption that thought was rational, later research failed to provide much insight into the non-rational or irrational nature of thought. What information the research did offer was largely negative (how people did *not* think rather than how they *did* think) and sketchy. The elaborated definition of political reasoning required for the analysis of the implications of this finding for the functioning and development of political institutions was not forthcoming. As a result, the attention initially received by the belief systems research has not been sustained and its impact on institutional analysis has been limited.

Politics may also be viewed from a social structural perspective. Here it is assumed that both politics and individual political actors are derivative, determined by a common underlying structure. Political ideology is regarded as an appropriate object of study, but only insofar as it is understood to be a social representation (a collective product) and is analyzed with regard to its place in a larger societal context. Given this definition of politics and ideology, it is clear that a theory of ideology which focuses on individuals can only be considered fruitless and misleading. Because an individual's political thinking is only a fragmentary, momentary reflection of a collective ideology, it will exhibit neither the coherence nor the reliability required of an object of theoretical description. Furthermore, insofar as an individual's political thinking is merely a reflection of a collective ideology which is itself a product of collective forces, it does not make sense to focus on the qualities of individuals when seeking to explain the politics of either individuals themselves or the group of which they are a part.[9]

In sum, a psychologically oriented theory of ideology cannot be of heuristic value to analysis based on a sociological conception of politics. However, this is not to say that a psychological theory is necessarily without consequence for such an analysis. Integral to a sociological conception of politics are certain psychological assumptions. The two most critical are: (1) that an individual's thinking is not coherent unto itself; and (2) that an individual's political thoughts are externally rather than internally determined. To the degree to which these assumptions are not true, it may be argued that individuals exist (at least to some degree) apart from the collective or interactive environment and, therefore, that they are not simply determined by it. Given this independence, it may also be argued that individuals direct their own action and thus constrain and direct the collective life in which they participate. Through argument of this kind, the central theses of the sociological view of politics may be challenged.

To make this challenge, a theory of ideology must offer an explication of the internally coherent and self-determining qualities of individuals' political thinking. Moreover, it must be made clear how these qualities of political thinking shape the way individuals interact and, thereby, contribute to the determination of the structure of social and political life. Such a psychological theory of ideology raises a host of interesting and very difficult questions for sociological theorizing. As we shall see, the very sense of sociological description and explanation is called into question.

Sociological description focuses on the norms and institutions of social and political life. While these are understood to be realized through the regulation of interpersonal exchange and, therefore, through the thought and action of individuals, they are assumed to be collectively defined and constituted. Description focuses therefore on this collective definition. The introduction of strong psychological claims into this analysis significantly alters the problems confronted when describing political phenomena. The claim that thought and action are psychologically defined suggests that description must focus on individual rather than collective representations. Moreover, when the claim that quality of reasoning and perception may vary between individuals is also introduced, the analytical consequences extend beyond the description of representations to the characterizations of sociopolitical realities themselves. Insofar as institutions are realized in the regulation of action and people's understandings of those institutions and their purposes vary significantly, then the sociological assumption that social life consists of a single coherent form must be called into question. Indeed, psychological considerations lead to a very different conclusion – that social reality is a multidimensional phenomenon, a confluence of psychologically constructed realities. In this light, the sociologist's task becomes one of constructing a description which reflects this complexity.

As the introduction of strong psychological claims call into question sociological description, so it calls into question sociological explanation. The sociologist presumes that social causation proceeds along the following lines: social structure defines the parameters of social exchange which in turn delimit the possibilities and constraints imposed on individual action. Thus, the concerns of individuals are conceived as largely derivative and explanation focuses on the structure and dynamic of collective causes. Present social circumstances and historical trends are interpreted accordingly. The introduction of psychological assumptions transforms the analytical premises of the sociologist's explanations. Individual thought and action are not considered derivative but determining. In this light, interpersonal exchange and social structures must be explained with reference to the quality and direction of individual action.

As suggested by the foregoing, a theory of individuals' political thinking can only serve a sociology of politics by providing an analytical counterpoint, one which forces a broader and more complex vision of the polity. Indeed, some contemporary sociological theory has moved in this direction. In so doing, it has sought to establish a truly social psychological base for social and political theory. Among the most prominent examples are the recent writings of Jürgen Habermas and Anthony Giddens. Central to this social psychological theorizing is the claim that political thought and action are structured by both collective and individual level forces. These forces dialectically interact to delimit the form and substance of political life. In Giddens' work, this is elaborated as the recursive interplay between agent and structure (1979). In Habermas' project, the dialectic is between the cognitive and ethical constructions of the individual on the one hand and the structure of social discourse imposed by society on the other (1979, 1984).

To contribute to such an analysis, a theory of ideology must be able to satisfy three metatheoretical requirements. First, it must conceive of the political thinker as the structural cause of his or her own political understanding. As I have already argued, this is the only way in which political thought and action can be defined as an importantly psychological product. Second, a theory of ideology must offer an explication of the relation between individual and collective constructions of political meaning. In so doing, it must supplement (or better, integrate) its psychological definition of political thinking with a delineation of how that thinking is socially determined. Third, and related to the second, a theory of idelogy which seeks to explicate the social psychological nature of its object must create a vocabulary which captures both aspects of that object. That is, a single theoretical language must be created which can be used to describe both the psychological and social structural character of political phenomena.

To conclude, it should be noted that the attempt to craft a social psychology of politics remains an unfinished project. The attitude psychology underlying the belief systems approach has contributed little. It fails the first requirement, that the individual be conceived as the structure or cause of his own understanding. Other psychologies have contributed more. The most influential has been the psychoanalytical approach of Freud and his followers. More recently, the developmental psychology of Jean Piaget is beginning to have an impact. These approaches have contributed precisely because they offer an interpretation of thinking as a coherent, self-determined product. Despite their advantages, neither approach provides a satisfactory basis for the construction of social psychological theory. Both fail to recognize the self-constituting and constructive qualities of a collectivity and, therefore, neither adequately accounts for the social determinants of thinking. Social influences may be noted, but they are rendered theoretically peripheral and uninteresting. The result is a psychological reductionism (for classical examples, see Freud, 1972; Piaget, 1965a, 1966). The contributions of individual and society to the construction of political life must be balanced as well as integrated. Insofar as a theory of ideology contributes to the achievement of this end, it may provide the basis for the development of a truly social psychological understanding of politics.

SUMMARY AND CONCLUSIONS

Discussion began with the claim that the mainstream research on political ideology, the belief systems research, has failed to progress. The research was then reviewed in an attempt to discover its limitations, learn from them and suggest a more fruitful approach. To start with, the belief systems research was described in its own terms. From this perspective, it was argued that it is a remarkably homogeneous body of research with widespread agreement over basic descriptive and explanatory concepts. Although there is some debate over research method, this debate only revolves around issues of appropriate application of commonly accepted methodological principles. It was suggested that underlying this broad agreement on how to study ideology is a shared epistemology – a neo-Lockian mix of an empiricist concept of knowledge, an atomist concept of meaning and a universalist concept of human reasoning. In fact, the collage of concepts and methods adopted in the belief systems research may be regarded as a theoretical expression and empirical operationalization of this epistemological perspective.

Having described the belief systems research, a critical assessment was then made. Basic questions were raised regarding the quality of the evidence provided, the theoretical power of its descriptive and explanatory concepts, and the value of its contribution to the general study of politics. In response to these questions, the following conclusions were reached: (1) The data gathered are not satisfactory. They reveal little of what most people do and what they do reveal is inherently ambiguous. (2) The orienting conceptualization of political thought is not, and cannot be, theoretically powerful. Guided by these concepts, researchers have had little success in going beyond the data in hand. More importantly, an analysis of the underlying theory suggests that it cannot engender concepts which are sufficiently powerful to allow for the requisite generalizations and predictions. (3) The contribution of the belief systems research to general political inquiry is limited. Viewed from the perspective of an institutional conception of politics, the research initially provided some intriguing evidence. However, like institutional analysis itself, the research made assumptions regarding political reasoning rather than investigating its nature. Consequently, little of additional interest was provided and the initial discoveries which were of interest remain incompletely understood. Viewed from a social structural perspective, the belief systems research is at worst distorting and misguided and at best insignificant. At its worst, the methodological individualism of the research obscures the true nature and causes of both ideology in particular and politics in general. At its best, thirty years' research only succeeded in demonstrating what the social structural analyst knew at the outset.

In this light, it was concluded that the belief systems approach does not provide a fruitful framework for the study of political ideology. Significantly, the failures of the belief systems research were not explained as the result of insufficient ingenuity or effort on the part of individual researchers. Rather, they were understood to reflect basic inadequacies in the concepts and methods characteristic of the approach. Ultimately, doubts were raised regarding the epistemology upon which these concepts and methods depend. It was suggested that following the logic and assumptions of this epistemology will necessarily lead to the kinds of problems and inadequacies encountered in the belief systems research. In this context, the conclusion was drawn that the belief systems approach must be abandoned in its entirety and a radically different approach must be adopted.

An attempt was then made to determine what a more adequate approach to the study of political ideology must be like. The question posed was that of what form a theory of ideology must take if it is to yield (1) better data, (2) more powerful concepts, and (3) a greater contribution to the study of politics. With regard to collecting better data, it was concluded that empirical research must be designed to reveal how individuals define, search for and use information when seeking to understand or judge political phenomena. To provide the requisite foundation for this kind of research, a supporting theory of ideology must be developed. It must define political thinking to be a meaning-making activity and suggest the ways in which the parameters or logic of that activity may vary from person to person. With regard to constructing more powerful concepts, it was concluded that a more formalistic and structural approach to theory building must be adopted. The theory which is produced must then provide definitions of both the object that empirical research will address and the methods that may be employed. Finally, with regard to contributing to the study of politics, it was concluded that a theory of ideology must define ideology (at least partly) in dynamic psychological terms. Rather than concentrating on attitudes or beliefs, the focus must be on the process whereby political understandings are constructed and judgments are made. This process must itself be defined, at least in the first instance, as a subjectively directed and self-structured activity.

In sum, our review suggests that the future study of political ideology must adopt a radically different approach. A new epistemological orientation must be adopted. Thinking must be viewed as a structuring, subjective activity. Further, it must be recognized that the nature of this activity may vary from person to person and, therefore, so may the structure of their understandings. In this context, it is also necessary to recognize that the activity of thinking operates upon and represents phenomena which are real and interpersonal. As a result, it is shaped by objective and real constraints as well as subjective ones. To fully understand thinking, the relationship between these external and internal structural regulations must be understood.

Building on this base, a new theory of ideology must be developed. To begin with, ideology must be viewed as an understanding, the result of reasoning about political phenomena. It must be regarded as a subjectively constructed and a structurally coherent way of defining and making sense of specific people, issues and events. In this context, possible differences in ideology must be explicated. These differences must be characterized in formal structural terms and explained with reference to differences in the structure of the sociopolitical environment to which individuals are exposed. Such a theory of the structure and development of ideology must be formulated with reference to some concept of the relationship between the subjective construction of political understandings on the one hand and the interpersonal or collective construction of political realities on the other.

The design and methodological sensibilities of empirical research on ideology must reflect the aforementioned theoretical considerations. The first goal is to discover the way in which different people think about politics. Empirical research must be designed accordingly. The focus must be on individual persons, rather than on people in the aggregate. Given the theoretical interest in structure rather than content, it is clear that the empirical investigation of each person must be an interpretative enterprise. An attempt must be made to go beyond the individual claims a person makes and discover the logic which ties one to another and, at the same time, to reach behind the cultural definition of the terms a person uses and uncover their subjectively constructed meaning. Methods of collecting data must be crafted in this light. Interviews and experiments must be designed so as to ensure (a) that all subjects are provided with the opportunity to demonstrate how they make sense of and attempt to resolve a problem or judge an issue and, (b) that the investigator is provided with the opportunity to probe subjects' reasoning whenever there is uncertainty about the connections being made. The most important methodological concern here is the need to collect sufficiently rich and unambiguous data from each subject to allow for the requisite interpretative analysis. Given the assumption that an individual's thought mediates all environmental influences similarly, worries regarding the comparability of stimuli to which different subjects are exposed become secondary. Therefore, the investigator is free to modify the interview or experiment so as to maximize each subject's opportunity to reveal the logic of his thought.

The second goal is the explanation of the genesis of political thinking and the examination of the relationship between the structure of individuals' political thought and the nature of the environments to which they are exposed. The research strategy here will reflect more traditional concerns regarding experimental or quasi-experimental control over environments and an examination of their impact on a population of subjects. There is, however, one way in which this research diverges from convention. Both dependent and independent variables must be defined in structural terms. Thus, both individuals' thought and the environments to which they are exposed must be interpretatively defined prior to any causal or correlational analysis.

In the following chapter, the epistemology and cognitive psychology of Jean Piaget are presented. Although never articulated as a theory of ideology, the approach he adopts meets most of the requirements we have outlined here. In chapter 4, an attempt is made to build on his work and construct a new and more fruitful framework for the study of ideology.

3
The Structural Developmental Approach: A Piagetian View of Epistemology and Psychology

Our review of the current research on political ideology suggests that it has reached the limits of its fruitfulness. For further progress to be made, a new epistemological orientation must be adopted. The empiricism, atomism and universalism underlying the current research must give way to a view which focuses on the subjective and stuctural qualities of thinking and captures how these may differ from one person to the next. As a first step in this direction, the genetic epistemology of Jean Piaget is introduced. His view meets many of the requirements outlined in chapter 2 and therefore provides a good basis upon which to build. Despite its advantages, his epistemology is not completely satisfactory. It is built upon and amended in chapter 4.

Jean Piaget's psychological theory and research is widely recognized as among the most influential of this century. Less well known, however, is the fact that his work is as much epistemological as psychological. In fact, his psychology and epistemology depend on one another. Together, they represent a major departure from the conception of thinking and the theories of cognition and learning adopted in most of the research on political thought and behavior. Unaware of the fundamental difference of his epistemology, many social scientists who have sought to apply or interpret Piaget's psychology have unintentionally redefined it according to their own theoretical and epistemological presuppositions. To avoid this confusion, Piaget's epistemology is introduced in the context of other more familiar ones. The point here is not to offer a critical review, but rather to provide a basis for comparison. His position is presented first as a departure from these others and then in its own terms. Finally, its implications for the conduct of psychological research are considered.

CLASSICAL EPISTEMOLOGICAL QUESTIONS
AND ANSWERS: A PIAGETIAN PERSPECTIVE

Philosophical analysis of knowledge focuses both on its absolute nature and the process whereby it emerges. For the most part, it is oriented by two critical sets of distinctions: the absolute distinction between a person's understanding of the world and its real nature, and the dynamic distinction between the activity of learning and the state of knowledge. Accompanying these distinctions is a recognition of their unification: that of subjective meaning and objective reality in knowledge, and that of learning and knowledge in the process of coming to know. It is this awareness of these distinctions and unities that defines the problematic of most epistemological inquiry. Thus, the questions posed are: (1) Given the difference between subjective meaning and objective reality, how are we to understand their relation in knowledge? (2) Given the difference between learning and knowledge, how are we to understand their common participation in the process of coming to know?

In the speculative philosophy of the seventeenth and eighteenth centuries, these questions are answered by emphasizing unities and minimizing differences. For present purposes, we may distinguish two grand traditions of speculative analysis, Baconian and Cartesian. Despite their opposition, they employ a common strategy in the analysis of the absolute relationship between subjective meaning and objective reality. In both cases, analysis entails denying the distinctiveness of one element and reducing it to the terms of the other. In the Baconian or empiricist tradition, the subject–object distinction is overcome by assuming that people have direct experience of the reality of their environment. In this view, subjective understanding consists of bits of information which are 'given' to the individual as sense data. Meaning is thus a mere reflection of the reality to which it refers. The 'problem' of the unity of meaning and reality is resolved in that the former is simply determined by the latter. An opposing reduction and explication of the unity of subject and object is offered in the Cartesian tradition. From this perspective, it is the fact of subjective meaning or understanding which is given. Objective reality must be understood in light of its compatibility with the nature of human subjectivity. Thus, again the unity of meaning and reality is explicated by denying the difference between them.

This reductionist strategy is also evident in the speculative conception of the dynamic relation between the activity of learning and the state of knowledge. In the empiricist tradition, the unity of the process of coming to know is defined with regard to learning and thus as the incremental accumulation of bits of data gathered in the course of experience. As the product of this activity, knowledge consists of the set of accumulated observations and learned associations. It is thus defined in terms of learning. Those operating in the rationalist tradition offer a very different view. Within their framework, it is the state of knowledge which is primary. It is explicated with reference to its inherent organization or categories. These are assumed to be characteristic of all intellectual activity. In this context, the process of coming to know simply becomes one of elaborating pre-existing structures. Thus, activity of learning is defined in terms of the state of knowledge. In both cases, an understanding of the dynamic of knowledge is achieved by reducing one of its distinguished aspects, either the process or the final state, to the terms of the other.

Both speculative traditions find expression in the contemporary social sciences. The empiricist tradition underlies associationist or behavioral psychology. With its reduction of subject to object and knowledge to learning, it minimizes the role of grand theory and focuses on the experimental study of the effect of environments on behavior. Its impact on political science is evident in the study of political socialization and much of the work on attitudes. The rationalist tradition provides the underpinning for much of cognitive psychology, especially that which focuses on perception, transformational grammars and reasoning. Its impact on the social sciences is evident in a variety of ways, such as the rational actor modelling of economists and political scientists (e.g., Samuelson, 1938; Downs, 1957) and in the structuralism of Saussure (1977) and Levi-Strauss (e.g., 1963, 1966).

The problem of the unity of knowledge in light of the difference of its aspects has been dealt with rather differently in more contemporary analytical philosophy. The tendency here is to assume the unity of the aspects, but to predicate analysis on their difference and to defend their investigation in isolation. There is an acceptance of the relation between subjective meaning and objective reality in knowledge, but this is coupled with the recognition that this relation cannot be meaningfully analyzed. Meaning and reality are therefore left to be investigated separately. Meaning becomes the preserve of the philosopher and reality the preserve of the scientist. In this vein, a correspondent notion of truth is abandoned. To guide the analysis of meaning, new criteria of evaluation are invoked. Meaning is judged not with reference to objective fact, but rather with reference to what is commonly understood or agreed, that is, the common sense as revealed in language. [1]

In a similar vein, contemporary analysis is predicated on the assumption that meaning may be examined independently of the process whereby it is attained. The argument here is that a concept may be arrived at in a variety of ways and, therefore, exists independently of the manner in which it is attained. The analogy invoked is that of the distinction between the point of arrival at the end of the journey and the various paths which may be taken in getting there.[2] Again the terrain is divided between the philosopher and the scientist. The final product, meaning, is allocated to the philosopher, whereas the process, learning, is allocated to the scientist. The philosopher's task becomes one of explication and interpretation, and the scientist's task one of causal explanation.

Like its predecessor, contemporary analytical philosophy has also had its impact on contemporary social science. Most important, it is reflected in the self-conscious attempt to free empirical research from the philosophical vagaries of interpretation and moral judgment. The aim is a wholly objective, ahistorical, value-free research. This position has dominated the orientation of the American social sciences from the 1950s through to the present. The contemporary analytical view is also reflected in the way in which the social sciences tend to discriminate clearly between description and explanation. The former is generally regarded as a simple matter of access and the latter as the more theory-laden and difficult matter of analysis.[3]

Piaget's philosophical roots are dialectical and materialist. While not Marxist, he is perhaps best characterized as a Hegelian realist.[4] Consequently, his view of knowledge is quite different from those of the speculative or contemporary analytical philosophers. On the one hand, he accepts the emphasis on unity found in speculative philosophy but argues against the reductionism to which this leads in the Cartesian and Baconian traditions. While rejecting the solution offered by both these traditions, he does see each as having its analytical advantages. He appreciates the realism and geneticism of empiricism and its emphasis on historical analysis and the impact of environments. He also appreciates the idealism and structuralism of rationalism and its emphasis on interpretative analysis and the qualities of mind. However, given the partial nature of each view, he abandons both as inadequate and distorting. He criticizes empiricism as a 'geneticism without structure' and rationalism as a 'structuralism without genesis'.[5] This extends to his consideration of the psychologies which have emerged out of these two speculative traditions. While allowing the importance of culture and learning, he rejects the atomism of associationist psychologies. Similarly, while acknowledging the value of an interpretative analysis of mind, he rejects the nativism of structural psychologies.[6]

At the same time, Piaget does not adopt the more current analytical position. While he accepts that the difference between meaning and reality must be acknowledged, he denies that this difference justifies ignoring their unity in knowledge and conducting the investigation of each in isolation. Piaget argues that the nature of analytical philosophical investigation limits its ability to address the problem of the relation between meaning and reality. In his view, however, this recognition does not lead to the denial of the question, but rather to a denial of the method which cannot properly pose or answer it. Thus, he claims that the complexity of knowledge as a unity of differences requires that analysis be genetic as well as structural and empirical as well as philosophical. Consequently, he rejects a purely analytical investigation of meaning as inadequate and stipulates that 'the first principle of genetic epistemology is to take psychology seriously.'[7] Similarly, he rejects empirical psychologies which attempt to divorce themselves from philosophical analysis. Because the apperception of reality is infused with meaning and judgement, experimental research is necessarily interpretative and evaluative. If it is to be well designed, these aspects of research must be recognized and properly taken into account.[8]

It is important to note that Piaget's critique of analytical philosophy extends beyond the denial of its assumptions to a rejection of its method of analysis. His argument is that knowledge is at once meaningful and real. It is a complex whole, a unity of different and independent parts. Philosophical inquiry, by its very nature, is unable to capture the nature of knowledge in its full complexity. It is handicapped in two respects. First, and less essential, it is based on the philosopher's own observations and reflections. Most often he is confined to his own knowing and a relatively unsystematic exposure to those of a few around him. As such, he loses sight of the possible differences in the forms which knowledge takes among persons of different ages and cultural backgrounds. Drawing on a limited sample, his analyses will necessarily be too narrow.[9] Second, and more fundamental, Piaget also argues that the very structure of philosophical investigation has a determining effect on the philosopher's rendering of his object and, in the case of knowledge, this rendering is inadequate. This is a more fundamental and sophisticated criticism and deserves closer examination.

Piaget's position is based on the claim that how one knows determines what one knows. This may be illustrated by the comparison of the efforts of two men, one blind and one deaf, to describe a bird. Limited to his hearing, the blind man describes the bird in terms of its song while the deaf man, limited to his sight, describes the bird in terms of its appearance. In each case, the men render the real object of their investigation according to the manner in which they come to know it. The case of the analytical philosopher is no different. He understands an object by rendering it meaningful. That is, he knows it by defining it according to the common sense and seeing the interrelationship among its various aspects so distinguished. Like the deaf man, the philosopher is bound by his method. The former's understanding is determined by his vision; the latter's by his systematic and common definition. As the deaf man denies or ignores the audible aspects of his object, the philosopher denies or ignores those aspects of his object which are uncommon or unsystematic (e.g., that which is apparently idiosyncratic, childish or irrational).

In this light, it is clear that the validity of one's method of inquiry depends on its relation to the reality of that to be known. The structure of the inquiry must be compatible with the structure of its object. To the degree to which it is not, the real nature of the object will be distorted or its existence will be overlooked entirely. For example, in the case of the blind man seeking to understand the nature of a symphony, the mode of inquiry and the real object share a common essence, sound. Therefore, his mode of inquiry may be considered appropriate to his object, and valid. In the case of the blind man's attempt to understand the nature of a stage play or pantomine, it is clear that his mode of inquiry is inadequate to his object. In the first instance, that of the play, the blind man's research will produce a reductionistic and thus distorted view of his object. In the second instance, that of the pantomine, the blind man's methods are entirely incompatible with the nature of his object and therefore it will be missed entirely.

Similarly, the philosopher's analysis may be more or less appropriate depending on the nature of his object. From a Piagetian perspective, it is too narrow. The limits of philosophical analysis are apparent when its structure is compared to that of knowledge itself. Philosophical analysis involves the construction of a definitional system. It entails a complementary definition of the whole to be examined and its component parts. The coherence of the whole is defined by the integration of its parts and the nature of each part is defined by its articulation in the whole. In constructing such a definitional system, philosophical analysis is guided by its companion criteria of meaning and non-contradiction.

The structure of knowledge is very different from that of the meaning constructed in the course of philosophical analysis. This is apparent at both macro and micro levels of definition. At the macro level, that of the whole to be examined, Piaget claims that knowledge does not necessarily consist of an integrated, systemic unity. It incorporates both an objective reality and a subjective meaning under a single umbrella. These two dimensions are not only defined by their relation in knowledge, they are also independent and self-constituting. As a result, they may not be defined elements of an integrated whole, but rather self-defining forces which may differ from and contradict one another. As the conjunction of these different and possibly opposing aspects, knowledge does not consist of the simple integration of a philosophical system. The incompatibility of the structure of philosophical analysis and the nature of knowledge is also apparent at the micro level, that of the elements of the whole. The complex nature of the unity of knowledge implies that its component aspects, objective reality and subjective meaning, do not have a simple existence. On the one hand, each is articulated in the whole of knowledge and its nature is determined accordingly. On the other, each exists unto itself and its nature is self-determined. Determined in this complex manner, the components of knowledge have a dual (and possibly self-contradictory) nature and not the single and simple form of the elements defined in the course of philosophical analysis.

In this light, the sense of our earlier claim that the philosophical study of knowledge entails the reduction of knowledge to meaning may be elaborated and its implications made clearer. The philosopher's reduction and distortion of knowledge is a result of his description of it as a system. Bound by his systematic form of inquiry, he cannot account for both the unity of knowledge and the difference between its meaning and reality. As mentioned earlier, he must therefore proceed either by denying the difference of the aspects of knowledge (as in speculative philosophy) or by ignoring the encompassing quality of its unity (as in modern analytical philosophy). In either case, the critical question regarding the nature of knowledge, how meaning and reality are related in knowledge given the nature of their difference, is never addressed or answered.

It is with these considerations in mind that Piaget rejects the efforts of philosophers as narrow in their scope and inappropriate to their object. This is not to deny completely the value of philosophical inquiry and the study of meaning. Rather, it is to stipulate that the study of knowledge must examine the interface between meaning and reality and therefore place itself at the intersection of philosophy and empirical psychology. Piaget views his own theoretical and methodological position as interposed between empiricism and rationalism on the one hand and between analytical philosophy and cognitive psychology on the other. His aim is to avoid the ambiguity normally associated with such attempts at integration and to present a tractable conception of the whole. This is elaborated in a complementary fashion in his redefinition of epistemology as genetic epistemology and his reconceptualization of psychology as a developmental science. [10]

GENETIC EPISTEMOLOGY AND CONSTRUCTIVISM

Piaget's aim is to explicate the nature of knowledge in its full complexity. To this end, he attempts to maintain the distinction between subjective meaning and objective reality. He acknowledges their difference and self-defining qualities. At the same time, he recognizes the fact of the unity of these diverse aspects in the totality of knowledge. In this regard, he recognizes that not only are meaning and reality externally related to one another, but that this relation penetrates the constitution of both. To reconcile the distinctiveness of meaning and reality with their unification in knowledge, Piaget offers a genetic conception of knowledge.

Knowledge as an absolute: resolving the dilemma

The philosophical approaches to the study of knowledge discussed earlier are predicated on the assumption of either the unity of knowledge or the distinctiveness of its aspects. The problem is that they are unable to incorporate both at once. In Piaget's view, the key to the problem is the definition of knowledge in absolute terms. This is a critical mistake both because it creates an insuperable obstacle to the conceptualization of the complexity of knowledge and because it ignores the evidence of the evolution of knowledge in the history of science and in the development of the child. [11] Piaget's solution to the problem is to define knowledge in dynamic terms. He abandons the notion of knowledge as a state and instead argues 'that knowledge is essentially active.' [12]

To develop Piaget's position, we begin with a preliminary definition of knowledge in light of the aspects it unifies. On the one hand, knowledge incorporates an objective reality. In Piaget's view, physical reality has a structure which regulates how objects can act on one another. [13] Knowledge pertains to and reflects this objective action. As a result, it has an operative or transformational quality and is delimited by the structure of the physical universe which the individual acts upon and observes. On the other hand, knowledge incorporates a subjective dimension. It reflects the abilities and aims of the individual and his attempts to understand and operate on the world. In this regard, it is meaningful and purposive. Taken in its entirety, knowledge is an activity which is both objectively and subjectively directed and therefore at once real and meaningful. The unity of these two aspects is ensured by the singularity of the individual's purposive action in which both are manifest.

As the totality or unity of knowledge reflects the different aspects it includes, so these different aspects must reflect their articulation in that totality. Thus, our concept of the reality and meaning of knowledge must be redefined. As incorporated in purposive action, the reality of intellectual activity is not simply the product of reality itself. While constituted by reality and bound by the structural determination inherent in it, intellectual activity is a differentiated aspect. It is limited by its subjective coordination and direction, and thus its meaning. In other words, intellectual activity cannot be more than what the individual is capable of thinking and doing.

As the reality of knowledge is infused with its meaning, so that meaning must be infused with its reality. Thus, in Piaget's conception, meaning cannot simply be defined as a subjectively determined relational system. To view it in these terms would be to lose the distinction between fantasy and knowledge. The latter reflects the articulation of meaning in the whole of knowledge and its consequent continuity with an external reality. This continuity is evidenced both in the form and substance of meaning. In its substance, meaning reflects its tie to reality in that its units (its relations) are not simply abstract and inert, but rather are constituted by the real irreversible transformations or actions performed by the individual in the course of his activity in the world. To quote Piaget, 'the essential character of logical thought is that it is operational' and these 'operations are indeed actions and do not consist of merely taking note of or apprehending relations.'[14] Thus, meaning is not simply a juxtaposition of relations, it is a coordination of actions or transformations. The formal link between meaning and reality is reflected in the way in which the subject's coordination of action is bound to its real coordination. The meaning constructed by the subject interrelates actions or transformational relationships which are already articulated in the structure of reality. They are already objectively defined and directed. Therefore, to achieve its own internal coordination or to effectively direct action on the real world, the meaning constructed by the subject must parallel that of reality itself. In Piaget's words, 'logic is not isolated from life; it is no more than the expression of the operational coordinations essential to action.'[15]

Having redefined the different aspects of knowledge in the context of their relationship to one another (the reality of knowledge as subjectively directed and hence meaningful, and the meaning of knowledge as a coordination of objective action and hence real), we are in a better position to define the nature of knowledge itself. The unity of these aspects, knowledge, encompasses both the subjective and objective coordinations which regulate an individual's intelligent or directed action. As the point of integration of two systems of coordination, knowledge itself becomes a force for their joint equilibration. In this light, we can understand the meaningful and real dimensions of knowledge as parallel systems whose content and form are dictated by the terms of their conjunction in the equilibrated whole of knowledge.[16] The key question then becomes: Given the unity of meaning and reality in knowledge, how are we to understand the nature of their difference?

To answer, we must consider their genesis. In the case of reality, the structure of the physical world is given. It exists prior to the relationship between the subject and his object and remains constant as that relationship develops. No matter how the meanings constructed by the individual may differ or evolve, his action is always subject to the same real constraints. In this sense, the structure of the real aspect of knowledge is simply determining and unchanging.[17] In the case of meaning, the structure of the subjective coordination of action is not simply given or innate, it is constructed. This is true in two senses. First, it represents real action and thus builds on something other than itself. Second, it not only precedes the subject's purposive behavior, it is also achieved in the course of a pragmatic exploration of action and its consequences. In the course of his experience, the individual discovers how actions are or are not linked to one another. He then elaborates or modifies his subjective coordination of action accordingly. As a result, the meaning he constructs is determined as well as determining and its structure may evolve.

This genetic difference between meaning and reality affects their relationship in knowledge. In the course of his construction of meaning, it is possible that the subject will coordinate his purposive action in a manner which is incompatible with its real structure. In Piaget's view, this will necessarily occur at the outset of the subject–object relationship. As a result, the unity of meaning and reality will be plagued by contradiction and tension. Where the structural integration of meaning and reality in knowledge implies an equilibrium, the genetic difference between them creates an opposing disequilibration.

In light of this reconceptualization of the difference between the subjective and objective aspects of knowledge, the question must again be raised as to how we are to understand their unity. Thus, the problem of the complexity of knowledge as a unity of differences is once again raised. In the present context, however, a resolution is available. In recognition of the difference between meaning and reality, Piaget posits that a concept of disequilibration must be incorporated into any theory of knowledge. In recognition of their unity in knowledge, he also argues that a concept of equilibrium must be similarly included. Considering both these dimensions of knowledge together, Piaget conceives of knowledge as a developmental progress motored by the disequilibration of the subjective and objective dimensions of intelligent action toward a final state of equilibrium. He thereby incorporates both the implication of contradiction inherent in the difference between meaning and reality and the implication of resolution inherent in their unification.

In sum, Piaget overcomes the problem of conceptualizing knowledge as a union of different and contradictory aspects. He does so by first conceiving of the unity of knowledge in dynamic terms – that is, as subjectively directed action in the real world. In a similar manner, he conceives of the aspects of this unity, subjective meaning and objective reality, as structures or coordinations of that directed action. Building on this base, Piaget defines knowledge as a force for the equilibration of the meaningful and real coordinations of an individual's action. At the same time, he assumes that these two coordinations are engendered differently and therefore may be incompatible with one another. This leads Piaget to recognize that while necessarily intertwined, the meaning and reality of the individual's action can be structured in contradictory ways. Reconciling the equilibration inherent in the unity of knowledge and the disequilibration inherent in the contradiction of its aspects, Piaget views knowledge as a developmental progress which is motored by the contradiction of subjective meaning and objective reality through a series of partial equilibria (or stages) toward a final and complete one. He thus resolves the difficulties inherent in more absolute or static philosophies of knowledge by offering what is truly a genetic epistemology.

Taking a genetic point of view

Thus far, Piaget's position has been presented as it relates to the questions of a perspective quite different from his own. As a result, some of the coherence of his vision has been sacrificed. Here, Piaget's genetic epistemology is reconstructed on its own terms.

In Piaget's view, the maturation of children and the history of science dictate that knowledge is not an absolute, but rather is a dynamic entity which evolves over time. Both in childhood and in science, individuals create the terms whereby they understand the world, apply them to their experience, discover their limits, and then construct new ways of understanding. For Piaget, the study of knowledge must recognize the fact of this developmental progress and aim to explicate its nature.[18]

Piaget conceives of this development as a process which begins at birth with the unity of the self and other in the reality of the individual's action. In his view, the individual starts life without meaning. Rather than subjectively directed, his action is reflexive and thus merely a physiologically conditioned response to environmental stimulation. To be sure, these reflex responses are not random. They reflect the structure of the individual's physical organism and are thus biologically coordinated.[19] While this biological coordination bears an important relation to intelligence, it does not have the reflective qualities of adult thought and meaning. In this context, the first concern of a developmental analysis of knowledge becomes the explication of the emergence of the self as subject.

Piaget views meaning as an extension of biological coordination and explains the emergence of the subjective self accordingly. Working backwards from the end to the beginning of intellectual development, he discusses the continuities between intelligence and biological functioning as follows:

> Verbal intelligence or cognitive intelligence is based on practical or sensorimotor intelligence which in turn depends on acquired and recombined habits and associations. These presuppose, furthermore, the system of reflexes whose connection with the organism's anatomical and morphological structure is apparent. A certain continuity exists, therefore, between intelligence and the purely biological processes of morphogenesis and adaptation to the environment. (Piaget, 1952, p. 1)

In this view, intelligent action, like all the activity of a living organism, is essentially adaptive. Its basic purpose is to create and maintain a life-sustaining relationship between the organism and its' environment. Initially, the individual's adaptive behavior is only reflexive and thus determined by the reality of the interaction between the organism and the environment. However, as soon as a reflex is stimulated, the infant 'discovers' the behavior and experiments in order to gain some control over it. At first, this involves the simple repetition of a particular behavior. Later, it extends to the linking of that behavior with others which precede it or follow from it in temporal chains of activity. The process culminates when the child can initiate an action and then reverse it so to cancel out the effect initially produced. Having created this transformational relationship, the child is able to use the time and direction of one behavior to deny the time and direction of the other. He thereby establishes an atemporal frame of reference which exists independently of, and yet applies to specific behaviors in, time. The result is the individual's first subjectively constructed basis for the meaningful representation, coordination and direction of action. [20]

According to Piaget, this first subjective coordination of action is necessarily incompatible with its reality. This is explained in terms of the initial partiality or egocentricity of the individual's point of view. The reality of action has a definition and place which is determined by the structure of reality itself. [21] This automatically integrates and is thus independent of the various views of that action that may be taken from particular positions in space or time. The problem confronting the individual is that initially he can see only through his own eyes. Consequently, rather than seeing action from multiple perspectives, he is limited to a view which reflects his own particular vantage point. A reflection upon this partial view, his attempts to represent and coordinate action will be undermined by the particularistic and egocentric quality of his perspective. The meaning he finally constructs will therefore be quite different from, and ultimately incompatible with, the reality he attempts to know.

The difference between the meaning initially constructed by the individual and the reality of his action sets the stage for the ontogenesis of knowledge. While they are incompatible, subjective meaning and reality remain united in the singularity of the individual's purposive action they both coordinate. Consequently, an initial contradiction is established and the need for further development is created. Whereas this development is one of knowledge itself and thus entails the transformation of both the meaning and reality of an individual's action, the focus is on the subjective dimensions of this process. Development is stimulated by the contradiction between meaning and reality, but it is achieved in the course of the subjective construction and reconstruction of meaning. [22]

The meaning the individual constructs is a subjective product. Initially, it consists of his view of actions and how they are related to one another. At the same time, however, that meaning is linked to a reality. As a coordination of action, it provides direction and thus is actualized in the course of the individual's attempt to act or operate upon the real world. To the degree to which the individual's subjective coordination of action is incompatible with its real coordination, the individual will not be able to achieve his purposes. His action will produce unexpected results and his intentions will be frustrated. Because of this failure, the individual is led to consider how he coordinates his action. In other words, he is led to question the terms of his own understanding.

It is at this point that Piaget's conception of the difference between intellectual and biological functioning is clearest. In the case of the physical organism, if the terms of biogenetically determined coordination are not sufficiently well coordinated with the reality of action, then the organism dies and adaptation can only be achieved through species evolution. In the case of intelligence, development does not depend on species evolution. According to Piaget, the individual is able to reflect on his coordination of action and thereby deny and supersede it. As a result, evolutionary reorganization or development can occur purely within the plane of knowledge. Piaget refers to this process of reflection and reconstruction as reflexive abstraction and defines it as follows:

> Reflexive abstraction is simply taking your means of organizing as object. Differentiating them out from the object world to understand them and take them as object. It is always a matter of separating out action from object . . . reflexive abstraction derives its substance, not from objects, but from operations performed on objects, even when the latter are themselves products of reflexive abstraction. (Piaget, 1970b, p. 28)

Reflexive abstraction involves focusing not on the normal objects of one's thought (actions as one perceives them), but rather on the ways in which one interrelates or coordinates them. Based on establishing a perspective on one's own way of perceiving, it leads to a decentering of the individual's initially egocentric view of the world. As a result, the individual's view of action is reconstructed as is his mode of coordinating it. Development occurs and new meaning is created.

Seen in this light, the development of meaning consists of a series of attempts to coordinate action subjectively. Motored by failure and guided by reflection, it leads to a decentering of the individual's perspective through ever greater abstraction. In the context of the ontogenesis of knowledge, this subjective development may be regarded as successive attempts by the individual to negate the way in which the meaning he constructs differs from reality and thereby as leading to an ever greater equilibrium between these two initially contradictory aspects of his purposive activity. Viewed from this perspective, the equilibration of the whole (knowledge) is reflected in the negation of the particularity and difference of one of its constitutent aspects (meaning).

This development has three distinguishing characteristics. First, it is periodic rather than gradual. Each reflexive abstraction yields a new mode of operating on the world, a new way of thinking. Following this is a period of coordination. During this time, the consequences of developing this new way of thinking are discovered. New dimensions of experience are observed and new kinds of relations among them are forged. A new subjective coordination of action and a new understanding is elaborated. In the process, the developing individual may think about different objects or issues in varying degrees of detail or elaboration. Despite this quantitative variation, however, the formal quality of his thought is constant throughout. His mode of thinking and consequently the structure of his understanding remain the same. Development continues as this subjective coordination is completed and its limits are recognized. This engenders another reflexive abstraction and a new period of coordination. As a succession of these periods each of which is internally homogeneous and structurally different from the others, development consists of a series of distinct steps or stages. In his own research, Piaget defines four such stages: sensorimotor, preoperational, concrete operational and formal operational.[23]

A second distinguishing characteristic of Piaget's concept is that development follows an invariant sequence. In all cases, development starts at the same point and proceeds through the same sequence of stages. It begins with the unity of subject and object in the reality of the initial interaction between the organism and its environment. Because all members of the species share the same basic genetic constitution and are all confronted with a reality governed by the same basic rules, this starting point is the same for all. All individuals begin with the discovery and subsequent coordination of their sensorimotor reactions to the environment. Development continues with a series of reconstructions of the individual's mode of coordinating his action. Each successive construction depends on the objectification of the preceding one and provides the foundation for the following one.[24] In this regard, the sequence in which the various subjective coordinations of action emerge is invariant. Beginning at the same point and progressing through the same sequence of stages, the progress of cognitive development is universal.

A third distinguishing charactcristic of development is that it necessarily culminates in a final point of equilibrium. Although guided by the reflexive abstraction of the subject, development is ultimately stimulated by the contradiction between the individual's meaningful coordination of action and its real determination. The impetus to develop only disappears when this contradiction is finally overcome. From the perspective of the subject–object interaction, this occurs when the subjective coordination of action parallels its real coordination. The capacity to know is finally achieved. From the perspective of the subject, the meaning he constructs is completely coordinated and its relation to the environment is essentially noncontradictory. His ability to understand is complete. Propelled by the same objective and subjective demands, all individuals achieve the same final level of development, that of formal operations.

In sum, Piaget takes a genetic view of the nature of knowledge. Rather than assuming that knowledge is simply given and absolute, he views it as an entity which evolves over time. In so doing, he is able to offer a conception which retains the unity of knowledge and at the same time captures the difference and opposition of its meaning and reality. Knowledge is conceived as a developmental phenomenon – one which is motored by contradiction and guided by successive attempts to coordinate action subjectively and then to overcome the limits of that coordination through reflexive abstraction. This conception is teleological. Development leads to the decentering of the individual's subjective perspective and the concomitant equilibration of meaning and reality in knowledge.

> On the plane of knowledge, the subject's activity calls for a continual 'de-centering' without which he cannot become free from his spontaneous intellectual egocentricity. This decentering makes the subject enter upon, not so much an already available and therefore external universality, as an uninterrupted process of coordinating and setting reciprocal relations. It is that latter process which is the true generator of structures as constantly under construction and reconstruction. (Piaget, 1970b, p. 139)

Taking this view, Piaget reorients the study of knowledge. The focus is no longer on the formal philosophical question of how meaning and reality are related in knowledge nor the substantive empirical issue of how knowledge is acquired or elaborated in the course of experience. These are the concerns of those who define knowledge as an absolute. Redefining knowledge as a dialectically constituted activity, Piaget establishes a new problematic. For him, the key question is: What are the forms knowledge takes during the course of its development? In the attempt to answer, Piaget moves away from the separate concerns of philosophy and psychology to the empirico-philosophical terrain of his structural developmental psychology.

STRUCTURAL DEVELOPMENTAL PSYCHOLOGY

Piaget's genetic epistemology can yield a general definition of the nature of knowledge. However, it cannot reveal the particular qualities of the subjective meanings individuals construct. This is a matter of discovery, not of definition; it can only be answered in the course of empirical research. This is not to suggest that Piaget's empirical research is independent of his philosophy. Quite the contrary, both its aims and methods reflect his epistemological vision.

The nature of meaning

In concert with the dictates of his genetic epistemology, the aim of Piaget's empirical research is to study the nature of the meanings individuals construct. To understand his research, it is therefore important to clarify the nature of subjective meaning as it is viewed from his genetic epistemological perspective. As suggested in the preceding section, meaning has to be considered in the context of its dialectical relationship with the objective reality it is intended to comprehend. Practically speaking, however, this cannot be done. In the first instance, the researcher is limited to a view of the subject's constructions at a particular moment in time. To guide his research, he therefore needs a static concept of subjective meaning. To meet this need, we abstract a concept of meaning from its dialectical relationship to reality and thus define this developing phenomenon in absolute terms.

As one element in a dialectical relationship, subjective meaning has a bipolar quality. On the one hand, the quality of subjective meaning reflects the force of the reality it confronts. It is defined by, and realized in, the context of the individual's interaction with his objective environment. Insofar as the organization inherent in this meaning is incompatible with that of the reality of the action it directs, its terms of organization will be objectified and thereby transcended. In the process, the individual's way of thinking will be reconstituted and the basic nature of the meaning he constructs will be transformed.

Seen in a static frame of reference, subjective meaning is manifest in different ways. Insofar as different individuals are at different stages of cognitive development, the meanings they construct will differ from one another. The meaning constructed at each stage must therefore be defined in its own terms. Despite their differences, however, these various meanings are related to one another. They emerge as successive steps in a progress motored by reflexive abstraction. Each builds on the preceding one and lays the foundation for the next. Consequently, to be properly understood, they also must be defined with respect to one another. They therefore must not only be defined in their own terms, but also relative to their place in a developmental hierarchy.

Subjective meaning also has a second and contradictory side. It is not only determined by reality; it is also self-determining. In Piaget's dialectical conception, meaning is not a mere reflection of reality, it is also constructed by the individual. At any given stage of development, an individual has a general way of thinking about or operating on the world. This capacity is realized as it is applied to specific circumstances. During this process, the individual's way of thinking is differentiated into a set of substantively distinct transformational acts. These acts are then coordinated relative to one another: actions are placed in meaningful relationship to one another and a framework for understanding is created.

Viewed from a static frame of reference, this self-determining aspect of meaning is reflected in two important ways. First, meaning is very much a subjective entity. It is not only constructed by the individual, it also mediates his interaction with his objective environment. In this vein, Piaget writes:

> . . . reality data are treated in such a way as to become incorporated into the structure of the subject . . . According to this view, the organizing activity of the subject must be considered just as important as the connections inherent in the external stimuli, for the subject becomes aware of these connections only to the degree that he can assimilate them by means of existing structures. (Piaget and Inhelder, 1969, p. 5)

As the framework within which experience is assimilated, this subjectively constructed meaning effectively delimits what the individual can experience and how he will experience it. The individual becomes aware of different aspects of his environment in the course of his attempts to operate upon it. Therefore, only those objects which can be incorporated in this activity are included in his considerations. Moreover, these objects can only be interrelated in a manner consistent with the quality of his operational activity. For example, consider the case of the child at the first stage of his development. At this point, he can only think or operate through physical action. To use Piaget's terminology, the child's intellectual activity consists of sensorimotor operations. He can only become aware of those aspects of the environment which are within sight, reach or earshot. Objects which are removed or abstract cannot be considered. Furthermore, the child can only interrelate what he does experience according to the connections he forges in the course of his sensorimotor operations. Insofar as these may only consist of placing one's own actions together in a currently enacted sequence, the connections he forges will be concrete and sequential or irreversible. The sensorimotor child may be exposed to an environment which is extended and abstract, but he will only be able to assimilate that which is immediate and concrete. Similarly, that environment may be governed by abstract rules and principles, but the sensorimotor child will only be able to understand these in terms of the concrete sequences he enacts.

A second characteristic of this subjectively constructed meaning is its formal nature and structure. Piaget is quick to acknowledge that the substance of an individual's experience and understanding is a product of the environment to which he is exposed. Externalities determine the particulars of what an individual knows and the specific associations he makes between one object and the next. For example, whether one knows a great deal about another's habits or very little, or whether one associates an event with positive things or negative ones is largely a function of exposure. At the same time, Piaget asserts that understanding has a formal structure and this is subjectively constructed and determined. It is the qualities of this structure with which he is concerned. Thus, the focus is on the quality of the elements and relations of the subject's understanding. In the case of one individual's understanding of another person, evidence of particular associations or knowledge is probed in an attempt to discover the quality of the relations and elements structuring the apparent understanding. Thus, the focus is on whether the individual thinks of another person's action only as it is incorporated in the individual's own activity, or whether he considers the various acts the other performs in relation to one another. Similarly, there is an interest in whether the individual considers only such concrete observable qualities of the person as things he does or the way he looks, or whether he focuses on such abstract phenomena as the ideas expressed in his words or implicit in his action.

In accordance with the pragmatic action-oriented terms of his constructivist analysis, he defines the structure of meaning as follows:

> A structure is a system of transformations. Inasmuch as it is a system and not a mere collection of elements and their properties, these

transformations involve laws: the structure is preserved or enriched by the interplay of its transformational laws, which never yield results external to the system nor employ elements which are external to it. (Piaget, 1970b, p. 5)

As suggested by our earlier discussion of sensorimotor thought, the transformational acts delimit the formal qualities of the objects of one's thought and the transformational laws delimit the qualities of the relations one forges among them. It is with reference to these formal structural qualities of an individual's operational thinking that the claim is made that the individual's thought at any given stage of development constitutes an integrated and coherent whole.

Consequences for the conduct of empirical research

What then are the consequences of this definition of meaning for the conduct of empirical research? First, it is clear that such research is necessarily a psychological, not a sociological enterprise. Because meaning is a subjective construction rather than a collective or intersubjective one, the focus must be on the individual rather than on culture or social structure. Piaget's position here is somewhat confusing. He has argued that sociology and psychology are closely related disciplines. Indeed, he has claimed that there is no contradiction or incompatibility between the two forms of inquiry. None the less, his theoretical statements and his empirical focus clearly indicate that psychology is the root discipline and sociology is derivative. The issue here is an important one and deserves closer examination.

The most powerful of the sociologies are built upon a organismic or holistic conception of society. Examples include those of Marx or Durkheim. Piaget does not accept this view. Instead, he argues that society is best conceived as a system of social relations. In this vein, he writes:

> It is necessary for sociology to envisage society as a whole, even though this whole, which is quite distinct from the sum of the individuals composing it, is only the totality of the relations between these individuals . . . the whole formed by society is not so much a thing, a being or a cause as a system of relations . . . In sociological thought, it might even be asked whether it would not be better to replace the usual global language by an enumeration of the types of relation involved. (Piaget, 1973, pp. 156-7)

The social relations to which Piaget refers are ones of exchange between individuals. Rejecting a macrosociological perspective, he defines these relations in dyadic terms and views their structure without regard to questions of societal structure or culture.

According to Piaget, social relations consist of a 'co-operation' between individuals who are 'operating' on one another.[25] The basic structure of this 'co-operation' does not vary. It consists of a 'general coordination of action' which pertains to all relations and across all cultures.[26] Piaget argues further that the operations and coordination of a social relationship are isomorphic to the cognitive operations and coordination of the individuals participating.

> In the realm of knowledge, it seems obvious that individual operations of intelligence and operations making for exchanges are one and the same thing, 'the general coordination of action' to which we have continually referred as being an interindividual as well as intra-individual coordination. (Piaget, 1971c, p. 360)

He then concludes that 'there are no more such things as societies *qua* beings as there are individuals. There are only relations; these relations must be studied simultaneously from outside and inside (there being no possible conflict between psychology and sociology).'[27]

Despite his attempt to create this middle ground between sociology and psychology, it is clear that the latter is more basic. Development remains at its core a subjective and hence psychological phenomenon. Whereas the demands for cooperation may stimulate development, its nature and progress are determined by the internal activity of the subjective construction and reconstruction of meaning. Similarly, the products of this development, the structures of coordination constructed at each stage, are psychological rather than social constructions. In Piaget's view, the quality of the meanings constructed must be understood with reference to 'the fecundity of the subject's thought processes (which) depend on the internal resources of the organism.'[28] He argues that even language and mathematics, often regarded as critical examples of a social construction of knowledge which provides the framework for individual understanding, are best understood as ultimately dependent on the subjective constructions of the individual himself.[29] Thus, Piaget concludes:

> Any explanation of the child's development must take into consideration two dimensions: an ontogenetic dimension and a social dimension. However, the problem is somewhat analogous in both cases, for in both the central question is the (internal) mechanisms of all constructivism. (Piaget and Inhelder, 1969, p. 157–159)

The primacy of psychology is also reflected in Piaget's analysis of social relations themselves. In his view, the possibilities for social interaction (both at any given moment or over time) are always constrained by the subjective abilities of the individuals involved. An example here would be the way in which the cognitive abilities of a three-year-old delimit the structure of the co-operative exchange that can occur between him and an adult.[30] In this vein, Piaget has even speculated about the mentality of the tribe as a 'generalized' form of preoperational thought.[31] In sum, although social analysis may be co-extensive with psychological analysis, their relationship is uneven. Psychological analysis is fundamental and sociological analysis is necessarily derivative.

A second implication of Piaget's definition is that empirical research must be an interpretative enterprise. As he defines it, the subjective meaning constructed by another person is twice removed from the researcher. To begin with, there exists the possibility that the researcher and the people he studies are at different stages of development and therefore mean different things by what they do and say. They may have a common language and participate in socially structured exchange, but none the less understand what is transpiring between them in completely different ways. A good example is the conversations between a teacher of political theory and an interested student. In the brief exchanges they may have in the classroom or after class, the student may appear to understand the particular theory discussed. The conversation may be lively and fluid, the two using the same terms and even reaching agreement on critical points. Both may assume a common understanding. Then an examin-ation is administered where the student is required to provide an explication of the theory discussed earlier. Reviewing the student's essay, the teacher may discover that the student failed to understand (or understood differently) the basic logic of the theory in question. The key point here is that a shared language or norms of exchange can obscure fundamental differences in the understandings and purposes of the people involved, differences which become apparent when novel circumstances or probing questions leave the participants free to act or express themselves in their own terms.

The subjective meaning constructed by another is also removed in a second sense, that is by virtue of its inherently abstract quality. As defined by Piaget, the manifest organization of a subject's meaning is governed by an underlying structure. Although implicit and abstract, a knowledge of this structure is critical to a proper understanding of what a subject does or says. The problem confronted by the researcher is that he is not exposed directly to the structure of his subject's thought, but rather to the particular attitudes he expresses or the behavior he performs. Stripped of their underlying structure, these particular statements and behavior are essentially undefined. This is often not recognized and the observer unself-consciously assimilates the behavior into his own framework of understanding and thus defines it in his own terms. The problem is well illustrated by the example of the teacher–student exchange discussed earlier. Exposed only to isolated statements and remarks, the teacher readily misjudges his student's meaning. Only in the context of the elaborated essay does this become clear. For the purposes of research, however, it is not enough simply to discount the student's understanding as flawed or incomplete. Rather, it is necessary to try to construct a model of his reasoning, of the underlying structure of his thinking, in an attempt to comprehend the logic and coherence of his apparently illogical or fragmented presentation.[32]

In sum, Piaget's concept of meaning dictates that empirical research attempt to discover the various forms which meaning takes in the course of its development. It suggests further that the research focus on the individual and that the analysis consist of a structural interpretation of the meaning he constructs. The latter requires that the researcher recognize that people's meanings may be fundamentally different from his own and that he seek to uncover the structure of both their meaning and, by implication, his own.

The practical implications for the design of research are clear. To capture the full panorama of the kinds of meanings constructed, it is necessary to study individuals at all stages of the developmental progress. Piaget himself focused on children from birth to adolescence.[33] In so doing, he adopted one of two strategies: using a longitudinal design and following the progress of a given child or children over an extended period of time, and using a cross-sectional design and comparing children of different ages. Apart from capturing the full range of meanings constructed, it is also important to reveal the structure of each. To avoid confusing form and content, this is best achieved by studying the performance of single individuals across a wide variety of substantively very different tasks.

In addition to determining the design of research, Piaget's concept of meaning also dictates the methods to be used in the gathering of the data. The demands of structural interpretation require that subjects perform tasks which lead them to make a number of related claims or judgements. As discussed in the introductory chapter, the problem faced by the psychologist investigating a child's understanding of the world is analogous to that of a historian of philosophy who is trying to make sense of the writings of a particular philosopher. In both cases, the investigator is confronted with the problem of discovering the logic and coherence of his subject's position without unself-consciously reducing the subject's meaning to the researcher's own. Such an interpretive enterprise necessarily involves the bootstrapping activity of inferring the logic of the subject's position from a set of related claims and then testing the adequacy of one's inference by applying it to another set of remarks or actions. There is, however, one important and obvious difference between the enterprise of the historian and the psychologist. The psychologist has the additional problem of making his subjects express themselves or act.

The problem of leading subjects to reveal their implicit 'philosophies' has been solved in two ways. In his research, Piaget has addressed this problem using his method of 'clinical experimentation'. This involves presenting the subject with a reasoning task such as determining what makes a pendulum swing faster. The subject is provided with all the requisite materials to discover the solution and is encouraged to experiment with them and discuss his strategies and conclusions as they evolve. Researchers following the Piagetian tradition have also turned to the analysis of open-ended interviews.[34] They present the subject with a dilemma (e.g., should you steal to save a life) and ask the subject to argue for a solution, or they present a complex subject matter (e.g., the nature of one's best friend) and then ask for an elaborate description. In both the clinical experimentation and the open-ended interview, the aim is to get the subject to make a number of related claims or judgements. To facilitate subsequent analysis and interpretation, the experimenter or interviewer is always left free to probe the subject's responses and thereby force him to provide further judgement, explanation or justification.

To conclude, Piaget's genetic epistemology leads to a psychology which is quite distinctive. On the one hand, the assumption that meaning is subjectively constructed and structured requires that research be an essentially interpretative activity. On the other hand, the assumption that meaning develops requires that research focus on the differences and continuities among the various understandings people construct. Building on this base, Piaget creates a psychology which is a fundamentally structural developmental enterprise. In the next chapter, this enterprise is extended. First, it is modified in light of a more careful analysis of the social dimension of meaning-making. The resulting social psychology of development is then applied to the study of political ideology.

4
Ideology and the Forms of Political Reasoning

In the preceding chapter, much of the epistemological foundation was laid for the present analysis of political ideology. Building on this, I regard ideologies as subjective constructions, the result of the individual's effort to make sense of his or her social and political environment. Going beyond Piaget, I argue that this political reasoning is itself a product not only of the individual subject, but also of the larger society. In my view, these two forces, subjective and collective, are dialectically related – each defines and is defined by the other. As a result, both individuals and societies may develop. The product of such a relationship, political reasoning, may take several forms, each of which reflects a particular stage in the progress of this psychosocial development.

This theory of ideology is developed in three parts. First, the requisite epistemological foundation is constructed. This is accomplished by modifying Piaget's epistemology in recognition of his failure to account adequately for the social and cultural bases of thinking. A more differentiated concept of social environments is adopted and they are accorded a more central role in the individual's social and political development. Second, a theory of ideology guided by this Neo-Piagetian vision is presented. Defining ideology with reference to political reasoning, the focus here is on the nature of this political reasoning. Finally, a description is offered of the forms which political reasoning takes at three stages of development – sequential, linear and systematic.

BEYOND PIAGET:
TOWARD A SOCIAL PSYCHOLOGY OF DEVELOPMENT

The belief systems research was reviewed in chapter 2. There it was argued that this research has failed to provide a comprehensive, powerful or fruitful characterization of how people think about politics. It was further argued that the problem does not lie with any particular concepts, methods or applications, but with the basic theoretical framework itself. The conclusion was drawn that future studies of political ideology must adopt a radically different approach, one based on an alternative understanding of the nature of thinking. In particular, it was suggested that thinking must be viewed as a subjective activity which: (1) mediates between the individual and his environment and thus structures his understanding of it; (2) has formal qualities which may vary from person to person; and (3) operates upon and represents social events which have their own structure and is therefore shaped by collective constraints as well as personal ones.

In chapter 3, Piaget's concept of thinking and his psychology of cognition were presented. This was done because his approach satisfies many of the epistemological requisites outlined in our critique of the belief systems research. He assumes that the individual is an active agent who thinks and thereby constructs his under- standing of the environment. In addition, he claims that the nature of this thinking may be transformed in the course of the individual's attempt to act effectively on things and other people. Guided by these assumptions, he provides a psychology which yields structural descriptions of the various ways in which people think at different stages in their cognitive development. Sensitive to differences in the forms which thinking may take, his psychology provides a basis for a more comprehensive description of how people think. Formal and abstract, it provides a basis for the construction of concepts which are theoretically powerful. In these two respects, Piaget's approach is well suited to the requirements of the study of ideology and my own efforts have been guided by it.

Despite its advantages, Piaget's work does have a serious drawback. It does not provide an adequate account of the dialectical interplay between personal and social constructions of meaning and action. The influence of sociocultural environments on intellectual develop- ment is noted, but the focus is on the relationship between subject and object, not subject and society. In this regard, Piaget's approach does not satisfy the final criteria established in chapter 2. Insuf- ficiently sensitive to the social dimension of thinking, Piaget adopts a psychological view of what is in fact a social psychological phenom- enon. As a result, he does not adequately represent the nature of meaning-making and the dynamic of its development. He fails to recognize how subjectivity is socially structured and does not anticipate developmental differences in adult thinking. Thus, while

Piaget's theory has its great strengths and offers good ground upon which to build a theory of ideology, it remains importantly flawed. My own approach is designed with this in mind.

The social dimension of cognitive development

The theoretical perspective I adopt to analyze the nature of ideology is strongly influenced by Piaget's work. His structuralist concept of meaning, his pragmatic view of the relationships between thought and action, and his dialectical analysis of the development of thinking are all retained. However, in recognition of the limits of his theory, I pay greater attention to the social dimension of thinking. The resulting view differs from the classical Piagetian one in two basic respects. First, it adopts a more differentiated view of social environments. Second, it attributes to those environments a much more central role in the individual's intellectual and political development. As we shall see, these differences have important implications for how the dynamic of development and the stages of its progress are conceived.

Let us consider first the difference between Piaget's conception of social environments and my own. Piaget views social environments in rather narrow and undifferentiated terms. For him, social environments consist of individuals engaged in relationships of exchange. To be successful, these relationships require that the actions of the individual participants be coordinated relative to one another. This is the single essential structural requirement of any exchange relationship. It holds equally well for the social relationships of the most primitive tribe and those of the most complex metropolis. This sociological claim is relevant to the developmental psychologist because it suggests something of the world to which the developing individual must adapt. Social environments require individuals to cooperate with one another. In so doing, they place cognitive demands on the individual. To cooperate, the individual must transcend the egocentricity of his own perspective, recognize the perspectives of others and the group, and coordinate these with his own. This in turn requires that he represent social actions and events in a way which extracts them from the concrete specificity of their reality and locates them relative to another in an abstract conceptual space of his own construction. Placing these demands on the individual, the social environment fosters his development.[1]

Adopting this view, Piaget clearly recognizes that social environments play a role in the development of individuals. However, because he does not assume that these environments vary in any significant respect, they are regarded as a constant which must be assumed, but then may be ignored in the analysis of development. Consequently, in his own work, he focuses on individuals and the personal dimension of their thinking and ignores any particular qualities of the social environments in which they live.

I regard social environments in less individualistic and more differentiated terms. In my view, the social exchange between individuals identified by Piaget is itself embedded in a larger social and cultural context. This context has its own inherent structure, one which determines the formal qualities of the kinds of social interaction and discourse which occur within its boundaries. Because it shapes the nature of social exchange, this social structure influences the cognitive development of the individual members of a society. This point becomes particularly important when coupled with the claim that the structure of social environments to which individuals are exposed may vary from society to society. Different societies may create conditions of everyday exchange which pose different kinds of problems, problems which require different levels of conceptual sophistication in the individuals trying to solve them.

To illustrate how different environments may require more or less of individuals, let us consider the problems associated with conditions of social exchange in an illiterate tribal society and a more extended one in which formal schooling is introduced. For present purposes, let us assume that in an illiterate tribal society, most social exchange is so structured that action and conversation occur in a context where the object of concern is present and available to all participants (or refers to a past experience of the object they share). Here, the demands of social exchange are minimal. The individual is required to represent objects which are immediately present both to himself and another with whom he is familiar, and then to coordinate their two perspectives on those objects for the purposes of cooperative action. The conditions of social interaction change significantly when formal schooling is introduced. In the classroom, the focus is often on nonpresent events, on what has happened in places one has never been, at a time before one was even born. The exchange itself may occur between people who do not know each other well or come from dissimilar backgrounds. What one has experienced directly and finds familiar, the other may never have seen and find completely strange. In this setting, more is required of individuals to insure effective cooperation and communication. Each must develop a conceptual framework which can support both representations of absent and never experienced phenomena and an appreciation of the differences between one's own and another's experiences. Such an environment makes greater demands and therefore is likely to foster greater intellectual development.[2]

The general point here is that the structure of social environments may vary in ways which influence individuals' cognitive development. When structured differently, social environments will pose different problems and offer different opportunities to solve them. For the most part, when an environment is structured in such a way that everyday life presents individuals with problems which involve large numbers of people and objects which are remote in space and time, it forces individuals to achieve higher levels of cognitive development. Social environments which present problems which involve fewer and more immediate considerations require less of individuals. Consequently, they foster relatively low levels of cognitive development.

In this context, it is important to note that the structural quality of the environments which individuals confront may vary not only from society to society, but also within a single society. Consider the environment of the president of a company which owns a factory and that of a line worker in that factory. Each presents problems of a very different nature which must be solved. The company president's environment is forever posing problems which require the integration of a large number of disparate factors to be considered within an extended time frame. The line worker is usually confronted by problems which involve relatively few factors and a much shorter time horizon. Both are members of the same society, yet their environments differ in ways which should have significant consequences for the level of cognitive development each achieves.

My perspective also diverges from Piaget's in its view of the role played by social environments in the actual process of meaning-making itself. The issue here is to what extent these environments penetrate the activity of the constructing subject. According to Piaget, the construction of meaning is an essentially psychological phenomenon – the activity of the individual struggling to objectify his own terms of understanding and to coordinate or meaningfully interrelate the terrain he thereby creates. His environment is significant, but its role in the process is a negative one. As an objective organization of action, it can negate the meanings an individual constructs and thereby force another round of development. However, the positive aspects of the process – that is, the quality of initial understandings, the consequent terms in which environmental negations are recognized, the activity of self-objectification and the final process of conceptual coordination – remain subjectively directed and determined.

In my view, the individual's social environment penetrates the construction and development of meaning much more deeply. Beyond negating the terms of his current understanding, it also provides concepts and experiences which guide the process of constructing a new understanding. A society consists of an organization of action and a complementary weave of cultural definitions. Coordinating the purposes and understandings of individuals, the organization of a social environment is necessarily structured at a higher level than the subjective coordinations of the individuals themselves. Social life is therefore a collective product. Social organization and cultural definition are not a product of the individuals nor is their true nature understood by them. None the less, the individual does become aware of these collective constructions and is affected by them. They regulate his exchange with others and therefore apply to actions and definitions as he understands them. Consequently, they pertain to experience as he construes it and are recognized by him. Through his recognition, these collective constructions enter the individual's meaning-making activity. They do so in two ways. As suggested by Piaget, they play a negating role. They present the individual with events which are unexpected and discourse which is incomprehensible and therefore undermine his subjective understandings. In addition, I suggest that society and culture also play a constructive role. They provide patterns of action and categorizations of phenomena which lead the subject to view and think about his environment in a way which he could not on his own. They lead him to see connections which he himself could not construct. In so doing, they set the goals which orient his attempt to reconstruct his understandings and provide guidelines for his coordination of the new ones which are created. Thus, while the subjective process of objectifying one's own understanding pushes and directs meaning-making from below, the penetration of the social environment pulls and orients it from above. The construction and development of meaning is therefore not simply a psychological process, but rather a profoundly social psychological one.[3]

The relationship between collective definitions and personal understandings in the subjective construction of meaning can in part be illustrated by the example of a student in an introductory class on political philosophy. Let us assume that our student is somewhat politically interested and holds a number of particular attitudes and beliefs. For example, he may be against social welfare programs, favor recruitment of elites into government and be against affirmative action policies. He may also harbor strong religious beliefs. Of importance here is his understanding of these various attitudes. In his mind, they are independent concerns, each of which has its own specific, concrete point of reference. Thus, his lack of support for social welfare may mean that he is against pouring money into black neighborhoods because all they do is waste it anyway. Similarly, his religious belief may simply reflect his sense that the world is a complex, confusing place which only a superior being could possibly understand and control.

Armed with this understanding of his own views, our student enters a political philosophy class. In the lectures and readings, he is exposed to a discourse which imposes a higher order construction on the meaning of the beliefs he holds. In the classroom, beliefs are no longer defined as discrete entities which bear relation to specific policy alternatives or particular private confusions. Instead, they are seen as expressions of a general political point of view, in his case, conservatism. These political viewpoints are themselves linked to general epistemological positions. Thus, our student may have his conservatism presented to him as the political expression of the epistemological rejection of the rationalism and universalism of eighteenth century liberalism.

Clearly the meanings implicit in the discourse presented to the student are structured differently from his own. The objects defined are more abstract and the relations among them more complex. As a result, the student will misrepresent the classroom discourse by assimilating it to the terms of his own understanding. None the less, insofar as it speaks to attitudes as he understands them, this discourse may have an impact. It can directly deny the student's own under-standing of his attitudes as independent entities which are meaningful only with respect to particular policy initiatives. In so doing, it can stimulate development. Alternatively, the classroom definitions can facilitate and direct this development. By suggesting how various attitudes (as they are defined by the student) are grouped together, these definitions can present the student with novel configurations of evidence and thereby orient the student's attempts to create a new understanding. They may also guide his efforts by providing new concepts. Although initially misunderstood, they provide hooks upon which he can hang new ideas and set specific goals to be reached in his general attempt to make sense of the discourse in which he is attempting to participate. In sum, the dialogue the student conducts with the lecturer facilitates a development in his ideas both by undermining his faith in his old understanding of what it means to have a political perspective and by guiding his attempt to construct a new one.

The differences between Piaget's and my own view of social environments and the role they play in the individual's construction of
meaning have important ramifications for how the results of that construction, the stages of cognitive development, are conceived. In both
formulations, a single stage of development may be characterized as
evolving through two phases, one of new definition and one of con-
solidation. The first is a period of instability, active exploration and
partial knowledges. The second is one of more complete integration
and understanding. The first moment drives the individual on, the
second allows rest until the next round of development. Together,
they cohere as two moments of a single stage, as two expressions, one
more simple and the other more elaborated, of a single structure.
Piaget's conception and my own differ with regard to how these
moments are characterized and how they cohere as part of a single
structure.

Piaget's conception is a strictly structural and psychological one.
Meanings are constructed, elaborated and ultimately coordinated
within the context of the thinking individual's own constructions.
Given this psychological formulation, Piaget views the period when
the individual takes his own understandings as object as the first
phase. During this time, the individual is just beginning to recognize
a new terrain and reconstruct his old understandings relative to it. His
new understandings are fragmentary and uncoordinated with one
another. The second phase is one of conceptual coordination. The
individual begins to place his new concepts in relation to one another.
In the end, a new structure of reasoning is elaborated. In his
descriptions, Piaget sometimes refers to these first and second phases
as the 'A' and 'B' substages of a given stage of development.

My conception is more dialectical and social psychological. In my
view, meanings are always constructed and coordinated at two levels,
intersubjective as well as subjective. While each level is an independent structure with its own coordinations and definitions, each is also
dependent on the other. The subjective depends on the intersubjective for the higher order terms of its own integration and the
intersubjective depends on the subjective for the lower order terms of
the knowledges in response to which its constructions will emerge. In
this light, I regard the construction of meaning as the result of the
interplay of subjective and intersubjective constructions each of which
penetrates the activity of the other.

Let us examine the consequences of this conceptualization for the
subjective construction of meaning. In so doing, we must consider
both the personal and social dimensions of how an individual thinks.
This leads to a different conception of the nature and cohesion of the

first and second moments of a stage from that offered by Piaget. For us, the first phase of a stage is one of subjective coordination, not objectification. Moreover, this coordination is regarded as destabilizing, not stabilizing. It lays bare the limits of the individual's ability to integrate what is known and to make sense of social action. The second phase begins a dual process of appropriating social definitions and objectifying the terms of one's own understanding. While itself based on a partial understanding of higher order meaning, this second phase yields a subjective sense of full understanding and the public appearance of social skill.

During the first phase, the individual begins to elaborate and then coordinate the personal dimension of his construction of meaning. As a result, he constructs an increasingly clear vision of the world and a more adequate basis for directing his actions. However, he cannot fully coordinate his understandings at this level and his knowledges remain fragmentary. Most important, his partial coordination reveals to him the limits of his own understanding. Having partially coordinated his thinking, he develops clearer expectations of action and its consequences and is able to better observe events as they are consistent with his own terms of understanding. Given that his thinking has not developed to the point where it is consistent with the structure of his environment, his expectations will not be realized and he will observe configurations of events he cannot comprehend. The result will be a personal sense of confusion and an attendant need to develop further. At the same time, social pressure for development is also created. Entering a new stage of development and having begun to coordinate understandings at this level, the individual appears to be a more effective social actor, capable of more complex social interaction and higher level discourse. Acting and speaking in ways which suggest greater ability and insight, he is allocated greater power and responsibility by other people. However, insofar as his new understanding is only partially coordinated, it is defined with reference to particular situations. It therefore lacks the flexibility and scope that it initially appears to have. In other words, the individual does not yet understand the how and why of the new activity in which he begins to engage nor does he understand the full meaning of the new concepts he begins to use in his discourse. He is therefore frequently unable to initiate action or respond in ways which are properly coordinated with the requirements of social exchange. His specific knowledge of how to act and talk creates new expectations of him, but their lack of integration prevents him from meeting those expectations. The result is increasing pressure for development placed on the individual by those around him.

As suggested by our analysis, both the psychological and social pressures for further development created in this first phase are a result of the individual's increasing coordination of the personal dimension of his thinking. Dependent on the higher order definitions inherent in the social environment, this personal coordination cannot be completed. This is accomplished in the second phase, when personal coordinations are integrated with appropriated social definitions. Until then, the ongoing effort to coordinate thinking only increases both the individual's and others' awareness of the limits of his understanding. In a sense, the more he understands what he knows, the more he is aware of what he does not understand and cannot know. Similarly, the more socially able he appears to be, the more fully he will be allowed to participate in social life and thereby reveal the extent of his inadequacy.

A more personally satisfying sense of understanding and a more socially appropriate mode of interacting is achieved in the second phase. Here, the individual begins to find superordinate direction for resolving the difficulties which emerged in the first phase. This involves the interdependent activities of objectifying one's own terms of understanding and recognizing (but not integrating and thereby understanding) the higher order meaning implicit in the organization of social events and cultural definitions. These twin activities provide the superordinate direction needed to fill in the intellectual gaps and to avoid the social mistakes revealed in the first phase. On the one hand, a subjective sense of complete understanding is achieved. Because they are of a higher order, the new definitions provide boundaries and internal order for the individual's effort to coordinate his lower order knowledges. Although these definitions are themselves fragmentary, they are not themselves objects of understanding or coordination. Therefore, the individual remains unaware of the bases of his new success or its intrinsic limitations. On the other hand, the individual becomes a more competent social actor. Aware of particular rules of interaction and discourse of a higher order, the individual can use them as guides to action intended to achieve lower order ends. In a piecemeal fashion, he can learn what these rules are and when they apply, and thereby act in a manner consistent with the expectations placed upon him. Because these rules are not themselves objects of understanding and hence a basis for defining purposes, the individual does not extend himself beyond what he knows nor does he suggest any such ability to others. Therefore, he is not led to commit any new kinds of mistakes. In the end, this second phase yields both a subjective sense of understanding and an objectively more appropriate basis for engaging in social interaction. It is, therefore, a natural resting point in a developmental progress.

In sum, unlike Piaget, I view thinking to be the result of collective and intersubjective forces as well as personal and subjective ones. The meanings constructed at each stage of an individual's cognitive development reflect a union of recognized social constructions and coordinated personal understanding. Given this psychologically decentered view of an individual's understanding, I regard the moments of coordinating personally construed experiences and then reaching for a partial knowledge of socially constructed meaning as two phases of a single stage. Translating this into the Piagetian focus on personal defined meaning and using his terminology, I regard what he views as the 'B' moment of one stage and the 'A' moment of the following stage to be, in reality, two moments of a single stage. I expect people's thinking to cohere accordingly.

The divergence between my view and Piaget's is not a matter of theoretical hairsplitting. On the contrary, it produces important differences in the overall view of cognitive development and in the design of empirical research. As already noted, Piaget assumes that: (1) development occurs in response to environments (social as well as physical) which despite their apparent differences, all create essentially the same demands; and (2) this development progresses according to its own internal psycho-logic, a logic which is shared by all people. These assumptions lead him to the twin conclusions that all cognitive development is driven to a single end and that as fully mature adults, all individuals think in basically the same way. Consequently, in his research, he focuses on children and the psychologic of their development. To describe the stages of this development, he uses the language of mathematics and symbolic logic. In this context, little attention is paid either to the social conditions or consequences of individuals' development or to the exploration of possible differences in thinking among adults.

Given my social psychological orientation, my conception of development and my research focus are different. I assume that: (1) the structure of social environments may vary in ways which are relevant to cognitive development, and (2) the social organization of action and discourse importantly penetrates the process of the subjective construction of meaning. Given these assumptions, I am led to conclude that when exposed to different environments, different adults may reach different stages of development and therefore reason in fundamentally different ways. Consequently, I am more interested in the analysis of the social conditions of development and the exploration of the developmentally produced differences in thinking which may exist among adults. To describe the various stages of cognitive development, I abandon Piaget's mathematical language in favor of the more socially and politically relevant language of action to describe the various stages of cognitive development.[4]

A THEORY OF IDEOLOGY

Here, I offer a structural dialectical definition of ideology – one which builds on the foregoing social psychological revision of Piaget's genetic epistemology. The resulting theory of ideology and approach to empirical research is quite different from that adopted in most political studies. In this section, we focus on questions of theory. In the following chapter, we will address questions of method.

As indicated in chapter 2, most current research on ideology is guided by a liberal epistemology. In this liberal view, there is a clear distinction between ideology on the one hand and reason on the other. Ideology is regarded as a set of learned attitudes or preferences. These attitudes are defined in terms of their specific content, that is, in terms of the particular issues and policies to which they refer. It is assumed that they are shaped by social custom and tradition. In this sense, ideology is viewed as a culturally and historically relative product. Reason, on the other hand, is regarded quite differently. It is regarded as a process which is defined in abstract terms and is structured by the qualities of the human mind. It is a universal phenomenon. Where ideology divides people, reason provides the basis for a common understanding and an avenue to objective truth.

My own view is based on a structural and dialectical tradition which emerged in part as a response to the perceived inadequacies of the liberal epistemological tradition. It yields a very different conception of the nature of ideology and reason. According to this view, the foregoing distinction between ideology and reason is a false and misleading one. Ideology is not simply a set of learned preferences. More basic, it is a way of making sense of politics – of defining who and what is involved, what they do, and how they relate to one another. In this regard, it is a form of reasoning and therefore a subjective process which has certain abstract or formal characteristics. As such, it is not simply a product of environmental forces, but is, in the first instance, a subjective construction which reflects the general qualities of the individual's thinking. As ideology is regarded as reasoned, so reason is regarded as ideological. This is to suggest that the activity of reasoning is pragmatically tied to an external social environment. As a result, the individual's reason is itself structured by the terms of social interaction and discourse to which he is exposed. Determined as well as determining, reason is historically and culturally relative and, in this sense, ideological.

In this context, I adopt a more integrated view of reason and ideology and use the single concept, political reasoning. In my view, political reasoning is a structured activity which, in the course of making sense of particular experiences, yields a coherent understanding of oneself, of others and of politics. It is a social psychological phenomenon, a product of both the thinking subject and an organizing social environment. These two forces combine to determine the nature of reasoning at any moment in time and establish the conditions of its transformation and development.

Central to this view are two key assumptions. The first is that one's political understanding is structured and, therefore, constitutes a coherent whole. Its structure and coherence is understood with reference to the nature of the activity of political reasoning. Like any reasoning, political reasoning consists of the individual's attempt to operate upon the world and then assimilate the results achieved. Thus, political reasoning provides the medium of exchange between the individual and the political environment. In so doing, it determines the structure of the individual's social and political experience. How the individual thinks (his or her capacity to operate and reflect) delimits both the nature of what the individual can experience (the quality of possible objects of thought) and how the individual will organize those experiences (the type of analytical relations between objects established). The activity of reasoning produces the structure of the individual's ideological thought. This structure then defines the terms (both relational and elemental) in which the political environment will be rendered subjectively meaningful.

This first assumption, that an individual's political understanding is structured and coherent, reflects the highly subjectivist and psychological aspect of my theory. It is a characteristic of the individual, his mode of reasoning, that dictates the quality of his experience. When interacting with the environment, the individual imposes the formal properties of his way of reasoning (the quality of the elements defined and relations established) on his experience of that interaction. Although the content of his experience is dictated by an external sociopolitical reality, its structure is the result of the individual's own subjective construction. Thus, the way in which experience is organized and defined is more a matter of subjective than of objective or cultural determination.

Consider the example of an individual who reasons by placing observed actions in a linear causal relationship to one another.

Thinking in these terms, he understands politics as an arena for action in which some people initiate acts which force others to react. Based on observation, the patterns of this action are discovered and are regarded as given or natural. An array of causes and effects, the political arena is understood in hierarchical terms. People are defined by their place in this hierarchy. Those who act as causes are ascribed greater status and privilege. Those who merely react are viewed as subordinates and are attributed lesser status. According to the theory, this way of thinking about politics will shape all of the linear thinker's attempts to make sense of his experience of particular political actors, events and institutions. Even where the external or social realities of political phenomena are defined differently, they will none the less be experienced by the individual in his linear causal terms. For example, he may be exposed to a liberal democratic culture in which laws are defined as social creations which are subject to personal evaluation and individuals are defined as abstract human beings who are equal in their humanity. These definitions are inconsistent with the structure of his own thinking. Consequently, he will continue to regard the practices of his liberal democratic society as the only natural and appropriate way to conduct politics. Similarly, he will continue to view individuals in terms of the specific things they say and do and ascribe their status accordingly.

The second basic assumption underlying this view of political understanding is that it develops. Like its structure, the development of political understanding is understood to be a necessary result of the activity of political reasoning. Political reasoning is a fundamentally pragmatic activity. It both emerges as a reflection of what the individual can do and leads to the formulation of strategic action. Thus, political reasoning provides the individual with an understanding of situations and a knowledge of how to act and what to expect. Drawing on this, the individual directs his own action and forms appropriate expectations. In so doing, he relates his subjectively constructed ideology or political understanding to the realities of social and political life. These realities are themselves structured, a product of the objective and intersubjective coordinations of collective life. Accordingly, social and political environments exercise their own independent effect on the interaction between individuals who participate in them. As a result, each individual's action is subject to social as well as subjective regulation. Consequently, the reasoning the individual uses to direct that action and the understandings which result will be constrained, in part, by the manner in which his social environment is organized.

The recognition that subjectively directed action is subject to constraints imposed by the sociopolitical environment is central to the developmental view of political understanding. It is the interaction between these two structuring forces, subjective and social, that constitutes the developmental dynamic. To the degree to which the individual's subjective construction of his political experience is inconsistent with the real constraints imposed on that experience by the environment, the individual's understanding of the world will prove unworkable. Self-directed action will end in failure and unexpected outcomes will be frequent. In addition, cultural definitions and explanations will not be understood. The combination of the failed actions, unexpected outcomes and misunderstandings will give rise to a sense of confusion and self-doubt. The individual will begin to wonder about the adequacy of his understanding of the world. At this point, his concern may shift from what he knows to how he knows; he reflects.

There are two dimensions to this reflection. On the one hand, it is a purely subjective activity. It involves building on the rejected terms of a prior political understanding. The conceptual relations characteristic of the rejected understanding become the objects of reflection. As a result, reflection is not arbitrary. The focus (and indirectly, the structure) of the reflective activity is in part determined by the old understanding being objectified and transcended. This self-objectification leads to the construction of a new mode of reasoning. The act of taking one's way of understanding as object entails the consideration of an object of thought which is not constructed in the course of one's normal thinking. As such, the consideration of this new object prefigures the emergence of a new mode of reasoning, one which includes this new object within its normal range of operation. On the other hand, reflection is an environmentally directed activity. When subjectivity fails, it is because it encounters objective regulations of action and cultural definitions which are incomprehensible. These not only destabilize old understandings, they provide a framework for the new. Although only poorly recognized and half-understood, these collective constructions provide objects of understanding which are not, and yet clearly must be, understood. Thus, they both lead the subject away from old concerns and provide a sketchy outline of new ones. Put in figurative terms, as self-objectification pushes reflection from below, the recognition of social patterns and cultural definitions pulls it from above.

In the end, reflection leads to the emergence of a new mode of reasoning. With this, the structure of political understanding is transformed and political experience is reconstructed. New objects of political concern are defined and new kinds of relations are formed among them. In essence, a new political subjectivity is created. The change achieved is both fundamental and directed; it involves a rejection of old knowledges and an incorporation of those which are yet to be understood.

To exemplify the process, consider again our linear causal thinker. Assume for a moment that he is embedded in an immediate environment organized along liberal democratic lines. Here, several factors conspire to destabilize his understanding of politics. First, he is confronted with certain political facts which cannot really be understood. For example, political regimes change with great frequency. With that change, not only do the holders of power change, but the rules of what is desirable or acceptable also appear to change. His notion of politics as given and immutable ritual is confounded. In addition, power is clearly distributed more complexly than he anticipates. The electorate chooses who will have power and exerts influence accordingly. Power and control seem to flow up as well as down. At the top, power seems divided and chains of command are unclear. Where the linear thinker expects government to speak with one voice, he is confronted with a constitutional division of powers producing a cacophony of different voices. Second, our linear thinker is confronted with a host of definitions and explanations he cannot understand. Political discourse is filled with references to such intangibles as systems of beliefs and ideologies or individual rights and some abstract equality among men. It is also rife with analyses which focus on the interactive relations among individuals or the systemic qualities of political environments. Together, the unexpected and confusing quality of the facts and the parlance of politics serve to undermine the linear thinker's sense of the world. They engender self-doubt and, in so doing, foster reflection.

Through reflection, our linear thinker is led to think less about specific political activity, the normal object of his understanding, and more about the relationships he constructs when thinking about that activity. Consequently, he thinks less about specific actions and how each particular one is linearly related to another. Instead he focuses on the linear relationships themselves and tries to determine how they are related to one another. For example, rather than simply noting that a government official can force a citizen to perform a particular action or that a citizen votes and thus can force officials to attend to his desires, our struggling thinker now attempts to juxtapose these facts in an attempt to understand how they are meaningful relative to one another. This creates a concern which is novel and demands a form of analysis which has yet to be constructed. This process of reflection is further advanced by the unexpected configurations of behavior and cultural definitions with which the political environment confronts our developing thinker. The apparent cultural and historical relativity of forms of political action and organization enjoin him to consider sets of political rituals relative to one another and as they are embedded in a given society or epoch. Similarly, references to the social production of politics and concepts such as system and principle also lead to the consideration of new phenomena and provide novel means for understanding them.

In the end, this process of reflection leads beyond reasoning which operates by placing actions in linear relation to one another, to the development of a mode of reasoning which involves juxtaposing these linear relationships and placing them in some general context or framework. As a result, our thinker's understanding of politics is reconstructed. Where there were sets of specific political rituals, there are now systems of political action. Where there were simple hierarchies, there is now complex organization. Where actions were conceived in specific terms and by virtue of their specific effects, they are now exemplars of a class of actions defined by the function they perform in the polity. Development has occurred.

As suggested by the foregoing analysis, political understandings are embedded in an ongoing process of subjective construction, denial, reflection and reconstruction. In this sense, they are the moments or stages in a developmental process. The dynamic of this process is such that development has the following characteristics. First, because each stage builds on the preceding stage and creates the foundation of the succeeding stage, the order of development is invariant. Everyone passes through the same sequence of stages in the development of their political understanding. Second, because each stage emerges as a reflective response to the inadequacies of thought at the preceding stage, development leads to an ever greater cognitive sophistication. At the same time, because these inadequacies are relative to a given political environment, development also leads to a more appropriate adaptation to the political environment. Third, because environments stimulate development and the structure of environments may vary, different individuals may reach different stages of development. As a result, the manner of their reasoning and the structure of their understanding of political life will differ.

In introducing this second assumption, that of development, it is important to note that the subjectivist and psychological emphases of my structuralist view are complemented by objective and sociological considerations. This is true in two respects. First, the assertion that experience is subjectively structured is tempered by the recognition that the individual's interaction with the environment both contributes to, and may force structural transformations in, how he thinks. Second, the claim that the structure of thinking may differ across individuals is supplemented by the understanding that these differences are a product of variations in the structures of the social environments to which those individuals are exposed. In this regard, my structural developmental theory of ideology reflects a deeply social psychological view of political reasoning.

In the following sections, the different types of political understanding that emerge during the course of development are defined. They are sequential, linear and systematic. True to their developmental conception, each type is seen as a stage which builds on the preceding stage and sets the foundation for the emergence of the succeeding stage. When development is arrested at a given stage, the structure of understanding remains unchanged and gives rise to a type of adult thinking. Each type of thinking is defined in terms of its characteristic form of reasoning and constituent structure. The political understanding associated with the type is regarded as an expression of that essential structure.

Each type of thinking is presented in the following manner. First, the general nature of the reasoning characteristic of the type and the structure of thought that this reasoning generates is described. The structure of thought is analyzed in terms of its constituent conceptual relations and units. Second, the general qualities of the political understanding associated with the stage are discussed. This is followed by a more specific examination of how a thinker at this stage would make sense of the space, time, players and action of political life. Finally, the nature of the social conditions which promote and inhibit development are specified. At times, the descriptions offered are quite difficult and abstract. To assist the reader, a summary table is presented in the Appendix.

SEQUENTIAL POLITICAL REASONING

The sequential thinker reasons by tracking the world which appears before him. His focus is on the immediate and concrete events he observes and the memories of earlier ones they evoke. He understands these events as moments of an unfolding sequence. The questions which guide the intellectual activity of the sequential thinker are: What does this look like? What happens next? The answers to these questions are found through personal observation, either of one's own or another's experience.

The structure of sequential thought

Tracking the world as it appears to him, the reasoning of the sequential thinker is mediated by appearances. Dependent on the raw material of his own observation, his attempt to link events is guided by their apparent overlap – that is, either by how one appears to lead into the other in a sequence of events, or by how a current event appears to share common physical features with one observed in the past. This provides the basis for the conceptual linkages he forges and the objects he considers. His conceptual relations retain the temporality of appearance and his conceptual objects retain its particularity and concreteness.

The conceptual relations constructed by the sequential thinker consist of either a sequential ordering of events or a match between similar ones. Relations of this kind have several distinguishing qualities. First, they are synthetic without being analytic. They join events together, but the union forged is not subject to any conceptual dissection. In the case of a sequential ordering, events are joined by virtue of their temporal contiguity. However, no analysis follows on this synthesis. The observed activity is not abstracted from its spatiotemporal context and then disassembled into its constituent moments and their interrelations. Consequently, events are not extracted from real time and causally analyzed nor are they abstracted from real space and categorically defined. Rather, the representation of an observed sequence retains the temporal and unfolding features of the observation itself. In essence, the subject creates a subjective moving picture of a train of activity, one which can be used later to recreate the effects initially observed. In the case of a matching relation, two phenomena are joined when an aspect or the whole of one is apparently the same as that of another. Here again synthesis is not followed by analysis. Sequential thought lacks the atemporal frame of reference needed to hold either present and past events, or a feature of an event and the whole of it, as simultaneous objects of analysis whose similarities and differences may then be compared and contrasted. Rather, the mind passes from one to the other, fusing the two and identifying the first with the second. While this may lead to an appropriate identification of a present object with earlier observations of that object, confusions of part and whole and the failure to subject the phenomena being identified to true comparison often engender distortion.

A second feature of the conceptual relations constructed by the sequential thinker is that they are mutable. On the one hand, learned sequences can be readily extended when they share recognized overlapping events. This increases the flexibility and power of sequential thought. On the other hand, a single sequence of events which is learned and subjectively represented can readily be changed. Using his understanding of an earlier sequence of events, the sequential thinker can attempt to recreate the effects observed. If the effects are not obtained, he will experience frustration. Despite this, he will see what has transpired and his representation of the new chain of events will readily override that of the old. In this sense, the relations of sequential thought engender expectations, but do not create subjective standards of normal or necessary relations between events.

A third feature of the relations of sequential thought is their concreteness and particularity. When a relationship is forged, it is between particular events which are constituted by a particular set of concrete objects. The understanding obtained from this circumstance remains limited to it. The sequential thinker learns that particular objects are involved in a certain order of events which produce a given result. His learning generalizes only insofar as identical objects (where identity is constructed in the manner described above) are observed. These may then substitute for the originals. However, it is only in this limited way that his conception of the relationship among events generalizes. As a result, the sequential thinker's understanding of his environment is rather strictly constrained to the particulars of his experience and only expands in a slow, piecemeal fashion.

Reasoning by tracking also delimits the quality of the conceptual objects of sequential thought. Thought of this type can only incorporate those objects which currently are, or have been, observed. Objects which have never been experienced or objects which are abstract and therefore have no visual or tangible existence cannot be addressed. The objects of sequential thought are also regarded individually. Their identity is a product of their particular concrete appearance, not of any subjectively constructed relationships between any one object and others. This appearance-mediated definition is, however, somewhat fluid. Because the consideration of an object may focus on the whole object or on one of its particular aspects, its appearance and consequent definition may be readily altered. The objects of sequential thought are understood as they are identified with memories, or as they are observed to be nested in sequences of action or located in a given setting.

Political understanding

Like the general nature of his reasoning, the political reasoning of the sequential thinker is grounded in the concreteness and temporality of his observations of the social and political activity. It involves identifying phenomena by matching current observations with memories of earlier ones and understanding their use by observing how they are articulated in a sequential order of events. This political reasoning is bereft of causal analysis or categorical definition. Sequences of actions are merely recorded. Possible cause and effect relations are not explored and normative standards of appropriate procedure are not applied. Social groups, such as classes, ethnic groups, political parties or nation states, are not naturally constructed. To the degree to which they are understood, the general features of the whole are lost in the particularities of a present or remembered representative of that group. The objects of this reasoning are restricted to observable entities, e.g. particular political leaders, that have actually been seen. Unseen actors and abstract forces and principles are not the objects of sequential political thought.

Reasoning in this way, the sequential thinker constructs a view of politics as concrete, real and immediate. In so doing, he fails to distinguish the political from the social. He does not recognize that there is a collective coordination or an intersubjective agreement implicit in the daily exchanges in which he participates. Moreover, he does not understand how the domain of politics extends beyond his moment and place. For him, politics is simply the particular people he sees doing particular things. As such, it is an indistinguishable part of his own immediate and concrete daily life. With time he can learn that certain of the objects (people and symbols) he observes are labelled political and he can come to understand that these objects are in some sense remote, rarely entering the reality of his personal environment. Thus, politics is viewed as inhabiting the grey world of the not-here, not-now. It is largely ignored and little valued.

It should be noted that not only is politics regarded as an aspect of the social, but the social itself (and politics along with it) is not adequately distinguished from the real. To the sequential thinker, people, animals and inanimate objects all have a similar status. They are all understood as they are articulated in sequences and are valued as they are instrumental to the attainment of personal ends. The social only becomes distinguished insofar as people are observed to be unusually active and satisfying elements of one's environment. The achievement of sequential thought is the distinction between the individual subject's own representation of an object and its reality. This is not complemented by any of the understanding of the nature of subjectivity and the differences between subjective perspectives that is essential to the distinction between the social and the real. The sequential thinker can recognize that other people also have a perspective on the concrete world. However, he assumes that they see what he does. Only through experience does he learn that they may see it differently. This is understood as the result of being in a different place and therefore having literally seen a different side of the events in question or simply having seen less or none of those events. Even this is hard for the sequential thinker to keep in mind. Consequently, his discourse and behavior will frequently reflect an inadequate recognition of the different perspective of his listener.

The space of politics   As we have mentioned, the politics constructed by the sequential thinker is concrete and real. The space in which this politics exists is an immediate and fragmented one. It is immediate in the sense that it is limited to what has been observed. Thus, the political space of the sequential thinker includes particular people who have been observed to do particular things. It does not extend beyond personal experience to include people or places that have not yet been, or may never be, encountered. The sequential thinker has difficulty making sense of events reported by others and is unable to generate or understand hypotheticals. Limited to what has been observed, his political space also does not provide a place for what is inherently intangible or abstract. Thus, it cannot adequately incorporate collectivities such as classes, institutions or nations, or abstract objects such as freedom, rights and obligations. The limited boundaries of this political space are matched by the minimal quality of its internal order. Tied to appearance, it is organized according to the observed contiguities among event/spaces. One event is viewed as leading to another in space and time and a subjective relationship between them is forged. This yields a localized organization of the particular spaces involved in a given sequence of events. However, these sequences are not located relative to one another. As a result, the sequential thinker's political space consists only of a disconnected set of knowledge fragments.

   In the era of television, the domain of the sequential thinker's political space is extended beyond the range of his personal experience to include that captured by the cameraman's lens. Disparate and remote phenomena such as the offices of Senators, the statements of Ronald Reagan and the posturing of Libyan and Iranian demonstrators enter his thoughts. Although his universe is thereby expanded, it is represented in essentially the same terms. Only that which is actually observed is included. Therefore, only objects which are actually seen on television (e.g., Presidents, buildings and demonstrators) can be incorporated into the sequential thinker's political space. Nothing else can exist for him.

The organization of this expanded space of politics depends on the qualities of its presentation to the observer. In this context, it should be remembered that the world presented on the evening news lacks the coherence and routine of the sequential thinker's immediate social environment. Except in the most discordant of times, his immediate environment has a visible order. The same people doing the same things in the same places are seen again and again. This gives the sequential thinker ample opportunity to observe the sequences and spaces of daily life and to learn how they lead into one another in a seamless web. The political domain depicted on television is quite different. To being with, it lacks repetition and routine. There are always new people in new places doing new things. This makes initial cognition and learning more difficult. Additionally, these novel events are presented incoherently. The visual presentations of politics on television are brief and fragmentary. The first two-minute segment flashes on the President speaking to a religious group in Ohio, the next focuses on pictures of a toxic waste dump in Pennsylvania and a third pictures 'contras' in Nicaragua. The lack of spatial or geographic organization to television politics is reflected in the representations of the sequential thinker. His political space consists of little more than a collage of persons and places that bear little relation to one another except that they were seen on television and are not here.

The time of politics   The limited and fragmentary quality of the space of politics is also reflected in its time. The relations of sequential thought yield a time which consists basically of a passing present. It extends from the initial moments of the sequence through to its conclusion. In this context, there is no clear sense of a future beyond the sequence nor a past before it. Both exist merely as the 'not now'. In this context, the past does have some substance; it is the time of memories. However, this substance has little order. The past is recalled when its particular contents, a moment or sequence of events, are evoked by current observation. With this evocation, the memory is fused with the currently observed events. Thus, the past has no elaborated identity independent of the present to which it is being related. The organization of the passing present and remembered sequences of events is itself minimal. It exists in the singularity of its appearance to the individual. It may be extended as sequences are connected, but otherwise the relative times of different sequences remain unrelated to one another.

This time constructed by the sequential thinker orders his own activities reasonably well. The events which transpire in his immediate environment have an apparent structure, one which is visible and available in terms which can be assimilated by the sequential thinker. First, many of these events occur in sequences which are repeated again and again in daily life. This gives the sequential thinker the opportunity to learn the order of individual sequences and to discover how they overlap and thereby combine to form longer chains of activity. Consequently, the time of his passing present is extended. Second, these sequences transpire only in the time of the sequential thinker's observation of them. Consequently, his sense of time is unified by the singularity of his egocentric vision. Third, the personal and immediate time of these sequences itself occurs in a larger context, that of the recurring sequences of day and night and of the changing seasons. Thus, the sequential thinker's construction of time acquires a broader, circular frame of reference.

While the objective characteristics of the events of his personal life lend his construction of time greater extension and integration, the objective order of the politics he observes does not. Limited to contact through television, he is presented with a political time which is fragmentary and disconnected. There is no extension of this time to the present. Individual events rarely last longer than the two minutes of the standard news item presentation and there is no apparent overlap between temporally contiguous events. One moment a President is talking, the next Afghan rebels are fighting and in the third we are worried about missing children. Moreover, there is no clear unity to this time. Egocentric perception is confounded with that provided by the television. Consequently, events occur according to their own times. A President may take an unbearable infinity to drone through to the end of his speech and several days' events in Nicaragua can be compressed into just a few moments. In the end, the sequential thinker is left with a subjective understanding of politics which consists of a collection of event sequences with little integration. He may remember each with considerable vividness and accuracy, but will be unable to integrate them into any coherent history or project them into the prediction of a future.

The players   The sociopolitical universe of the sequential thinker is populated by observed, concrete objects, each with its particular appearance and place in a sequence of events. These entities are truly objects, not subjects. They are the accoutrements of events, not the agents which give those events their dynamic and direction. So conceived, the objects which are seen to participate in social and political life may include things as well as people. For example, concrete symbols which commonly accompany political rituals (e.g., the flag or the crown) may be viewed as involved in similar and as important ways as political leaders themselves. Of course, the sequential thinker may observe how much more leaders do (or are involved in) than cultural symbols or icons, but the latter will continue to occupy a significant place in his dynamic political universe. In this regard, the sequential thinker's reasoning may seem infused with magical thinking and superstition.

Animate or inanimate, these objects of social and political life are understood with reference to their appearance and the specific things they are observed to do. For example, a sequential thinker may understand President Reagan to be a nice-looking older man who wears a blue suit, gives speeches and tells people what to do. His conception of the President will not include anything the President has said or done which he has not had the opportunity to observe nor will it include anything which is inherently unobservable such as the President's general beliefs or understandings. He may hear statements of belief and be able to repeat them. However, he will understand them only as accompaniments of a particular event or action he has witnessed.

Conceived in these appearance-mediated terms, the inhabitants of the sequential thinker's world are not themselves subject to self-conscious definition. Their features are not analyzed and then ordered according to some subjective standard. Rather, people and things are really regarded only as markers for distinguishing the moments of a sequence. A single person may be observed to be a participant in a number of events. However, no global conception of the person is constructed which incorporates all of these activities and places them in some internal relation to one another. Rather, the sequential thinker's conceptualization of other people is fragmentary and fluid. On one occasion, a person may be conceived with regard to one aspect of his appearance or in terms of a particular thing he does. On another occasion, circumstances may direct the sequential thinker's focus to a different aspect of that person's appearance or a different behavior. Thus, the same person may be different things at different times to the sequential thinker. Evaluations of that person will vary accordingly.

As an individual is not given any integrative definition, so different individuals are not compared and grouped according to any abstract categorical standards. In sequential thought, people are considered as singular entities. They are not defined in terms of certain abstracted features of their appearance or behavior and then self-consciously identified with some people and differentiated from others on this basis. Conceptions such as class, race, ethnicity or nationality are not, therefore, a natural part of the sequential thinker's construction of politics. He therefore lacks the conceptual structure to support adequately such in-group loyalties as patriotism and such out-group hatreds as racism.

Again, the inherent structure of the sequential thinker's exposure to this immediate social environment supports a somewhat richer representation of persons than does his exposure to politics. His immediate social environment presents him with many people whom he encounters daily. As a result, he may acquire a great deal of fragmentary knowledge about these familiar others, knowledge which is tied to a host of cues present in his immediate environment. Therefore, his conceptualization of these familiar people will be relatively rich. Still, he cannot conceive of them as self-directing and creative subjects nor can he define them in an integrative manner. Thus, his conception of even his close friends will remain concrete and fragmentary. The sequential thinker's political environment generally gives him less support. The people presented by the media are seen rarely, do only a few things and appear to have little direct effect on one's life. As a result they are easily forgotten and, when remembered, are understood in only the sketchiest terms. The sequential thinker has little to say about even the most ever-present political figure, the national leader.

In this context, it is worth noting that the world of politics often requires the sequential thinker to consider groups or institutions. The news frequently focuses on ethnic groups and political parties or on the Congress, the Supreme Court and the various departments of the executive. As suggested earlier, the sequential thinker cannot make sense of the whole of a collection of people, either as a group or an institution. Groups and institutions cannot be seen, only individual people can. Moreover, the internal relations that characterize the organizational structure of a collectivity are not apparent in any simple observation of an array of people or the sequence of their actions. Consequently, the sequential thinker will tend not to think about groups and institutions. To the degree to which he must, he will focus on a particular symbol or representative and understand the group in these terms. Thus, when trying to understand Libya, he will do so by considering only Gaddafi or when trying to understand blacks, he will do so in terms of a particular black to whom he has been exposed. Although the sequential thinker observes people in a social or political context, he does not define them contextually – that is with reference to their relationship to one another.

Political action   The action of the players in this sociopolitical universe consists of what is specific, concrete and actually observed.

The focus is on the particular things people are observed to say and do. Characteristically, this focus does not extend to what the sequential thinker is unable to observe. He does not extrapolate to consider what occurred beyond the particulars to which he has been exposed. Therefore, when hearing of an event or series of events, he does not consider what may have occurred earlier or what is likely to follow. (The exception here is when the events in question match a known sequence and this is then used to go beyond the information given.) He also does not construct hypotheticals. He does not consider a variety of alternatives which might have transpired or might be explored. Therefore, in his judgement of social and political affairs, he is limited to a consideration of what has occurred and judges it simply on the basis of whether the outcome is a desirable one.

An action is understood with reference to its place in a sequence of actions in which it is observed to appear. These sequences may be learned and remembered, but they are not analyzed. There is no atemporal juxtaposition of antecedent and consequent events and no consideration of a possible causal connection between one or more aspects of the earlier event and the event which followed. Nor is there any construction of a system of interrelated activity and a consideration of the role or function of an action in this context. Consequently, the sequential thinker's reasoning does not lead him to explain other people or their action, nor does it lead him to interpret that action with reference to some general group or political context. They simply are who they are observed to be and they do what they are observed to do. The object of reasoning is rather to observe and remember the place of particular people and their actions in a particular sequence of events.

Bound by this conception of action, the sequential thinker perceives and accounts for political activity in a very limited way. Typically, he will perceive only specific acts and statements. He will note that Carter sent the helicopters as part of the failed rescue mission in Iran, that Gaddafi threatened Reagan and Gary Hart spends time in the mountains. These actions are in turn linked to little sequences in which they have been observed to be played out. Generally, these sequences are not long – mere shreds of activity which are not related to one another. There is no causal analysis, no determination of why something occurred and no prediction of where events will lead. The explanations and predictions provided by other people (or generally prevalent in the culture) may be repeated when something of the sort is required of the sequential thinker by someone to whom he is talking, but their rationale is poorly understood and never justified. As there is no causal analysis, there is no interpretation of action in any

framework nor does the observation of action lead to such a framework. For example, sequential thinkers will tend not to use information on who does what to whom across a variety of circumstances to
make inferences regarding a social hierarchy to account for the behavior observed. Rather each sequence of activity is noted in all the
richness and limitation of its particularity.

Social conditions of adaptation and development   The sequential
thinker can successfully adapt to some environments and not to
others. Given the nature of his reasoning and the quality of the
political understandings he can construct, he can readily adapt to a
social life which orients around phenomena which are real and concrete. Problems such as where to go to get food, what piecemeal tasks
must be done on the job or the meeting time to perform a particular
task or game, are readily addressed within the framework of
sequential reasoning. The issues involved are understood when their
solution is provided by experience. The sequential thinker needs the
opportunity to observe the specific patterns of events or interpersonal
exchange which provide answers to the questions of when, where and
how. Thus, he can best adapt to social conditions wherein the activity
he is required to perform is modelled by others and the rewards
associated with successful or unsuccessful performance are immediate
and clear. Adaptation is further facilitated when the people, places
and instruments of social exchange are recurring and therefore
familiar and well-learned features of daily life.

The question then is what kind of societal configuration would
confront the sequential thinker with such a congenial environment. It
is clear that the relevant domain of social exchange would be limited
to the confines of a small group. In this context, individual members
of the group would have regular face-to-face contact with one
another. The structure of such a group would be simple and fluid. To
the extent to which there are role differentiations and power hierarchies, these would be implicit and reflect concrete differences in the
talents and strengths of particular individuals as they are relevant in
particular situations. With changing situations and passing time, the
relevance and very existence of these differentiating qualities may
change and the implicit structure of social life would alter accordingly. The activities of such a group would be oriented toward the
present, but in such a way that they tend to reproduce the past.
Things will tend to be done as they have been done before, but at the
same time specific practices (as they are embedded in global event
sequences) will readily be changed in the light of what appears to be
transpiring in the present. As a result, the group's pattern of exchange

creates anticipations, but they must be supported ongoingly by realities. Such a group would develop little in the way of a history and/ or future orientation. At most, it might produce a collage of stories which are evoked by their connection to specific events and ordered only by their place in the cycle of days and seasons.

These small, simple and fluid social environments provide a context in which the sequential thinker can adequately adapt and develop a subjective sense of the adequacy of his own understanding. As a result, they do not encourage development beyond this sequential stage. One example of a social group of this kind may be the primitive tribe. Closer to home are the isolated and powerless subpopulations of a modern industrial society. Examples of these might include the fluid, experience-bound and individually anchored society of Elliot Liebow's *Tally's Corner* (1967). Although embedded in a complex, modern society, the poor are insulated by their lack of access to the bases and tools of power needed to encounter such a society in its full complexity. Consequently, their lives revolve around the immediacy of their neighborhood as it is now. In this context, it is interesting to speculate on the cognitive bases of the so-called 'culture of poverty'. It may very well be that the apparent impulsiveness and limited horizons of those caught by poverty and their inability to conceive a path of escape can be best understood with reference to the inherent potential and limits of sequential reasoning.

Whereas such relatively simple social settings are comprehensible and manageable, the settings created by more complex and differentiated societies are not. The latter force the sequential thinker to make sense of a world which is not simply concrete, but one infused with subjectivity. He must not only observe the reality of what people do and its consequences for him, he must also recognize other people's points of view and the consequences which events have for them. At the same time, to act effectively, he must make sense of people and places he has not seen, and may never see. He must also draw on relationships evidenced in the past and project into a clearly conceived future in order to plan an appropriate course of action. In addition, more complex societies also require that the sequential thinker make sense of social phenomena relative to one another. Thus, he is led to define individuals with reference to their place in a hierarchical order or their membership in a categorical group and to understand behavior with reference to the social and political rules which govern it.

Exposure to these demands and definitions of a complex society lead the sequential thinker onto an unfamiliar cognitive terrain and demand a form of reasoning different from his own. His attempt to make sense of it can only yield partial and ultimately distorting images of the world around him. He will not understand his environment and, therefore, will not respond to it appropriately. This will be evidenced both in his failure to get what he expects and in his inability to perform in the ways expected of him. The result will be personal frustration and discomfort on the one hand and social reproach and punishment on the other. From the perspective of the sequential thinker, the problems are difficult and unsettling. To address them, he needs an environment which encourages his development, one which gives him the freedom to make his mistakes and yet demands that he learns from them. In particular, he must be given the opportunity and direction needed to work with what is novel, remote and abstract. He must be accorded the power to engage in action which incorporates numbers of new and removed objects and people over an extended period of time. In the end, he must also be rewarded for his successes. To the degree to which all of this is provided, the sequential thinker is likely to develop. His reasoning will become linear. To the degree to which his social environment fails to provide the requisite encouragement, opportunity and direction, he may not develop. Faced with personal frustration and social rejection, he may withdraw from the larger and more complex polity. In so doing, he will actively consider only his concrete, immediate social environment and do so in his sequential manner. Thus, he will escape the larger society as best he can. Depending on a variety of factors, the more sophisticated and adapted members of that society may come to regard him as crazy, criminal or merely stupid.

Even where the sequential thinker fails to develop and attends only to his personal social environment, he will continue to have some exposure to the larger society. For the most part, he will ignore what he cannot understand. Insofar as he is led to make some sense of it, he will do so according to the structure of his sequential understanding. He will thereby redefine that socially constructed reality in his own, ultimately inappropriate, terms. To illustrate, let us consider some examples of what may result. First, there is the problem of making sense of references to political actors whom the sequential thinker has never seen. Again, the most probable result here is that he will simply ignore these references. Where conditions force some attempt to understand, it is likely that he will use some aspect of the reference to the actor (either a verbal label or a reported recognizable physical feature) to forge an identification between this unseen person and one he has already observed. With this fusion, the unknown comes to share features of the known and, thereby, has meaning for the sequential thinker which it could not otherwise have. For example, the reference to the President as 'father' of the country may provide a basis for understanding the President as the same as one's own father. In this context, it is important to remember that the sequential thinker's understanding of his father is fragmentary, partial and concrete. Made meaningful in these terms, the conception of the President is likely to absorb only one or two perceived features of the father.

A second example is provided by the difficulties the sequential thinker encounters when attempting to make sense of the explicit hierarchicalization of political life. In more complex polities, there are a variety of relationships between leaders and followers and intervening levels of powers to be understood. The best the sequential thinker can do is focus on particular political actors and follow the ways in which one acts on another. In so doing, he can only construct a crude two-step hierarchy in which the person performing the antecedent act is seen to be higher than the one performing the succeeding one. Moreover, the hierarchy thus constructed has only limited application. It applies only to a specific case of particular individuals involved in a particular activity.

A final example is provided by the sequential thinker's attempt to make sense of social and political groups. Lacking the means of constructing a classificatory schema for grouping individuals and defining their common characteristics, he can only focus on the particular individuals presented to him as members of the groups in question. He will then fuse the group label with the observed representative and think of the group accordingly. Thus, he will think of a political party with reference to a particular party member he has observed or he will think of a nation in terms of its leader. In both cases, not only is the whole not greater than the sum of its parts, it is reduced to only that one part currently under consideration. Because the focal point of an individual's reasoning about a group may vary (according to the substance of what the environment presents him at any given moment), so his image and response to the group may also vary.

The vision of the sequential thinker in a complex polity can be illustrated by the metaphor of the naive stargazer. He looks up into the night sky and sees a host of stars. They appear to do nothing to each other and nothing to him. Occasionally, one may be observed to move, but never in a way that has personal consequences. If forced to think about the stars, to understand them, the stargazer will think of them with reference to things he knows and view them accordingly. Left to his own devices, he will think of the stars very little. The only thing he will really comprehend about them is that they are located up above and next to one another. For the sequential thinker, politics is the domain of the night sky.

LINEAR POLITICAL REASONING

Linear thinkers analyze the sequences of activity they observe. They do so by focusing on specific actions and then placing one in relation to another. Three kinds of questions guide their intellectual activity. The first are those of external relation. The basic questions here are what was the cause of an observed effect or what future effect will an observed cause produce? The second kind are those of identity. The orienting question is what group of actions produces the same effect or is the result of the same cause? The third kind of question is normative. The issue here is what is the correct or proper sequence of actions which should take place? The answers to all these questions are discovered either through one's own observation or through another's report.

The structure of linear thought

When reasoning about a sequence of events, the linear thinker creates an atemporal frame of reference within which to examine them. The result is a concrete abstraction of those events from the time of their sequential unfolding. He is thus able to consider several individual actions at the same time and to examine how each leads to or follows another. In this manner, he can decompose and reassemble a sequence of events which he observes or has reported to him. Metaphorically speaking, the linear thinker can take the motion picture of an event, analyze it into its individual frames of activity and then examine their relative places in the overall order of the film. In this sense, the reasoning of the linear thinker is both analytical and synthetic. However, these two aspects of his activity are not themselves integrated. Rather than occurring simultaneously, one follows on the other. As a result, both linear analysis and synthesis are guided by the qualities of the objective phenomena as they are presented. Therefore, while linear reasoning goes beyond what is apparent, it remains anchored in the concreteness of the objective environment upon which it operates. It allows for imaginative recombination, but not directed a priori or hypothetical thought.

The conceptual relations produced by this linear reasoning are abstracted from ongoing events and thus have a subjective definition which is independent of them. These relations are unidirectional

– that is, when connecting units, they assign priority to one, and the others are defined relative to it. To illustrate, let us consider the linear thinker's understanding of the relation between a person's work and its product. In the context of their linear relation, either the work activity or the product is given priority. Where the activity is regarded as primary, the product is defined relative to it. It is understood as an attribute of the person working, as his property. Where the work product is thought of as primary, it is the person's work activity that is defined in relative terms. It is conceived as an attribute of the object transformed or produced. The person himself may be defined in these terms, that is, with reference to his occupation. The general point here is that whether the focus is on the work or its product, one of the objects related will be considered primary and constitute the basis for defining the other. The two are not reciprocally related or understood with reference to some general principle or abstraction in terms of which both may be defined.

So structured, these conceptual relations have a number of distinguishing characteristics. First, they are experientially based and concrete. They derive from the quality of events as they are directly observed or described. This is true in several respects. On the one hand, they depend on the presentation of events to guide the dissection of a sequence into its parts. The determination of the components of the phenomenon observed will reflect what is visually or verbally distinguished. On the other, linear relations depend on the presentation of events to guide the connection of these components. The links made are based on what is observed to be contiguous in space and time or on what is verbally related in others' reports. The characteristics of the situation observed and the focus of other people's descriptions also determine which of the components so linked will be used as a basis for defining the others.[5]

Second, despite their concreteness, linear relations do have a certain generality. Relating specific actions to one another in the context of a specific event or set of events, linear relations reflect the particulars of the initial observation situation. However, once established, these relations exist in an atemporal space of the subject's own construction and are thus freed from the specific context in which they were observed. As a result, the linear relation established in one situation may be self-consciously applied in an attempt to anticipate or understand novel situations in which the same actions may be involved. For example, upon observing that person A's smile is followed by person B's friendly nod, the linear thinker may infer a causal relationship. Then when examining C smiling at D, he will anticipate that D will respond with a nod. The actions related are specific, but the relation between those actions is itself applied generally across persons or circumstances.[6]

Third, linear relations may also be extended or combined in ways not directly dependent on their objective presentation. Within the atemporal frame constructed by the linear thinker, relations not directly related in the unfolding of one's experience may be linked to one another. This occurs when the person recognizes that relations based on different contexts share common objects. It may happen in two ways. Several different linear relations may be observed to share one object in common. An example would be the several relations which involve a given person observed doing a variety of things at different points in time. The person may have been observed to speak in a low voice on one occasion, to lift particularly heavy objects on a second and to laugh boisterously on a third. Sharing a common cause, the person as agent, these apparently dissimilar effects may be combined to form a single category. In this manner, linear relations may be subjectively combined so as to form concrete, aggregative categories. Alternatively, linear relations forged under different circumstances may be linked when they are observed to overlap with one another. In this case, two relations may share the same action-object, but in one instance that object is an effect to a prior cause and in the second it is the cause to a subsequent effect. Where several linear relations are related to one another in this manner, each may serve to extend the rest as a link in a linear causal chain.

Finally, linear relations have a normative quality. While derived from experience, they are subjectively defined and thus retain an order and quality of their own. Largely independent of subsequent experience, they provide a standard whereby that experience may be judged. In this regard, linear reasoning yields concrete rules of normal action. These rules reflect social definitions of appropriate behavior and the personal observation of recurring sequences of action. If violated by subsequent experience, these rules will not be abandoned. Instead, the experience itself will be denied or denigrated. In this sense, the relations of linear thought yield stronger expectations and are far less mutable than those of sequential thought. A linear rule will be reconstructed only when an accumulation of contrary experience or a change in social opinion dictates.

Linear reasoning also delimits the qualities of the units it can address. These conceptual units are concrete, observable actions. They include the specific acts that the linear thinker has personally observed and those described to him by others. Where an action is not in fact present, it may none the less be inferred. These action-units are extensive. They are meaningful as they are related to one another. To create this meaning, a single connection will suffice. For example, consider the linear thinker's attempt to make sense of the waving of one's hand. Unto itself, the action is meaningless and a search for its unidirectional connection to some other act is conducted. This is satisfactorily completed when it is linked either to a cause which precedes it, say another person's wave, or to an effect it produces, such as another person's jumping back in fright. If no other act is observed, one will be inferred on the basis of prior experience or cultural dictate. The action will then be conceived relative to the other with which it is joined. In our example, the wave is thus seen as friendly greeting or aggressive gesture depending on the nature of the act to which it is related.

In this context, concrete objects, the focal point of sequential thought, are only subunits. Action is the basic unit of linear thought. Accordingly, objects are defined by virtue of their relation to action. Thus, they are no longer conceived as 'things-unto-themselves' but as 'that-which-acts' (actors) or as 'that-which-is-acted-upon'. As a result, objects are identified primarily on the basis of what they do (or have done to them). References to appearance are secondary and conditional. Articulated into linear relations among actions, several objects may be considered at once. Any one will be conceived by virtue of its external relation to others. This relation may be simple or, where a number of relations are intertwined, categories and hierarchies of actors may be established. Categories of objects are created when all share a common cause or produce a common effect. For example, all children produced by the same mother may naturally be combined to form a single category. It is noteworthy that the whole created, the category of siblings, of which the various dissimilar children are a part, is conceived with reference to an attribute they have in common and not (as in the case of sequential thought) with reference to the global qualities of any particular one of them. Hierarchies are established on the basis of how different objects are observed to be placed in a causal linear chain. Those that are placed earlier in the chain are accorded greater status.

Political understanding

The political reasoning of the linear thinker does not simply involve a recording of what he observes or has reported to him. Rather, he naturally analyzes the component features of an event and constructs relations between them. Thus, he thinks of social and political life in terms of its constituent actions and considers these as they are causally related to one another. In so doing, he not only reconstructs what is presented to him, but he also reaches beyond it. Using the relations between actions he has already constructed, the linear thinker can go beyond the observation of an action and infer the existence of a cause or effect which is temporally and spatially removed. Despite this power, the political reasoning of the linear thinker is grounded in his experience and retains its concreteness. Both his analysis of social and political events into their component actions and his subsequent construction of the linkages between them is guided by the way in which events are presented to him. Consequently, his political reasoning is powerfully mediated by the quality of his own experience and by the information other people provide. Given the unidirectional quality of his reasoning, the linear thinker does not consider abstract objects nor does he construct abstract, principled relations among them. Although he can build on his experience to understand subsequent and novel events, he can therefore never redefine or critically evaluate that experience. Consequently, the political understandings he constructs will necessarily be very much a product of the sociocultural environment to which he is exposed.

Despite these limits, the linear thinker is able to reason well beyond his particular social and political experiences. He can do so in two ways. On the one hand, he can generalize. Once he has understood the relationship among actions in one situation, he can use that relationship to anticipate and comprehend similar action as it is performed in new situations by different people. Here as always, his thinking is action-specific. The focus is on how particular actions follow one another. As a result, his generalizations are likely to produce a concrete and ritualistic conception of social and political life. His ability to generalize also has important normative dimensions. It provides the means whereby standards are generated and then applied. Insofar as the standards used are derived from experience, 'is' and 'ought' are merged in the mind of the linear thinker. For the linear thinker, to know that B follows A is also to know that B *should* follow A. One result is that his evaluation of political events will be guided by social conventions. On the other hand, the linear thinker is also able to go beyond the particulars of his experience by rearranging it along categorical and hierarchical lines. Thus, when thinking about politics, not only will he consider particular actors and actions, he will also think in terms of categories of actors and readily group them into classes, races and nationalities. Similarly, he will consider action in the context of causal chains of social and political command and construct hierarchies of individuals who are arrayed according to their places in that chain.

Reasoning in this way, the linear thinker constructs a view of politics as concrete and active. For him, politics takes place on an extended stage filled with actors, each pushing in his own direction. In this context, the linear thinker distinguishes between the subjective and the real. He understands subjectivity to consist of perceptions and internal motives. He also recognizes that it may vary. People may be exposed to events differently and therefore have different perceptions of them. Alternatively, people may be driven by different wants or purposes. Given these subjective differences, people will act and react differently.

While a clear improvement over the reality-bound conception of sequential thought, the linear thinker's notion of subjectivity is limited. It is always conceived in concrete and particular terms. Perception is understood with reference to its specific substantive content and motives or intentions are understood with reference to the specific acts they engender. In both cases, the subjective phenomena are understood with reference to external realities, perception with regard to its object and motives with regard to their consequences. No attempt is made to define subjectivity in its own terms or to consider its formal and abstract qualities. A person's attitudes, perceptions and intentions are never understood relative to one another, as expressions of an underlying understanding. Nor are they conceived as forces which define actions as well as direct them. Furthermore, no distinction is drawn between the constructions of the individual and those of society. The linear thinker has little awareness or understanding of collective or societal phenomena. He does not view the beliefs, values and rituals of daily life as expressions of a general social structure nor does he recognize that they are interdependent aspects of an abstract cultural whole. Exposed to a different culture, the linear thinker will only see an aggregate of particular actions and beliefs. He will understand them as attributes of a strange group of people and explain them as expressions of the inherent character of the individual members of that group. Failing to adequately distinguish or conceptualize the intersubjective and collective aspects of social life, the linear thinker will not adequately appreciate the role social structure and culture play in shaping the particular events and rituals of politics.

The space of politics   The political domain of the linear thinker is an extended staging ground for action. Guided by past experience and others' reports, the linear thinker constructs relations which can be used to reach beyond the limits of a present experience or report. Thus, observing or hearing of a particular action, he can make inferences about remote actors and actions which are causally related to the action in question. In this manner, the linear thinker can construct a political arena which extends beyond the borders of his immediate experience. Built on relations among actions, this construction is not simply defined in spatial terms. It is not simply a geography. It also maps social and political activity. Actors and actions are located by virtue of their active contact, causal influence and common behavior.

The linear thinker's construction of this political space has several distinguishing features. To begin with, its extension beyond the immediate is always dependent on past experience. To make inferences about what exists beyond what is before him, the linear thinker associates the immediate action with other actions with which it is already understood to be related. This prior understanding is in turn based on earlier personal experience or others' reports of how these actions are connected. In this manner, the linear thinker can go beyond the information given. However, he is able to do so only by drawing on past experience. As a result, his constructions of politics are ultimately, if not immediately, bound to events as they are presented to him. Two points follow on this. First, his conception of political reality will largely be determined by social and cultural factors. The purview of his own direct experience is necessarily limited to those people and activities he encounters in his immediate day-to-day life. Therefore, his understanding of the action relationships of a remote political system will largely depend on his exposure to others' reports and to culturally prevalent claims. His conception of the boundaries of politics (what are and are not political issues or events) and the nature of the domain so bounded (the relevant actors and actions and their interrelations) will be shaped accordingly. Second, the linear thinker's map of the political domain will be a fragmented one. The linear thinker understands those connections which he directly observes or which are drawn for him by others. He lacks the general conceptual framework required to make his own independent deductions of how activities may be linked. Therefore, he is unable to construct a single, integrated political reality. Rather, he reconstructs pieces of an objective political reality as they are presented to him. When a cluster of connected facts are made available on a specific issue, activity or place, pieces of his political map may be well elaborated. When few such associations are made, his representation of a piece of political reality will be spare. Similarly, when the connections are not made for him, these pieces will themselves be isolated from one another.

Another distinguishing feature of the linear thinker's construction is its shifting focus. As just noted, this political space is an aggregate of dissociated pieces. While his thought can move relatively freely among the weave of connections which constitute any one of those pieces, he can think in terms of only one piece at a time. To borrow Robert Lane's language, the linear thinker is a 'morselizer' (Lane, 1962, 1973). Which piece or morsel he will consider and the perspective he will take is objectively determined. His focus is directed to what he is personally experiencing or others are presenting to him and he will make sense of particular persons or activities as they relate to this focus. For example, when political discourse focuses on civil rights, this will engulf his conception of politics and direct the associations he constructs. With a shift in discourse, perhaps to a focus on national defense, the civil rights issue will evaporate and his view of politics will be dominated by the defense issue and its associations. As suggested by this example, the shifting focus of the linear thinker is powerfully determined by external circumstances as they are presented to him. In the language of the mass media research, he is very susceptible to 'agenda setting' effects.[7]

A third feature of the political space constructed by the linear thinker is its center–periphery structure. His present focus provides a center out of which peripheral considerations are built. In this context, the center retains a priority status and the peripheral considerations are understood as they relate to it. Even when prior knowledge suggests that this periphery is somehow more basic or important, the center–periphery structure is retained. In this instance, the center shifts to the new object of concern and all else is considered relative to it. An example of this structure is evident in the way in which the linear thinker conceptualizes the international arena. He may view his own country as the center. All other countries will then be conceptualized by virtue of their relationship to his own. They are the periphery. Little attention is paid to how these peripheral countries may relate to one another. In this sense, the linear thinker does not construct a decentered conceptual map of the international system relative to which all countries are similarly located. This is equally true of his construction of domestic politics.

So constituted, there are clear limits to the linear thinker's understanding of the space of politics. He has no sense of its systemic qualities. Political events, actions and actors are not reciprocally located and no weave of multiply intersecting relationships is constructed. In addition, the linear thinker has no sense of any abstract dimension of the political arena. No inferences are drawn regarding the existence of implicit structures which underlie the observed connections among actions. Thus, there is little sense of the collective as an internally differentiated, self-regulating entity. Finally, there is no element of the hypothetical in linear political space. The linear thinker is not able to construct an alternative vision of the world based on a logic of his own construction. As a result, his political reality is strictly conventional. It includes no aspect of the possible, the moral or the ideal beyond what is personally experienced or culturally defined.

The time of politics   The linear thinker's construction of time is extensive. Beginning with present action, he builds both a past and a future. Inferring prior causes, he creates a past, and divining subsequent effects, he creates a future. As suggested by our common usage of the terms, this past and future are distinct from the present, but are always conceived in relation to it. Neither is regarded simply unto itself nor are these segments of time distinguished by virtue of any internal logical or structural differences. The present itself is meaningful only by virtue of its relation to the past it follows and the future to which it gives rise.

So constituted, this linear conception of time has a number of related features. First, it has direction. It is a projection of action in the past through the present into the future. Second, it is concrete and grounded in the particulars of experience. Apart from its strong directionality, the qualities of linear time are determined by the objective presentation of particular actions following on one another in a particular order. Third, linear time is fragmented. Its internal connections reflect the real connections among actions as they are observed or reported. While interrelated among themselves in a sequence, the connections among the sequences themselves may not be presented. As a result, even if the linear thinker learns to mark these sequences relative to a single socially defined clock or calendar, they will be understood as separate trains of activity, separate lines of time. Fourth, linear time is inherently dynamic. It is motored by its own active nature. Each moment is produced and directed by one which precedes it or is drawn forward by one which will succeed it. These pushes and pulls are considered only with respect to their target and not relative to one another. There is no definition of an inherent structure to the dynamic of events which delimits the possible forms in which they might appear.

Within this frame of reference, the linear thinker is able to follow and make sense of an extended series of political events. He can readily understand what is remote and can use the conventions he has learned to fill in some of the gaps in his information. Thus, he can follow the particular events in an electoral campaign with interest and understanding. For him, it will be a sequence of concrete steps which lead finally to electoral success or defeat. In the vernacular of campaign politics, he sees it as a horse race. In this light, he follows the succession of trips, claims, attacks and counterattacks the candidates make and recognizes their impact on the final outcome. In a similar way, he can trace the history of national or international conflict. Following a confrontation such as that which occurred between Libya and the United States in the spring of 1986, a linear thinker can use television and newspaper reports to construct a sequence of events. In the case of the Libyan–American conflict, this might have begun with Libya sponsoring terrorism, Reagan reacting with a warning, Gadaffi returning with taunts and further terrorism and then Reagan ordering the air force attack. As suggested by these examples, the linear conception of the time of political events consists of an ordered set of particular concrete actions. These actions are links in a causal linear chain. Each produces the next or is predestined by it. In the end, the linear thinker constructs a political history of the events in question. Each of these histories is specific to the particular actions and events involved. Unless experience dictates otherwise, they will remain isolated from one another.

Not only can the linear thinker create a time which recaptures his observation of an extended series of events, he can also make inferences to unknown causes and effects. Thus, if he observes an event for which there is no evident antecedent, he will search for prior causes. For him, actions always have a history. To be understood, their antecedents must be discovered and the action explained. Similarly, the linear thinker will also consider the consequences of present action and thereby project into the future. In this vein, he can consider the implications of political policy, albeit in a crude fashion. Both his explanations and projections are necessarily limited. They are concrete. Only specific causes and effects are located. They also tend to be simple. The search for a linear connection may be completed by linking the current action to only one other. Thus, there is a tendency to explain events in terms of single causes and predict single effects. Finally, the linear thinker's explanations and projections are experientially based. The inferences upon which they are based always reflect the particular action relationships which he has observed or had reported to him.

The players   The players that populate the political universe of the linear thinker are conceived with regard to their participation in the action of social and political life. Unlike their conception by the sequential thinker, they are not simply regarded as an accompaniment of that action. Rather, they are seen as either its source or its target. In the first respect, players are the causes of action. They have internal drives and motivations which yield specific thoughts and behavior. As actors, they direct action. They are therefore regarded as more basic elements of political life and are accorded greater status. Players may also be the targets of action, their own activities directed by some other causal force. Acted upon rather than acting, they are regarded as derivative and are accorded less social and political status.

These player-actors are concrete. They include particular individuals or groups that have been seen or reported and others who have not actually been seen, but whose presence is inferred by action attributed to them. Actors who may potentially be, but never are, seen, such as gods or fates, are also included. Like observed actors, these unseen ones are conceived in concrete terms. Examples include the classic Greek conceptions of gods as particular people or animals and the anthropomorphism of more contemporary abstract gods. Like all others, these unseen actors have specific physical characteristics, hold particular attitudes and perform particular acts. As such, they play their own concrete role in daily social and political life.

When observing these concrete actors, the linear thinker defines them. His consideration is not simply limited to what they are observed to do (or have done to them) in a specific situation. Rather, he constructs a category of an actor as a cause or as an effect of a set of actions. As a result, a given actor is defined by the particular thoughts he expresses, the acts he performs, the results he achieves and by the particular ways in which others view, label and treat him. The actor is thus conceived as the aggregate of the specific things he does and has done to him. In his consideration of the actor, the linear thinker may draw on other experience and learning to extend this conception. In so doing, he may connect an actor's action with other actions and actors. As a result, he may come to think of the actor with reference not only to his particular behaviors, but also with regard to the additional actions or attributes with which that behavior is associated. These clusters of associated acts are themselves a product of personal experience or cultural definition. Articulated into the structure of linear thought, they are simple aggregates, not logically coherent wholes.[8]

To illustrate the terms in which a linear thinker conceives of particular social and political actors, let us consider how he would think of President Reagan. For him, Reagan is an actor who has been observed or reported to be involved in particular ways in a number of different situations. Thus, he would be conceived in terms of the specific statements he has made, actions he has performed and the ways he has been treated by other actors. The linear thinker may come to view Reagan as a man who warns Russia to respect American interests and as one who tells the poor that it is time for them to take care of themselves. He may also regard Reagan as a man able to get laws passed by Congress and who has survived an assassination attempt. Finally, he may think of him as well-liked by most Americans and as a president who simply does what others in his administration tell him to do. In the end, the linear thinker will conceive of Reagan as the set of all these particular ways he has acted and been acted upon. Importantly, the linear thinker's conceptualization of Reagan does not extend beyond this creation of an atemporal category within which to aggregate the concrete things Reagan has done. No attempt is made to further relate the specific acts thus grouped together or to interpret or explain them with respect to some underlying logic of Reagan's ideology, personality or place in a social structure.[9]

The linear thinker can also conceive of groups of individuals. Like individuals, groups consist of concrete categories. However, whereas an individual is an actor linked to a set of actions, a group is a set of actors linked to a common action. For example, the linear thinker may construct a category or group of individuals when they (1) behave in a common way or participate in a common ritual, (2) express a common belief, (3) command the same resources, (4) have a common appearance, or (5) have a common genesis or lineage. In this way, the linear thinker constructs a political universe which is not only populated by individual actors, but also by English-speakers, criminals, Catholics, conservatives, Democrats, blacks, the French and families.

This definition of social and political groups has all the trademarks of linear thought. First, groups are defined relative to action. This is true in two respects. On the one hand, the very definition of a group is based on the observation of a behavior or attribute which is shared by a group of individuals. Focusing on the group's membership, the linear thinker may recognize differences, but these are subordinated to the features common to them all. For example, if committing a crime becomes a basis for group definition, all criminals may be regarded as members of a common social category and the differences among them or their similarities to non-criminals will simply not enter into the linear thinker's political calculus. On the other hand, the group itself is regarded as an actor that performs in the political arena. Viewed with reference to others, the group is regarded in the same terms as an individual. It is an internally homogeneous force which evidences particular motivations and externally directed behavior. As in the case of the single actor, the various behaviors provide a basis for a more elaborated definition of the acting group. For example, having defined the French as a national group, the linear thinker may observe them or assimilate reports and come to regard them as preoccupied with food, well-dressed and stubbornly uncooperative with the United States.

Second, the social and political groups defined by the linear thinker are concrete abstractions. On the one hand, groups are concrete entities. Each one is constructed on the basis of the observation (or report) of a particular act or feature which is shared by all members of the group. The members are themselves observable, particular entities. Once constructed, groups are further defined in terms of the specific concrete action they take. On the other hand, groups are abstractions. They are constructed by abstracting particular features from a number of observations of global phenomena. The group is then defined relative to these features, features which all individual members share. Defined in these concrete and abstract terms, a group is both defined in terms of its members and yet is not reducible to any one of them. The confusion of the whole with its parts that is produced in sequential thought is therefore avoided. In addition, the now distinct whole provides a basis for the definition of the particular parts. With regard to social perception, the definition of a group provides a basis for conceiving that group's individual members. For example, it may be that a linear thinker may observe that in his town, blacks look the same and live in a single area of town. On this basis, he may define them as a social group. Having done so, he may then be exposed to culturally prevalent conceptions of blacks as lazy. Although he may have no personal experience of this, he may none the less ascribe this quality to the group and then view each of the members accordingly. Importantly, this view of blacks is not readily changed by subsequent experience. His views of blacks as lazy is a concrete abstraction and therefore not readily changed by the observation of particular blacks who are industrious. As suggested by this example, the linear thinker will generally think of groups in terms of stereotypes. These stereotypes will largely be the product of social report rather than direct experience and will remain impervious to the specific counterexamples which everyday life might present.

Third, whereas groups and individuals are defined with reference to one another, the linear thinker can only reason with reference to one set of considerations at a time. Depending on contextual cues, he will think either in terms of individuals or in terms of groups. Focusing on the former, the linear thinker will consider each one as the set of his unique attributes or as he is actively engaged in cooperation or conflict with others. Group membership is either regarded as one of many attributes or, where all are members of the same group, it may be ignored altogether. Focusing on the group, the linear thinker ignores individuals. They are lost in the homogeneous mass of the group to which they belong. Groups are then considered relative to one another.

This tendency to focus on either groups or individuals and its consequences for the perception of a group and its members may be illustrated by briefly considering Mueller's research on the effect of foreign involvement on presidential popularity (Mueller, 1973). One of his key findings is that the popularity of American presidents increases whenever the country is involved in an international crisis. This is true regardless of whether the president responds to the crisis well or badly. This strange result may be readily understood when considered in the light of linear thinking. Whenever presidents are considered in the context of domestic American politics, they are regarded as individual political actors who may or may not be pursuing a course a given citizen feels is desirable. As a result, many may disapprove of the President in this context. However, when presidents are considered in the light of international affairs, they are regarded only as group members, as Americans. As national leaders, they typically become symbolic of the group as a whole. Insofar as individual citizens have positive feelings about their country, all (including those who disapprove of the president when they think of him in the context of domestic politics) are likely to be more supportive when thinking of the president in this context.[10]

In addition to considering individuals as members of groups, the linear thinker can also place them in hierarchical structures according to their location in a linear causal chain of activity. The hierarchies which are thereby produced are unidirectional constructions. Individuals toward the beginning of the causal chain are regarded as more directive and are accorded more status. In the atemporal framework of the linear thinker, power emanates from the top down. There is no sense of power simultaneously flowing from the bottom up or of reciprocal relationships among members at any one level in a hierarchy. These linear hierarchies are also simple and concrete. They are forged in relation to specific action series. There is little attention to the relationship between different hierarchies nor is there any sense of a general social structure which permeates all these more specific hierarchies.

It is in these terms that the linear thinker makes sense of political institutions. For him, they are distinguished by the particular things they do. The Congress makes laws. The State Department takes care of foreign affairs. The Defense Department takes care of national defense. Each of these institutions is hierarchically organized. There is a man at the top who runs things. He issues instructions to those below him who in turn issue further instructions to those below them and so on. People at the same hierarchical level are regarded as an internally homogeneous group and are assumed to act in concert. There is little recognition of how the activity of the upper tiers of an institution may be influenced or at least subverted by that of lower ones. Additionally, there is little attention to the possible diversity of acts for which any institution is responsible and therefore to the possible ways in which they maybe intertwined. Thus, there will be no spontaneous consideration of the interplay among the Congress, State Department and Defense Department in the development of national defense policy. When external reports focus on this, the reported relations among the various institutions will not be well assimilated or understood. A likely result will be to ignore the information or construct a model in which the institutions themselves are regarded as simple groups of actors and are arrayed in a single hierarchy.

Political action   The players in this world perform observable acts. They do and say particular things. While conceived in concrete terms, these acts need not actually be observed by the linear thinker or reported to him by another. They may be inferred from their consequent effects or current causes. Thus, when circumstances or convention require, the linear thinker can consider such apparent intangibles as divine intervention or subjective beliefs and intentions. However, these are considered as though they are concrete particulars and, in principle, observable. Thus, it is assumed that in social life and politics, gods and fates concretely see people, prod and force circumstances upon them and tell them what to do. In a similar vein, beliefs and intentions are regarded as internal speech and therefore readily expressed in public ways. For the most part, these inferred actions are not considered relative to one another, but rather with regard to their concrete observable consequences. For example, beliefs and intentions are considered significant primarily with reference to the concrete behavior or policy initiatives which follow from them. There is little sense that these subjective entities are meaningful by virtue of their relationship to one another nor is there much attempt to interpret them accordingly.

For the linear thinker, this observable action takes place in an ordered world. Each act is a response to an antecedent act and a stimulus to one which will follow. It is a world of causes and effects. People and groups do things either because they are reacting to an external circumstance or because they are responding to some internal disposition. Causes of both kinds are specific: circumstantial causes consist of specific actions which affect the actor and dispositional ones consist of particular intentions to act and/or driving passions. Which causes the linear thinker identifies will depend on what is most available. Where the antecedent act of another is observed, it is likely that the behavior will be explained circumstantially. Where no antecedent act is observed, it is likely that the behavior will be explained dispositionally. As we shall see shortly, explanation under either one of these conditions is strongly influenced by cultural dictates and prior experience.[11]

The connections between cause and effect forged by the linear thinker are themselves concrete and action-specific: they are defined with respect to particular actions and apply to them. Within this limit, they do have a certain generality. While defining a relationship between two particular acts, the link between them is assumed to hold for whomever is acting under whatever conditions. In this sense, these connections constitute rules for action. Once formed, they direct observation and analysis. Confronted by an event, the linear thinker attempts to make sense of it. To do so, he draws on a relevant relational rule. This then orients his considerations. He tends to perceive, understand and remember the objective event in a manner consistent with his subjective, rule-oriented view of it. Frequently, this results in distortion. This occurs in a variety of ways. On the one hand, this distortion may involve the exclusion of relevant evidence or the mistaken inclusion of non-existent data in the analysis of a situation. For example, armed with the 'knowledge' that the English behave in a civilized, non-violent manner, the linear thinker is likely to ignore, misinterpret or forget evidence of the less civilized expressions of English culture (e.g., its punk culture or its football hooliganism). On the other hand, distortion may involve reinterpretation. Knowing that bad people do bad things and regarding the Soviet Union as bad, the linear thinker can only assimilate evidence of good behavior (e.g., disarmament overtures) by inferring improper motives, thereby rendering the good behavior bad and comprehensible.

Although they constitute the conceptual arsenal deployed by the linear thinker in his attempt to make sense of action, these causal linear rules of relationship are objectively determined. They are initially a product of his environment. The linear thinker learns the concrete relationships which then direct his thinking. He may do so by observing the regularity with which one act follows on another, regarding that relationship as 'normal', and then use it to guide subsequent inference. Alternatively, he may be exposed to culturally prevalent descriptions of what follows from what and use these to orient his thinking. For the most part, an individual lacks the ability, interest and exposure to come to his own understanding of most social and political relationships. Consequently, he relies more on the information provided by other people and the mass media.[12]

A product of learning and rather impervious to subsequent experience, the rules of action are understood as given. The linear thinker has no sense of them as products either of intersubjective negotiation or social structural construction. Consequently, he comes to regard social reality as a set of fixed rituals. So defined, these rules not only provide a basis for causal inference, they also suggest a standard for evaluating the appropriateness of behavior. What is normal dictates what one views to be good or desirable and this norm then dictates one's perception of what is actually taking place. In this manner, the moral and the real become intertwined in the context of linear thought.

Thinking in these terms, the linear thinker has no sense of any systemic qualities to what people do or say. Consequently, although he may identify a particular social cause for a person's action, he has no sense of a social structure which underlies the observed cause and effect relationship. Similarly, although he may view another's behavior as a reflection of his beliefs, he has no sense of an implicit structure to that person's activity or a logic to his thinking. This has a number of consequences for his reasoning. First, unaware of the systemic context in which a relationship holds, he will tend to overgeneralize what he learns. For example, he will tend not to anticipate how interactive patterns he has learned at home are unlikely to hold in a different culture. Second, he will not automatically consider how one sequence of events or one governing relationship is intertwined with others. Consequently, when searching for the cause of a given activity, he will tend to be satisfied with the first sufficient one he finds.

The linear thinker views politics as a stage filled with people, groups, institutions and nations doing and saying things to one another. Although there is obvious variety and conflict, this domain is an ordered one. It is regulated by a maze of concrete rules of how political action does and should occur. So ordered, social and political life is regarded as set of rituals, hundreds of little dances which reflect what is necessary and appropriate. The normal is both reified and used to define the good. There is, however, little understanding or even awareness of the manner in which these action-specific rituals cohere (except perhaps that they are dictated by some one person or thing) nor is there any clear sense of the nature and value of social change.

Confronted with a particular political action or event, the linear thinker will automatically seek to determine why it occurred and where it will lead. For example, upon observing the Republicans pushing for tax reform or the Democrats favoring tariffs, he will immediately wonder why they are doing so and what the outcomes of these policy initiatives will be. Throughout, his considerations will be guided by preexisting conceptions or schemas of what follows on what. Returning to the preceding examples, the linear thinker may 'know' that politicians do whatever they do so that they can stay in office. Consequently, he may conclude that Republicans support tax reform and Democrats favor tariffs simply because they believe these policies will get them re-elected. Similarly, he may 'know' that tariffs cause prices to rise and therefore conclude that the Democrats' initiative will make consumers worse off. Notably, both his explanatory and predictive efforts are satisfied by the discovery of a single cause or consequence. Unless forced by circumstance, he will go no further. When he is presented with a clear case where several causes may influence an event, he has trouble judging the relative or interactive effects.

Thinking about political action in these causal linear terms, the linear thinker can construct extended chains of events. Depending on the phenomenon he is tracking, this may take different forms. When viewing a conflictual interaction between actors, he may come to regard the events as something of a ping-pong match. For example, consider his understanding of the ongoing relationship between two countries. By following the sporadic news reports of events involving the two countries and by viewing later events as responses to earlier ones, he can reconstruct the pieces of information he receives into an integrated sequence. In so doing, he understands the relationship as an essentially two-sided affair in which one side makes a move which is followed by a counter move from the other side which in turn leads to a counter move from the first side and so on. While a considerable achievement, the result remains concrete, linear and isolated. It reflects little attempt to divine an underlying logic to what has occurred or to place it in relation to other ongoing events, either international or domestic. A different pattern emerges when the linear thinker attempts to understand a cooperative exchange. He will view such an exchange either as a case where equals speak in one voice or where those of greater control dictate the action of those with less control. Consider the linear thinker's attempt to make sense of how decisions are made within an institution or group. Typically, he can integrate the scattered information made available to him and construct a path of decision-making. Again the resulting conception is limited. Building from particular causal action to subsequent effect, the linear thinker traces a single and unidirectional line of command and directive. He will tend to do so, albeit in a more confused manner, even when information is plentiful and the organizational structure is complex.

Social conditions of adaptation and development   The linear thinker is a more capable participant in social life than the sequential thinker. Because of his ability to construct a more extended time frame, he is less dependent on immediate reward. Similarly, his expanded sense of social space allows him to consider actors and forces that are not immediately present. As a result, he does not need to be closely monitored to insure that he is behaving in a socially desirable way. In addition to orienting to an extended social time and space, the linear thinker is also able to recognize and respond to some of its internal complexities. He can readily understand that a social group may be differentiated into a set of roles and learn how to play his own and respond appropriately to others. Finally, the linear thinker is an inherently more social animal. He thinks in terms of rules or schemas which are largely products of his social environment. Thus, he is socialized not only because his behavior is regulated by social reinforcements schedules, but more fundamentally because his very way of making sense of the world is oriented by his cultural milieu.

Despite this greater social ability, there are certain environments in which the linear thinker is naturally comfortable and others in which he will prove inadequate. To function most appropriately and self-confidently, he needs a social environment which provides clear and concrete behavioral guidelines and social location. To lead his own life, he needs a social environment which provides a specific and elaborated code of behavior which he can learn and follow. Only when he knows exactly what his role is and what specifically is involved in playing it, can he be effective. He also needs to know his own identity. For him, this is a question of where he belongs or what he is part of. It is best answered by the designation of his membership in a group, one which he can clearly understand in terms of the common territory, practice and appearance of its members. He needs an environment where social labels are clear and loyalties are strong. Beyond specific direction and location, the linear thinker also needs guidelines for explanation and prediction. He understands the present events as occurring for reasons and leading to a future and he needs to know the answers to the questions of why and where. There is little room for uncertainty in his view of the world. The linear thinker's needs for clear, concrete direction, location and insight are best served by a social structure which is pyramidal and differentiated along task-specific lines. When control emanates from the top and people are differentiated by what they are supposed to be doing, the linear thinker can most readily understand what others are doing and why. In the light of his own political reasoning, such a structure is maximally comprehensible and legitimate.

In sum, the linear thinker is most personally satisfied and socially appropriate in an environment in which social life is traditional and ritualized, culture is elaborated and all-explaining, and politics is hierarchical. If the haven of the sequential thinker is the tribe, the natural resting spot of the linear thinker is the feudal kingdom.

If the certainties, direction and location inherent in feudal society fit the abilities and understanding of the linear thinker, it is clear that the ambiguities, freedom and social dislocation of the modern urban, industrial and democratic society do not. The debate over norms of behavior, the way they vary across subcultures and the rapidity with which they change present the linear thinker with a confusion of cross-cutting imperatives. He cannot meet the demands for self-direction and moral choice such an environment creates. The problem is exacerbated by the abstract terms in which these debates are often cast. The discussion of underlying logics that govern political thought and culture raises concerns which are not comprehensible within a linear mode of reasoning. Similarly, the analysis of abstract principles of allocation and the posing of hypothetical alternatives are activities which are not readily understood or valued. Not only does such modernity rob the individual of particular behavioral direction, it often also robs him of social location. Frequently, individuals are no longer considered in particular terms, that is by virtue of their group membership or role. Rather, they are conceived abstractly, as interchangeable and hence inherently equal social and political units. The linear thinker cannot understand such a conception and is left with a sense of loss of identity. The confusion is intensified by the peculiar metaphysics and epistemology which underlies modern discourse. Certainty is replaced by probability, and faith and knowledge are replaced by relativism and a clear sense of the unknowable.

All of this lack of direction, place, certainty and concreteness is institutionalized in politics. In general terms, an ethos of determination, convention and compliance is eroded in favor of one of possibility, creation and freedom. Social and political realities are not defined as given and universal, but as personal and collective products which vary across cultures and history. Personal identities are not ascribed and immutable, but are chosen and created. Conditioned by such a view, institutions are fashioned in the attempt (at least on the surface) to distribute control evenly and complexly. Power flows laterally and from the bottom up as well as from the top down. Tasks become more general and overlapping. The focus on individual obligations is complemented by one on individual rights. The demand for compliance is combined with one for critique and renewal.

A universe of abstraction, possibility, creativity and individuality, the modern world creates an environment which undermines the confidence, comfort and real effectiveness of the linear thinker. Insofar as he has power and responsibility in that society, he will be confronted with tasks which he cannot fulfill. Given the proper encouragement and guidance, his capacity to reason may develop. Robbed of opportunity or lacking the requisite encouragement and guidance, the linear thinker will withdraw rather than develop. Unlike the sequential thinker, he need not seek to isolate himself entirely. Rather, he only has to give up power and follow. As a result, he may lose status and prestige, but he may retain a position which is somewhat valued. After all, even in the modern egalitarian society, there is still a place for serfs.

Even when the linear thinker fails to develop in response to the demands placed upon him by the complexities of modern society, he may none the less be exposed to its institutions and discourse. Depending on circumstances, he will probably ignore what he cannot understand. Insofar as he is led to make sense of them, he will invariably do so according to the structure of his linear thought. As a result, he will redefine this socially constructed reality in his own terms. One example of this is the sense the linear thinker makes of the abstract principle so often invoked in American politics, that of justice or fairness. The linear thinker recognizes the issue is critical, but cannot understand it as it is embedded in a theory of individuals and the ideal conditions of their exchange. Rather, he can only understand it with reference to common or conventionally defined ways of acting in given situations. As a result, justice tends to be equated with the set of normal or legal ways of distributing rewards in a given society or culture. Such a conception has its problems. For example, when confronted with a situation in which several norms or laws apply in contradictory ways, the linear thinker lacks the principled construction needed to decide the relative importance of these various directives and deduce which is the just course.

Another example of the linear thinker's reconstruction of social phenomena defined at a higher level than his own, is the way in which he makes sense of such notions as ideology and culture. In modern discourse, these are generally defined as subjective or intersubjective entities which provide a basis for defining, and thereby ordering, social affairs. These entities are distinguished by their logic and have an existence which is neither concrete nor particular. The linear thinker does not conceptualize in these abstract, systematic terms. Given the concrete and aggregative quality of his thought, he regards these phenomena as sets of specific beliefs and preferences. Each belief is defined with reference to its concrete object or consequence and a set of beliefs is defined by association with the single individual or group expressing them. Thus, subjectivity is reduced to the idiosyncratic collection of beliefs voiced by an individual and culture is viewed as the beliefs and practices associated with a particular group.

Compared to the sequential thinker, the linear thinker is a far more sophisticated and capable political actor. His way of thinking allows him to bring politics down to earth and make it an integral part of the activity of daily life. For him, politics is something of a play, one already written by gods or nature herself. It is enacted by people and groups, some of whom he has seen and others he has not seen and will never see. These players are constantly acting on one another. The particular moves they make are understood as a reaction to another's action or as an expression of their inherent dispositional tendencies. By paying attention to the script, he can learn the parts that he and others are intended to play, what they are supposed to do and when. Because life is nothing more than the play, it is not that people simply play parts, they *are* those parts. Similarly, the script does not simply direct action, it defines the patterns of action that are at once necessary, normal and good. The play itself is an orderly one, filled with regularity and repetition. Watching it unfold, the linear thinker focuses on the action or discourse immediately before him. However, guided by the patterns he has learned, he can explain this as a reaction to a particular stimulus in the past and predict what future effect it will create. Bound to this play and focusing on its particulars, the linear thinker has no sense of alternative scenarios or even of the underlying logic of the one he has accepted.

SYSTEMATIC POLITICAL REASONING

Systematic thinkers juxtapose relationships among actions and beliefs. They recognize that these relationships are either objectively determined or subjectively constructed and therefore consider them relative to one another. Thus, they consider the general rules that govern how relationships may be associated, the particular context in which a given relationship will occur, and the function it serves in the larger system of which it is a part. The substance of the questions addressed by the systematic thinker vary with the domain of his inquiry. When considering objective phenomena, he thinks about interactions and asks the following questions:

1 What are the basic laws which govern the kinds of associations among interactions which may occur?
2 Under what conditions, real and hypothetical, will a given inter-active relationship hold?
3 What role does a given type of activity play in a system? What function does it serve?

When thinking about subjective phenomena, his focus shifts to propositions, but the questions he addresses remain essentially the same. They are:

1 What is the general rule in terms of which a particular prop-osition may be justified?
2 What is the subjective (or cultural) meaning of a particular prop-osition – that is, with what other propositions is it associated and how?
3 What role does a particular proposition serve in maintaining a person or a culture?

Finally, the systematic thinker also explores the relations between subjective and objective domains. In so doing, he may consider to what extent a hypothetical proposition meets the standard of an observed reality. Alternatively, he may consider to what extent an observed reality meets the standard of a proposition. In the first instance, his inquiry is scientific; in the second, it is ethical.

Systematic thinkers answer these questions in two ways. On the one hand, they rely on observation, both their own and others'. Aware of how the particular point of view of the observing subject and the specific conditions of an objective situation may influence the sub-stance of an observation, the systematic thinker attempts to control for these factors. In so doing, he aims to insure that the observations he relies upon are impersonal and the circumstances of those obser-vations are varied. On the other hand, systematic thinkers answer questions through reflection and argument. Here, concern focuses on issues of deduction and non-contradiction. Of note, there is a tension between these two modes of discovery.

The structure of systematic thought

When attempting to make sense of events, the systematic thinker begins by juxtaposing the phenomena he observes. He thereby considers a number of interactions or propositions simultaneously by placing them relative to one another in an integrated system of relationships. In so doing, he both breaks down a situation into its component parts and, at the same time, defines those parts with regard to their place in the system to which they belong. The process is one of coordinated analysis and synthesis. Reasoning in this way, the systematic thinker can induce the general from the particular, define those generalities in their own abstract terms, and then use them as a basis for redefining and constructing particular events. Thus, he can build a general model of a system of relationships and use it as a basis for interpreting observed events and for hypothesizing the conditions under which novel ones would occur.

A product of the juxtapositional quality of his reasoning, the conceptual relations constructed by the systematic thinker are bidirectional: they establish how units are reciprocally related. Unlike the connections of linear thought, they are not grounded in the particularity of how one unit bears on another. Interposed between units, they are not bound to any one. In this sense, systematic relations are independent of the specific entities they connect. Constituted in their own terms, systematic relations are abstract and general. The forms of connections created are differentiated not with regard to their substance, but relative to one another. Examples of the relations distinguished in this way include negation, implication, identity, inclusion, etc. While general, they are usually conceptualized with reference to a particular substantive domain of inquiry. For example, when reasoning about politics, general forms of relation such as authority, equality and citizenship may be constructed. Once defined, these relations provide a basis for discovering the terms of integration for any particular set of events. This leads to the construction of a system of interrelationships which in turn provides a basis for (1) locating a particular event relative to others and thereby interpreting its significance, and (2) for going beyond what is known (what has been observed, reported or learned) to deduce what must be the case – in other words, for constructing hypotheses.

Once constructed, systems may be subdivided into subsystems. These subsystems may be defined according to density of interaction. For example, in a society, the systematic thinker may perceive some actions and individuals to be more closely interconnected with one another and come to regard them as subsystems which have a certain order of their own. Thus, he may view the workplace or the family as subsystems embedded in a larger society. Subsystems may also be differentiated on the basis of their function. For example, the systematic thinker may regard the economic (function of production) and the legal (function of legitimation) as distinct arenas of exchange. Locating a given interaction in a subsystem, the systematic thinker can consider its place in two contexts at once, that of the subsystem and that of the larger system in which the subsystem is embedded.

The units of systematic thought are defined in this context. In part an objectification of the relations of linear thought, these units consist of the relationships between actions and beliefs. These linear relationships are, of course, reconstructed in the course of their objectification. In systematic thought, these concrete and specific relations are manifest in two basic forms. On the one hand, they consist of bidirectional relationships between particular actions. One is not defined in terms of the other. Instead, both are defined in terms of the overarching relationship which joins them. Where a linear thinker sees one action producing another, the systematic thinker sees an interactive relationship, itself a particular example of a more general type. For example, the systematic thinker may regard the case of a wife who offers help and a husband who accepts as an interaction of mutual obligation (or power) and view each actor and his or her action accordingly. Subjective phenomena, such as beliefs or knowledges, are viewed in similar terms. Consequently, they are not defined in terms of an action they produce or an object to which they refer, but rather in terms of how they are associated with one another. Thus, the unit for the analysis of subjective phenomena is not a belief, but a proposition or a judgement. On the other hand, the units of systematic thought consist of classes of beliefs or actions. Unlike their linear counterparts, these class-units are not defined in terms of any particular concrete attributes shared by their individual members. Instead, they are defined relative to the system in which they are articulated. Thus, actions or beliefs which play the same role in that molar system will be placed in a common class or category. In this sense, classes are defined by their function rather than any particular effect. Thus, stopping one's car at a red light, consummating a relationship by marriage and voting may all be considered acts of maintaining the social system.

Regardless of the particular form in which they are manifest, the units of systematic analysis are always placed in relation to one another in a system. They are interpreted and explained in this context. Thus, although a unit always has an intrinsic identity, it always has a relative one as well. For example, the interaction in which one person jostles another in an attempt to get on a bus has a certain inherent concrete identity. At the same time, this unit has meaning by virtue of its location in a system of social relationships. Thus, the interaction may be interpreted as insignificant or neutral in one social context (say that of New York) and as significantly dis-orderly or aggressive in another (say that of London).[13] The loci and boundaries of these systems are defined by observation or assumption. While these latter activities are not wholly independent of one another, they are quite different. The first depends primarily on the observation of the relative density of interactive or propositional relations among units – that is the extent to which they are observably intertwined. The second depends on the positing of some underlying regulative or organizing force (e.g., a culture or an individual's mind) which is credited with producing a set of outcomes. In this case, systematicity is assumed even when it is not at first observed.

The subunits of systematic thought are abstract objects or acts. Examples include unspecified action, the notion of people in general, or algebraic symbols. While they may identified with reference to particular concrete entities, they are not considered in these terms or regarded as meaningful unto themselves. Rather, they are defined relative to the interactive relations in which they are articulated and are considered in very general terms. In this vein, they are regarded merely as placeholders in a system and therefore as inherently abstract entities which are essentially equivalent or interchangeable.

In systematic thought, the relationship between conceptual relations and units is complex. This is a result of the way in which they are constructed. On the one hand, the conceptual relations are primary and the units are derivative. Systematic relations are defined without reference to the units related and thus are self-constituting and independent. At the same time, these relations generate a context in which the identity of the related units is defined. In this sense, the units of systematic thought are derivative. Some of the distinguishing qualities of systematic thought reflect these features of its underlying structure. The independent quality of its conceptual relations provides the medium for the directed abstraction and theory building characteristic of systematic thinking. The derivative quality of the units insures that the theories constructed apply across a variety of specific action situations, both observed and hypothetical.

On the other hand, the relations and units of systematic thought are so constructed that the units are primary and the relations are derived. The units of conceptual thought have an intrinsic identity (defined by their concrete particularity) which remains constant across the various relational contexts in which they may be articulated. In this sense, they are self-defined and independent. Moreover, they provide an empirical base from which conceptual relations are abstracted. With this reversal of the primacy of units and relations, we see another aspect of systematic thought. Insofar as the units are independently defined, it insures that all general claims (and hence all theories or subjective points of view) will share a common definition of the nature of particular interactions or specific propositions to which they refer. Consequently, the different understandings and theories constructed by systematic thinkers will share a common empirical ground and a common basis for discourse. Because relations are abstracted from units, the abstract constructions of the systematic thinker will not simply be flights of coherent fancy, but will be applicable to particular concrete cases.

In sum, the relations and units of systematic thought are constructed in two ways, one based on theoretical elaboration and definition and one based on observation and empirical abstraction. These two activities, the theoretical and the empirical, are not themselves coordinated. One result is the dualism characteristic of systematic thought. This is reflected in the difficulty the systematic thinker has in reconciling his conceptions of the general and the ideal on the one hand and the particular and the real on the other.

The relationship between the units and relations of systematic thought is complex in another sense. The issue here is one of form. Both the relations and the units of systematic thought are bidirectional and associative. This allows the systematic thinker to reflect on the terms of his own thinking without violating the structure of his reasoning. Reflection can thus be a normal feature of systematic thought and yet be limited such that it can occur without inducing any kind of qualitative development. The structural parallel between relations and units also allows the systematic thinker to construct relations at a number of different levels of generality or inclusiveness. Each level is formally the same. Each consists of a relation among units which are, at a lower level, themselves relations among units. Proceeding in this vein, the systematic thinker creates a pyramidal vision of the world as layers of abstraction which ultimately peaks in the self as thinker or other as inherently organized (e.g., systematic concepts of god as implicit in the organization of the universe).

So structured, systematic thought leads the individual to new considerations. Such concerns as systems and terms of integration, generalities and levels of generalities, and possibilities and hypotheticals are introduced. At the same time, methodological considerations of observational biases, interpretation, and non-contradiction are regarded as central.

Political understanding

The systematic thinker naturally constructs a very elaborated conception of politics, one which may go well beyond the particulars of his own experience and exposure. He focuses on the interaction between political actors and considers the system of political exchange in which that interaction occurs. In this manner, he understands political activity in terms of its inherent organization. The systematic thinker also focuses on the relationship between beliefs and makes sense of these relationships in light of the system of ideas in which these relationships are articulated. Thus, he understands political beliefs with reference to the system of meanings constructed by the individual subject or the political culture.

In this context, the systematic thinker distinguishes between systems of action and systems of meaning. With regard to the latter, he also distinguishes between subjective and intersubjective constructions. These two are differentiated with regard to the locus of their organization, in the mind of the individual or the culture of the society. Real, subjective or intersubjective, the dimensions of political life may be manifest in various forms. Thus, it is expected that patterns of exchange and belief will vary from society to society and person to person. This variation may be viewed in two ways. It may be assumed that this variation is essential and, therefore, that the possibilities for interpersonal and intercultural discourse are limited and all evaluation is relative. Alternatively, it may be assumed that these individual and cultural differences are variations of a single essential theme. This leads to the claim that discourse across individuals and cultures is possible and that some universal criteria for social and political evaluation may be generated.

As suggested by the foregoing, the systematic thinker has a dualistic conception of politics, one which reflects an essential dualism of all systematic thought. On the one hand, the systematic thinker reasons by abstracting the general from the particular. Building on the particular, this effort is necessarily oriented by the specific associations among interactions or propositions he observes. Consequently, his concept of politics is very much bound to the configuration of events to which he is exposed. Viewing different systems of belief and action, he will therefore regard them to be essentially different and conclude that politics is culturally and historically relative. On the other hand, the systematic thinker reasons by deducing the particular from the general. Structured by the nature of his abstractions, this effort is guided by the logic of his reflective and deductive activity. This produces an ideal conception of politics, one which is understood to be an essentially human product and thus not bound to culture. There is an uneasy tension between these two modes of systematic political thought. They rarely coincide and the question becomes one of which deserves greater attention or priority. Indeed, much of the classic debate between the two dominant Anglo-American ideologies, liberalism and conservatism, can be understood as an argument over the relative value of empirical and ideal conceptions of politics.

In sum, the systematic conception of political life is complex. While filled with activity, politics is not so much a matter of particular acts and their particular effects. Rather, it is a regulated system in which particular acts are determined and defined by the conjuncture of cross-cutting forces, both subjective and objective, which operate upon them. Thus, the linear view of politics as either a combat between competing actors or as a hierarchy of command gives way to a systematic one in which combat is seen to be choreographed according to collective rules and norms, and hierarchies are viewed as complex and legitimated organizational forms. Similarly, the linear view of politics as given and the normal as natural gives way to one in which politics is seen as a product, the result of interpersonal negotiation or cultural definition and a concept of the normal is supplemented by one of the ideal.

The space of politics   The political space constructed by the systematic thinker is an encompassing one. On the one hand, it has an objective dimension and provides a context for interaction and exchange. On the other, it has a subjective dimension and provides a context for propositions and judgements. In both cases, this space extends beyond what is immediate and known to that which may be deduced. In the latter regard, it includes the possible and the ideal as well as the actual and the real. This space is also an integrated one. Its diverse bits and pieces are woven together into a system. Regulating this system is a set of basic and general rules. These provide an underlying foundation for the patterns of exchange or configurations of meaningful associations which constitute the system. In so doing, they both provide a context for interpreting particular relationships and delimit what they actually are or can possibly be.

Such a political space can be differentiated into subsystems. These may be defined on the basis of the relative density of interaction within a system. Examples might be networks of association based on shared geographic location or common industry. Alternatively, subsystems may be distinguished on the basis of variations in the general patterns of exchange of the molar system. Finally, subsystems may be differentiated on a functional basis. For example, those interactions which serve a regulative or directive function might be distinguished from others which serve functions of material maintenance or integration. In this way, politics might be distinguished as a subsystem distinct from economic or social activity. Indeed, it is only with the emergence of systematic thought that a clear understanding of politics as a distinct domain is achieved. Notably, in all three instances, subsystems are not defined with reference to any particular features of individuals or acts.

So defined, the political space of the systematic thinker has a number of distinctive features. First, it is a decentered space. All points are located relative to one another. Unlike the constructions of linear thought, no particular one provides the center to which others are linked. For example, when making sense of international relations, the systematic thinker will not locate other countries relative to one particular one, e.g. his own. Rather, he will begin by understanding the international domain as one of a weave of forces related by conditions of geography, trade, culture and power. He will then locate both his own and other countries in this context. Second, this space is one in which all points are actually or potentially related to one another in multiple ways. Returning to the example of international relations, each country or alliance of countries is simultaneously related to several others. Third, this space has a strong hypothetical component to it. Considerations of the actual and real are always tempered by their relation to the possible and ideal. In this sense, the systematic space is constituted as much by what does not exist as what does.[14]

Given this conception of political space, the systematic thinker makes sense of a political phenomenon by first placing it in the context of the larger system in which it exists. In so doing, he not only locates objects and events, he also interprets them. Moreover, insofar as he can place the same concern in several systemic contexts, he may come to interpret its nature in very different terms. For example, when considering France, he may understand its nature quite differently depending on whether he chooses to conceive of it in the context of East–West relations, its membership in the European Economic Community or its role in the conflict between Britain and Argentina over the Falklands/Malvinas. One important consequence of this is that the systematic thinker's conception of situations and events is less dependent on circumstances as objectively presented than that of the linear thinker. Interpreting events, he is less immediately dependent on objective or cultural definitions of them. Locating them in context, he is less likely to have his attention directed by present circumstances. As a result, he is less susceptible to agenda setting effects.[15]

The time of politics Like its space, the time of politics is internally related and rule-governed. It consists of streams of activity or discourse. These are understood to be the temporal and concrete expressions of essentially atemporal and abstract relationships. Thus, reaction is seen to follow from action and conclusion from premise according to general rules. The various streams of activity are themselves interrelated. Consequently, actions are seen to have multiple causes and effects, and ideas to have multiple bases and implications.

Here again, the dualism of systematic thought is apparent. On the one hand, there is a tendency for systematic thinkers to assume that the basic rules which govern the ordering of political events are the same across all time. Thus, there is a presumption that a single set of sociological or economic principles may be used to explain the dynamic of all political life. An example is offered by liberal historians who assume that the specific events and conditions of the American, French and Russian revolutions may vary, but attempt to generate a single theory to explain them all. On the other hand, the systematic thinker may also recognize that the logic of events may be subject to different rules at different periods of time. An example of this is offered by those Marxist and conservative historians who argue that the basic dynamic of political life is transformed. To illustrate, they frequently refer to differences between medieval and enlightenment Europe.

Thinking in these terms, the systematic thinker analyses a linear sequence of events by linking it to other sequences with which it may be intertwined. For example, when making sense of Reagan's decision to respond to Libyan terrorism with the bombing of Tripoli, the systematic thinker would begin by linking that decision to a stream of activity which led to it and would flow from it. He might consider a variety of prior events such as Libyan-sponsored terrorist attacks or a growing willingness of the United States to leave the non-interventionist legacy of Vietnam behind. Similarly, he would consider the various events which have followed. In the course of these investigations, the systematic thinker would also consider those things which did not but might have occurred. In the present example, he might consider what the USA did not do to influence Gaddafi or what the USA has not done to other countries associated with terrorism (e.g., Syria). As he elaborates this stream of activity, he will also consider it in a larger context. Thus, he would examine how it is related to other streams of activity. For example, he might consider the relationship of Reagan's decision to respond by bombing to the emerging weakness of the oil market or to the ebb of his influence over the Congress. Throughout, the nature of the linkages made will depend on the systematic thinker's understanding of the general rules which govern the dynamic of international and domestic politics. Examples of such general principles would be that countries will react in concert with their economic interests, that political leaders act so as to maintain their own power or that the show of legislative power leads to even greater power.

The players   The players in this world as conceived as systems of action and belief. While they do act, they are not the actors of linear thought: they are not concrete entities nor are they defined by the collection of the particular things they do and say. Rather, they are abstractions which are defined by the terms of their internal integration. A system unto themselves, these players are their own source of organization of action and meaning. They structure the relationships among the various acts they do, or could, perform and therefore determine how particular acts may follow on one another in any specific sequence. Similarly, they determine how their ideas will be interrelated and therefore how they will understand particular concepts or situations. While external circumstance may dictate the particular situation which players must understand and to which they must respond, their perception and reaction will ultimately be mediated by how the stimulus is articulated into their internal system of action and definition. In this sense, these players are self-coordinating and therefore self-directing. They are agents in the full sense of the term.

The systematic thinker views individuals and groups in these terms. Both are conceived as loci of organization. An individual is viewed as a self-system, a personality. His personality regulates both his action and his thought. As an organization of action, it dictates how the individual will interact with others or react to external circumstances. It defines his character. As an organization of thought, the individual's personality dictates how he will perceive and make sense of events around him. In this regard, it shapes his social and political ideology. These two dimensions of his personality, his character and his ideology are themselves interrelated. The individual's way of thinking both directs his action and determines its meaning. At the same time, his thinking is affected by his personal organization of action. In the latter regard, his orienting aims and sensitivities reflect his character.

In this context, the particular things people say and do are made sense of in terms of their place in their character and ideology. For example, when confronted with the information that Reagan supports reducing government spending on welfare, the systematic thinker will begin to make sense of that action by first judging its meaning for Reagan. Having already determined that Reagan is a conservative, he may thus begin by interpreting his anti-welfare stance in light of his beliefs that (1) government cannot and should not intervene in the social and moral life of a community, (2) personal charity should be encouraged because it helps both the giver and the receiver and because it binds them together, and (3) different individuals have different abilities and therefore should play different, but equally respected, roles in society. This view may be tempered by his additional assumption that Reagan thinks in simple terms. In this context, the systematic thinker may further interpret Reagan's position with regard to the possibility that he may not appreciate the myriad of ways in which social conditions may prevent individuals from realizing their own potential or he may not understand how the factors of scale in modern urban society may render inappropriate a reliance on private charity rather than government subsidy.

Like individuals, groups are also regarded as regulative systems. They order the interpersonal exchange among their members. In this sense, they are defined not in terms of their location or the attributes shared by their individual members, but rather in terms of the nature of their social and political organization. This organization is conceived in relatively complex terms. Different levels of power may be differentiated. The resulting hierarchical conception is not the simple one constructed by the linear thinker. Power is understood to flow from the bottom up as well as from the top down. Moreover, it is recognized that power is exercised within a single level of hierarchy, often in cross-cutting ways. In this context, political outcomes are not seen as the simple expression of a leader's will, but as the product of complex and structurally constrained negotiation. Power is understood to inhere not in individuals, but in the organization itself. The organization of a group may also be differentiated along functional lines. For example, institutions may be defined by the particular purposes they serve in the overall maintenance of the political system (e.g., the judiciary as responsible for social integration, the State Department as responsible for external relations, etc.). Once distinguished, these institutions are seen in light of their place in the political organization. Consequently, the activity of each is seen to be potentially related to that of the others and all are understood to be subject to the general principles which govern action in the overarching political system.

A political organization also has a subjective dimension, its culture. This defines the terms of social or public meaning. It consists of a system of symbols (linguistic and extralinguistic) and values, and a logic for relating particular claims and beliefs. Thus, it provides a medium, a structure and an aim for discourse and understanding among its members. Any ideas expressed in the political system (by individuals as well as by institutions or collectives) acquire their meaning by virtue of their place in this frame of reference.

To illustrate the systematic thinker's conception of social systems, let us consider how he might try to make sense of a foreign country, say, Greece. Looking first to its objective aspect, he would not focus on particular habits such as eating late at night or common features of the population such as dark hair and skin. Rather, he would look to patterns of interaction and the organization implicit in it. Thus, he might note how strong relationships are among family members and how military postings are allocated on the basis of the recruit's social status. Gathering evidence such as this, he may make inferences regarding the particularistic quality of Greek life such that personal ties rather than rule of law mediate social and political exchange. Looking to the subjective aspect, he would not focus on particulars such as the the fact that Greeks talk about politics all the time. Rather, he would look to patterns of propositions and seek to understand the meanings which underlie them. Thus, he might note the weakness Greeks feel relative to other countries, their fear of their sea and their propensity to confront pain and difficulty directly. Seeking to see how these are interrelated, he might make inferences regarding the fatalism and pessimism of Greek culture.

It is important to recognize that there is a dualistic quality to the systematic thinker's conception of political players. As we have indicated, both individuals and groups are conceived as loci of organization and meaning. This conception is complicated by the fact that the activity of each kind of player penetrates that of the other in fundamental ways. On the one hand, the collective delimits what individuals can do and be. Its social structure defines rules of interaction which constrain how the individual can act and its culture defines the terms of public discourse in which his beliefs can be made meaningful. As participants in a social system, individuals are mere products of the regulations and definitions of the collective. Thus, they are regarded as derivative and evaluated with regard to their social function.[16] On the other hand, the personality of individuals delimits what the collective is and can be. Individuals playing out their purposes in the context of one another set the conditions of social interaction and the shared aspects of their private meanings structure public discourse. Viewed from this perspective, it is the collective which is regarded as derivative, and social and political outcomes are judged with regard to the needs of individuals.

There is a clear tension inherent in this vision of individuals and groups as at once organizing and self-directing, and organized and determined. In the extreme, it is reflected in the opposing visions of the conservative and the sociologist on the one hand and the liberal and the economist (or psychologist) on the other.[17] However, this tension is not merely between different systematic framworks. It is endemic in each and is reflected in the difficulties systematic thinkers have in fully integrating their understanding of individuals relating to one another in a social context. An example is the problem they have in balancing their recognition of the importance of fulfilling civic obligations with their appreciation of the value of respecting personal rights.

The nature of political action   Political action is conceived on two levels, that of general organizing forces and that of specific interactive relations. The organizing forces are basic. They are the source of regulation inherent in social and personal systems. On the one hand, they are regulative: they define the set of rules which govern interpersonal exchange. These rules are conceived in general terms: they constitute general laws or principles of interaction. These general laws then regulate specific interactive relationships. An example would be the laws (implicit as well as explicit) that govern contracts. These are defined in terms of the general qualities and constraints inherent in the agreements made between individuals. Thus, they are conceived with regard to abstract actors and the general conditions of their mutual obligation. These laws then apply to and regulate specific cases. In so doing, they determine how each participant can react to the other. On the other hand, these organizing forces are definitional. In this respect, they define the rules which govern the interrelationships among ideas. Thus, they delimit the way in which arguments may be developed and meanings may be constructed. In their generality, the rules produced by organizing forces delimit both the real and the possible. As a result, they not only provide a basis for interpreting and explaining the known, but also the unknown as well.

Political action is also considered in the more specific terms of particular interactions and propositions. Interactions are defined both with regard to the specific acts involved and with regard to the general rules of which the specific relationship is an example. For example, the instance of a husband helping his wife and her accepting is understood both in terms of the particulars of what each partner does and in terms of the relationship of mutual obligation which governs their exchange. Similarly, giving grades to students in a college class is understood in its particularity and with regard to the principles of meritocratic reward of which it is an expression. Ideas are also understood in terms of their interrelationship. Here, the focus is on propositions or judgements. Like interactions, they are defined with regard to the specific constituents, the ideas and beliefs which are involved, and with regard to the general principles their relationship expresses.

Given this conception of political action, the particular things which people say and do are never examined in isolation. Unto themselves, they are mere abstractions whose social or personal definition is inherently ambiguous. They only acquire meaning by virtue of their place in a system of action and ideas. Thus, to know what giving aid to Nicaragua means, it is first necessary to know with what other acts it is connected. For example, within the framework of Norwegian foreign policy it probably is an act of mercy and an attempt to foster the self-determination of peoples. However, within the framework of Soviet foreign policy, it is probably an attempt to destabilize the region and undermine American influence. Similarly, to know the meaning of the statement, 'I am against affirmative action policies,' it is first necessary to know something of the other beliefs with which it is connected. When linked to a belief in the inherent propriety of a workforce dominated by white males, it means one thing. When linked to a concern about the self-perception of those who are intended to benefit from those policies, it means quite another.

Explanation and prediction are crafted in light of this conception of action. First, the focus is on particular interactive relationships such as whether, given 'a', 'b' will follow. These are then considered in two ways: as an expression of a relational rule and as they are intertwined with other relationships in a system of exchange. In the first light, the interactive relationship is viewed as the product of the regulations of a particular social or psychological system. If systems change or new systems are examined, there is no expectation as to whether or not the underlying rule will exist and therefore if the interactive relationship will hold. In the second light, the relationship is seen as it relates to the host of other interactive relations with which it intersects. In this regard, a relationship is understood not to have a single cause, but to be multiply determined. Thinking in this way, the systematic thinker will explain activity, such as George Bush's decision to be a Vice-President who is subservient and loyal to his President, by searching for a variety of causes. Thus, he might consider such related phenomena as Bush's belief that his task is only to serve his President, Reagan's clarity about the role he expected the Vice-President to play, Bush's desire to benefit from Reagan's popularity in his own bid for the presidency, the real congruence between Bush's beliefs and Reagan's, etc. His search for the various independent and interdependent causes is of course guided by his understanding of the regulations and definitions inherent in the relevant systems, in this case, Bush's mind and American politics. Consequently, the explanations he will offer or any future predictions he makes will be confined to the case of Bush in the current American political context. He will not extend his understanding to the case of different political personalities or different political circumstances.

Viewing action at these two levels, the systematic thinker naturally regards the conduct of politics as a well choreographed dance. There may be points and counterpoints, but these are juxtaposed and resolved in the context of the dance itself. Similarly, the steps and rhythms may be varied but the essential theme remains the same. As with the definition of the players of politics, the integration of this conception of political action suffers from the dualistic nature of the systematic vision. To interpret or explain an act, the systematic thinker must relate it to other actions which are subject to a common regulation. The problem is that the act may either be related to the acts of other persons or to other acts by the same person. Thus, the same act may be articulated into two potentially dissimilar systems.

Let us examine the consequences of this dualism. On the one hand, the analysis of an action may be guided by the assumption that the collective is the source of regulation and definition. In this context, a person's act will be considered relative to the acts of others with which it is associated. Thus, it will be seen as an initiative or response in a social exchange and will be defined in public terms and explained with reference to social regulations. In this context, the rules of political life are regarded as given. They are not necessarily universal or unchanging, but they are an extra-individual phenomenon. They shape rather than are influenced by individuals' actions. On the other hand, the analysis may assume the individual is organizing and defining. Consequently, his act will be considered relative to other acts he performs. It will therefore be seen to be a product of his personality and will be defined in his subjective terms. In this context, the patterns of social life are regarded as a negotiated product. A creation of individuals, these patterns may be altered by those individuals.

Social conditions of adaptation and development The systematic thinker is a flexible, independent and able citizen. His thinking is guided by abstract rules which enable him to craft general analyses of social situations and deduce likely, hypothetical and desirable outcomes. He can discover the structures which govern particular arenas of social and political life and apply them to specific cases. As a result, he can appreciate the organizational complexities of a social system.

He can recognize the cross-cutting influences which bear on social outcomes and consider the multiple causes and effects of particular acts. He is also aware of the relativity of the meaning of social phenomena. He understands that the same actions may mean different things to different people and have a different significance in different cultural contexts. The systematic thinker also tends to take these complexities into account when planning his own action and therefore can be a very effective social actor. He can also be unusually self-directing. Aware of the general principles governing interaction, he can deduce what is appropriate or effective in a particular circumstance. Consequently, although he depends on the general terms of social exchange, he requires little specific behavioral direction. Finally, the systematic thinker can also be a creative and critical member of a social group. Understanding the basic terms of its organization, he can generate novel solutions to old problems and consider how new problems may best be addressed. On a similar basis, he can construct a clear conception of the ideal forms of exchange implicit in a social organization and then use this to critically consider present realities.

The systematic thinker conceives of himself as an independent entity. Unlike the linear thinker, he does not rely on his social location or definition. He does not identify himself as a group member nor does he view himself as others see him. Instead, he regards himself in his own terms. He is a coherent being, the purposive and rational force implicit in the system of things he says and does. He is a personality and thus distinguished on the basis of his character and his ideology (social as well as political). This is not to say the systematic thinker conceives of himself as isolated and asocial. On the contrary, he sees himself in relation to other individuals in the context of a larger social system in which they are integrated. Like all others, he has responsibilities within that system and may be identified by the functions he serves. While he is different from these fellow citizens, he retains an abstract sense of the common terms of their existence. In sum, the systematic thinker conceives of himself both as an individual unto himself and as a participant in a larger community.

The needs the systematic thinker brings to society reflect his self-conception and the thinking which underlies it. As an individual unto himself, the systematic thinker requires a sense of his own independence and the real freedom to think and act as he chooses. The freedom he requires is not an arbitrary one nor is it simply to insure he gets those things he wants. The systematic thinker needs to maintain his coherence. To do so, he must be able to rely on his own way of organizing his thoughts and actions to structure his exchange with others. Thus, freedom for him is a matter of self-expression and, through it, self-realization. As a participant in a community, the systematic thinker also requires a sense of his own contribution, of his ability to serve communal needs. In his conception, he is an element of a community which has a being unto itself. Consequently, by enabling that community to maintain itself and thrive, he further realizes himself.

In both the private and public dimensions of his self-conception, the systematic thinker depends on a sense of the coherence and law-fulness of thought and action. Unlike the linear thinker, he does not need any specific definitions or social rituals. He can deduce the particulars of social life on his own. However, he does require a set of regulative rules which define patterns of action and provide a basis upon which those patterns can be comprehended. There must be a general order to action and thus a meaning to what goes on around and within him. Without this, the world as it is becomes incommen-surate with the world as the systematic thinker is able to conceive it.

It is evident that modern cosmopolitan and industrial society meets many of the needs of the systematic thinker.[18] On the one hand, it offers much of the freedom he requires. Its industrial and technological requirements encourage change in specific beliefs and practices, and its multicultural composition provides a variety of cross-cutting and contradictory directives for specific action and belief. Together, these aspects of modern society create the openness and fluidity needed to foster personal freedom. This is supported by a liberal ideological agenda which acknowledges individual rights and fosters social criticism and debate. On the other hand, modern society encourages the participation the systematic thinker wants. There is a recognition that all individuals contribute to the social product and unpre-cedented opportunities for civic inclusion are made available. This grass roots liberalism is complemented by a conservative ethos which emphasizes social obligation and civic responsibility. Importantly, this freedom and opportunity are presented in a context which is structured in a manner compatible with the systematic thinker's way of making sense of the world. Underlying the diversity and complexities are general principles which govern action and discourse. Thus, there is a lawfulness to social interaction and a coherence to cultural definitions and beliefs.

As modern society provides an environment which is sympathetic to systematic thought, it also carries the seeds of frustration and confusion. This reflects the difficulties inherent in balancing the needs of the individual with those of the society at large. On the one hand, the attempt to preserve the freedom of the individual tends to produce a diversity which defies integration. The result may be a society which is more a set of minimally overlapping microcosms than a coherent system. In such a setting, each individual may find his own voice, but a sense of mutual understanding and common purpose is lost. This structural condition is reinforced by a culture in which the individual is defined as independent and self-directing and the society is regarded as a mere instrument for the realization of private ends. In this regard, the freedom society offers the systematic thinker may isolate him from others and destroy his sense of community. On the other hand, the attempt to preserve the integrity of the social system in the face of its internal diversity tends to produce an integration which denies the individual the opportunity to be a creative participant. The sheer scale and complexity of the ensuing social organization may remove real power from all but a very few individuals. This may be reinforced by cultural demands for a greater uniformity of social convention and a commensurately greater constraint on personal thought and behavior. For the individual, the resulting organization and coherence is achieved at the price of personal impotence and alienation.

Apart from its immediate consequences, this lack of balance in meeting the needs of the individual and the community has an even more fundamental consequence for the systematic thinker. The contradictions implicit in this imbalance suggest a fundamental fact: that modern society is not really a system governed by a single regulating force, but the asystemic product of two such forces. The abstract regulations which govern society clearly conflict. This conflict is reflected in the fact that the culture lacks real coherence and social exchange lacks real lawfulness. This is in turn evidenced by the fact that both the structure and culture of modern society are not stable, but appear to be in a gradual but constant state of evolution.

Viewed from the perspective of the systematic thinker, these essential facts may be recognized, but not comprehended. To be understood, they must first be considered with reference to the qualities of the organizing forces (both personal and collective) which yield the abstract regulations of social life. The systematic thinker cannot do this. The assumption of such a force structures systematic thought, it is not its object. Consequently, the best the systematic thinker can do is to define the activity of organizing and defining in the most general and undifferentiated terms. As a result, he will see all forces in the same terms, ultimately his own. To the degree to which their organization parallels that of his own thinking, he will recognize the systematic or logical quality of their product. To the degree to which their basic organization is different from his, he will not recognize their existence (and therefore view their product as random or irrational).

In addition to a consideration of the forces behind the regulations of thought and action, the understanding of modern society also depends on a consideration of the relationship that exists between them. This relationship is one of essential contradiction: the forces are at once independent and self-regulating, and dependent on one another and thus regulated by their exchange. The systematic thinker cannot conceptualize such a relationship. For him, forces either are integrated in a systematic context and thus interact in a lawful and stable fashion or they are not, in which case their exchange will be random and everchanging. Insofar as society is constituted by forces which are both, it will be incomprehensible to him.

As the sequential and linear thinker before him, the systematic thinker can either develop in response to this situation or withdraw. To develop, he will need to be exposed to an environment which forces him to address the contradictions inherent in everyday life. He must be led to consider the incongruities and instabilities present in society and himself. At the same time, he needs exposure to a cultural framework which offers concepts that can direct his attempt to reconstruct his thought along the lines suggested above.[19] Insofar as this is unavailable, the systematic thinker will not develop. Instead, he will simply misunderstand his environment in his own terms. In so doing, he may retain confidence in his systematic vision and try to avoid evidence of its internal contradictions or of its failure to capture social realities. To do so, he may adopt a more localized focus and then attribute apparent discrepancies to exogenous variables, limited information or a short time frame. Thus, he will continue to see essential stability where there is superficial change, basic coherence where there is apparent confusion and the power of ideals where the realities are largely unaffected by them. Alternatively, the systematic thinker may recognize his failure. In so doing, he may call into question both the essential nature of things and his basic capacity to understand them. This may lead either to the skepticism of the conservative or, more extreme, to a full existential crisis. In the latter case, all is regarded as meaningless and purposeless. Lost in such a universe, one can know nothing and therefore cannot reasonably act.

To conclude, the systematic thinker, like the linear thinker, sees politics as a play. His vision is, however, more complex. For the systematic thinker, the play is not simply the particular actors involved and the things they do to one another. More fundamental, it is the expression of the intentions of an author. The author has a set of themes he wishes to explore and these then define the basic structure of the play. They underlie its basic organization and provide a meaning to what transpires. The various roles created and the specific ways they interact are crafted accordingly. The actors and their action must not just be identified according to their particular features. Instead, they must be treated as abstract symbols and interpreted with reference to their interaction and the themes that interaction is intended to express. The systematic thinker's conception is also complex in a second sense. For him, the play is a very modern one in that it provides a medium for the self-expression of the actors as well as the author. Thus, although the script is provided, the actors are free to alter it in ways which reflect their own themes. What transpires must thus be interpreted and explained with reference to the individual actors as well as with regard to the overall structure of the play itself. In the end, the systematic thinker's conception is a difficult one. Indeed, it is one which extends beyond the limits of his own understanding.

5

Three Empirical Studies

The three studies reported here were conducted over the last several years. They represent a first step in the exploration of our structural developmental theory of ideology. The aim of these studies is to validate the typology of forms of political thinking. No attempt is made to examine the relationship between the structure of the individual's thought and that of his or her social environment. That relationship will be the focus of the next step in my research program.

All three of the studies address the general claims that (1) there is a structure to an individual's political thinking, (2) this may differ from individual to individual, and (3) these differences are well captured by the three-fold typology of sequential, linear and systematic thought. In this regard, the studies complement one another and their results are mutually reinforcing. They differ, however, in their focus. The first study investigates the hypothesis that there is a general structure to an individual's thought. It examines the way an individual thinks about political and nonpolitical phenomena. In the second study, the investigation concentrates on the individual's understanding of domestic American politics. Here, the individual's conception of the basic structure of government, the dynamics of political activity and the nature of citizenship are examined. In the third study, the focus switches to the individual's conception of international relations. Conducted shortly after the US bombing of Libya in 1986, the study explores the individual's understanding of the structure, dynamics and resolution of international conflict.

A product of a common epistemological and theoretical framework, the three studies share a common set of methodological considerations. The key assumption orienting the design of the research is that different individuals may understand the same act or statement in fundamentally different ways. This dictates that the research examine different performances of the same person and that the data be gathered in a way that facilitates a subsequent interpretation of their underlying structure. Two methodological caveats follow from this. First, aggregate analyses of a group should not be relied upon to make inferences regarding individuals. Second, a person's statement or act should not be considered without reference to that person's understanding of the behavior in question.

The research is structured accordingly. In all three studies, the focus is on individuals. To test the claim that an individual's thinking is determined by a single underlying structure, each subject was asked to perform a number of tasks. Both the nature of the task (the kind of activity the subject was required to perform) and the content of the task (the substantive area addressed) were varied. Because the aim of the research is theory validation rather than the description of a national population, a diverse but small group was studied. No attempt was made to construct a representative sample or to draw inferences about people beyond those studied. Two methods of data collection, in-depth interviewing and clinical experimentation, were used. Each method involves the presentation of a complex stimulus and gives the subject the opportunity to respond at length. In both instances, the subject's responses may be probed by the experimenter/interviewer so as to clarify the nature of the connections that the subject is making. This choice of methods reflects the need to elicit sufficiently elaborated responses (reasonings) to allow for an interpretative analysis of the structure of the subject's thought, and the desire to insure that the results obtained were not simply an artifact of a particular method used.

STUDY ONE:
THE STRUCTURAL BASES OF POLITICAL THINKING[1]

The aim of this first study is to examine the claim that there is a general structure which underlies all of an individual's thinking. The implication of greatest interest here is that an individual's political thinking is but one manifestation of the general quality of his thought. To test this proposition, I examined how people think about both nonpolitical and political phenomena. To provide evidence of their thinking about nonpolitical phenomena, subjects were asked to solve an elementary chemistry problem and a simple physics problem. To provide evidence of their thinking about political phenomena, they were asked to discuss first an issue of relevance to domestic American politics and then one of relevance to international relations. Responses to each of these tasks were coded according to categories defined on the basis of my characterization of sequential, linear and systematic thought. The consistency of individual subjects' responses across the four tasks and the differences between subjects were then examined.

Subjects

Given our choice to explore first the validity of our typology rather than to investigate the distribution of the types in the population at large, we conducted an intensive study of a relatively small group of fifty adults. To insure a fair range of different styles of political thinking were represented, subjects from a variety of cultural backgrounds were studied. Subjects were drawn from New Haven, Connecticut and southern California. They varied in age, sex, race, occupation and education. They ranged in age from eighteen to seventy-two. Half the subjects were male, half female. Three-quarters of the subjects were white, one-quarter black. Some of the subjects were unemployed. The others were employed in a wide variety of occupations (e.g., housewife, janitor, middle level manager, store owner, lawyer and factory worker). One-third of the subjects had received high school education or less; one-third had some college education; and one-third had two or more years of postgraduate education.

For a limited purpose, an additional forty subjects participated in one of the tasks. These subjects were second-year students at a California university.

Procedure

Subjects were told they were participating in a study of people's social and political attitudes. As part of a larger study, each subject was then asked to do the following (in order of presentation): (1) respond to an in-depth interview focusing on a domestic policy issue, (2) respond to an in-depth interview on American relations with Iran, and (3) solve two natural science problems. Each subject was tested individually either by the author or a research assistant in three one-hour sessions.

The in-depth interview and the problem-solving tasks are assessment instruments. They require the subject to make a large number of related assertions and, thereby, provide the kind of data needed to determine the structure of the subject's thought. Using the definition of types of thinking as a guide, each of these assessment instruments was analyzed to determine how a subject of each type would respond. This yielded a definition of three categories of response – sequential, linear and systematic – for each instrument. Subjects' performances were then coded accordingly. Coding was done by two raters who were blind both to each other's ratings and to the subject's identity. Inter-rater reliability for the 200 cases (four tasks for each of fifty subjects) was 84 per cent. A full description of the assessment procedure is provided in the following paragraphs.

The natural science problem-solving tasks Each subject partici-pated in two Piagetian problem-solving tasks, one which required solving a chemistry problem, the second which required solving a physics problem (Inhelder and Piaget, 1958). In response to the chemistry problem, subjects were asked to determine how a chemical reaction is produced. First, subjects were shown that a colorless liquid turns yellow when several drops of a clear agent are added. They were told that the initially colorless liquid came from one, or a combination of more than one, of four beakers of colorless and odorless liquids. They were then given the opportunity to experiment with the four liquids and the agent in order to determine the contribution of each liquid to the production of a yellow color. Subjects' performances on the task were classified in the following manner:

Sequential: Sequential thinkers merely track phenomena. They are unable to think causally. All they can do is follow the instruction to apply drops of the agent to the clear liquid. Generally, they will try each of the four liquids in turn and end by saying (despite evidence of the earlier demonstration) that they cannot make yellow. When prodded, they may attempt one or two combinations of liquids. If they happen on the correct combination, they will explain the reaction as the result of primarily one of the liquids involved.

Linear: Relating actions, linear thinkers do think causally. They test single liquids and combinations of liquids with the agent until they discover the combination that works. They understand that both agents interact to produce the result and both are equally necessary. However, when asked to discover the role of the two liquids which do not create yellow, they flounder. They tend to conclude the other two liquids 'do nothing'.

Systematic: Systematic thinkers can juxtapose relations. Consequently, not only can they work their way through the various combinations of liquids to discover the one that creates yellow, they can also determine the role of the remaining two agents. By examining the effect of the remaining agents on the combination which creates yellow, they can determine whether each has a neutralizing or neutral effect on the reaction.

In the physics experiment, subjects observed a swinging pendulum. They were asked to determine what influences the rate of oscillation. They were told that four factors may be relevant: the length of the string, the weight of the swinging object, the force with which the object is initially pushed and the height from which it is initially released. To discover the answer, subjects were encouraged to experiment with the pendulum using strings of varying length and objects of varying weight. Subjects' performances on this task were classified as follows:

Sequential: Sequential thinkers do not analyze causes or perceive multiple dimensions of a single activity. Thus, they randomly vary one factor (e.g., weight) and then another. They tend to vary several at once. They also tend to have a different explanation to account for the result achieved with each new combination of factors tested. Being unable to relate actions, they also have great difficulty understanding what the rate of oscillation is and confuse it with the speed of the swinging object.

Linear: Because they can relate actions to one another, linear thinkers understand the concept of oscillation and can detect changes in its rate. They tend to associate a single cause with an effect and have difficulty considering several causes simultaneously. Consequently, when examining the impact of one possible cause, they are unable to hold all other possible causes constant. Thus, they will inadvertently vary two factors at once.

Systematic: Systematic thinkers can reason in terms of a system of possibly interrelated factors. The problem for them therefore becomes one not of determining which has an effect, but of eliminating those which do not. By keeping in mind the juxtaposed set of factors, they can readily hold several constant to examine the effect of one.

American politics interview The focus of the interview was the subjects' understanding of the structure of government decision-making. Each subject was asked to suggest an issue which he or she felt to be of particular interest. The issue chosen provided the substantive concern for the remainder of the interview. The subject was then asked questions such as who is responsible for the problem, what is government doing about it, what role does the Congress, the President, the Cabinet or the bureaucracy play, and how do these various aspects of government relate to one another in the decision-making process. When the meaning of a subject's response was unclear, the interviewer probed further with questions such as what do you mean by that, why do things work that way, etc. Responses were coded as follows:

Sequential: The focus is on particular actors and one or two specific things they have done (e.g., make war, tell each other what to do, speak to the people, build highways). Contact between actors and their targets is immediate and direct. The leader of government (unless a specific alternative is presented) has personal responsibility for all government acts. Where the environment dictates the consideration of more than one actor, it is assumed that the two actors do the same thing or a two-level sequential hierarchy is constructed. The latter consists of little more than a leader telling a follower to do something. Event-specific, this hierarchy has no generality and may even be reversed from one instance to the next. In all cases, understanding is partial and fragmentary. There is virtually no sense of the dimensions of government beyond the specific activity being discussed.

Linear: There is clear, if limited, sense of the general organization of government. It is understood to have a simple hierarchical structure. Control is centralized at the top and flows down to the bottom. There is little regard for, or understanding of, the constraints on this control. Given the ideology of democratic countries, there is a strong emphasis on these complicating aspects of political structure. Reconceived in linear terms, these forces are often understood as follows: (1) the interaction of those of equal power is reconstructed either as an interaction between actors of unequal power or as an interaction in which all parties negotiate a common course and act as a unit; (2) power from the bottom up is either ignored or momentarily acknowledged and regarded as absolute (unconstrained power from below). The concept of government also reflects a recognition of the role of institutions and groups. When considered by itself, a given institution or group will be viewed like a government, i.e., as a differentiated entity which is organized in a simple hierarchical fashion. When considered in the context of other political units, an institution or group will be viewed as an individual agent, i.e., as an undifferentiated actor who speaks with a single voice.

Systematic: Government is viewed as playing a particular role in a larger political system. It is that institution which is designed to serve the twin functions of regulating behavior and being responsive to the needs of the community. Government is itself organized. It consists of an elaborate system of levels and substantive areas of control. The various places in the system are occupied by individuals, groups or institutions. A complex weave of reciprocal relations of power and influence exist among these elements of the governmental system. Within any given level of control, multiple actors' interests are identified and the congruences and conflicts among their actions are considered. Across levels of control, the limitations placed on the more powerful by the less powerful are recognized. In this context, political cultures and ideologies are seen as very significant. They are understood to provide direction for action and a basis for the interpretation of events and, thereby, sustain the coherence of a political system.

Foreign relations interview   The interview focused on American relations with Iran. It was conducted toward the end of the hostage crisis and *all* subjects demonstrated clear awareness of this aspect of international affairs and a command over a considerable amount of detail (e.g., who said what, what events had transpired recently, the exact number of the hostages, etc.). Each subject was asked to explain what exactly was going on between the two countries and why. Again, subjects' assertions and explanations were probed in order to discover the precise meanings of the statements made. Responses were coded as follows:

Sequential: The focus is on present or very recent events. Although subjects all exhibited a considerable knowledge of a variety of relevant details, this knowledge was specific and pertained to particular individuals and actions (e.g. the Ayatollah has a particular appearance, the President recently made a particular statement, the rioters in Teheran did something, etc.). These items of knowledge, while generally correct, remained isolated from one another. There was no sense of how events fit together, why they were happening or where they would lead.

Linear: Here there is a clear understanding of the existence of events in the context of a relationship of exchange between two nations. Thinking in terms of cause and consequent effect, this exchange was followed as something of a tennis match – the US did 'X' which caused Iran to do 'Y' which in turn caused the US to do 'Z'. Throughout there is a strong tendency to personalize the exchange, that is, to consider each country as a univocal actor.

Systematic: The relationship between the US and Iran is understood in context – either international, national or both. In the first case, the American–Iranian relationship is analyzed and explained in the light of the international system (e.g., American/Soviet, First World/Third World) in which that relationship is embedded. In the second case, the initiative of any country is understood both as a response to other countries and as a response to that country's domestic political situation.

Results

Two hypotheses were explored: (1) that there is a general cognitive structure which underlies a person's thinking about political and nonpolitical phenomena, and (2) that different people's thinking may be structured differently, in a way captured by the typology of sequential, linear and systematic thought. To test the hypothesis regarding the structure of thinking, each subject's scores (sequential, linear or systematic) on the chemistry task, the physics task, the American government interview, and the foreign relations interview were examined. *In forty-two of the fifty cases, the subject performed at the same level on all four parts of the study.* This result suggests that there is a single underlying cognitive structure that delimits how an individual thinks about both political and nonpolitical phenomena. To test the hypothesis regarding the differences in structure of thinking across individuals, the scores of these forty-two subjects were compared. *Nine subjects reasoned at the sequential level, twenty subjects reasoned at the linear level and thirteen subjects reasoned at the systematic level.* Five of the remaining subjects performed at the same level on three of the four parts. None performed at three different levels or at two levels apart, e.g., sequential on one task and systematic on another. This result suggests that there are differences in the structure of people's thinking and that these differences are well captured by the typology.

These summary results do not do justice to the richness of the evidence obtained through in-depth interviewing and clinical experimentation. To provide a sense of that evidence, some examples of subjects' responses to the in-depth interview on foreign affairs and the chemistry task are included here.

A sequential thinker: Lynne is twenty-seven years old, black, has a high school diploma and is a clerical worker. She regularly watches political news on television, but expresses little real interest in political affairs. None the less, she has accumulated a considerable knowledge of the specific, concrete facts regarding current political events. (Indeed, she corrected the interviewer's incorrect statements regarding certain details of then current political events.) Her understanding of politics is, however, extremely limited. It consists of fragments, bits and pieces of sequences of events, each of which begins with the first and ends with the last event observed. Thus, politics is understood as series of observed acts and the expressed emotions which accompany them. When circumstances force Lynne to go beyond the specific information given, she tends to do several things. Sometimes, she indicates that she did not realize events extended beyond her knowledge of them (Lynne was surprised to learn that the United States had relations with Iran prior to a year before the interview.) More frequently, Lynne responds with conventional knowledges (culturally provided descriptions) which she understands in her own sequential terms (see her remarks on freedom below). At other times, she makes sense of certain political events by incorporating them into the framework of her understanding of sequences of events which occur among her friends. She will then interpret and predict the political events accordingly. Therefore, although Lynne uses the abstract political language she hears, she has little understanding of the causes and context of international relations. Indeed, she has little sense of nations themselves and how they conduct their business. This is true even with regard to the United States.

The following are excerpts from the interview conducted with Lynne.

(A response to a general question on American involvement and goals in Iran.)

> (We want) Peace, I guess. Peace. We just want to make this a better place to live. One thing, they want all the people back, but I don't know how they are going to get them. They seem like to me that they're coming up with some kind of plan, because it seems like the Ayatollah he is not giving up. I think there is going to be a war. I think so.

(Why?)

> I think . . . well, that's my opinion. It has been too long.

(A later discussion of Iran's hostility toward the United States.)

> The Ayatollah is really angry with us because of the Shah, right? (Why is that?) Because he is over here for medical reasons and they are trying to get back at us. They're mad because . . . I don't know what the case was, he did something. I think he was unfair.

(A reply to the suggestion that the United States might bribe a few Iranian officials in order to gain their support for the release of the hostages.)

> (Shakes head.) We (the United States) are not going to be able to borrow that much money. Someone will find out and that will make matters worse.

(A response to a request to describe the Soviet Union to someone who knows nothing about the country.)

> Right now we are pretty close to them aren't we? I hope we never make them angry with us. Because they got a pretty much strong army and they have something to do with Pakistan, didn't they?

(A response to a request to describe the United States to someone who knows nothing about the country.)

It's a free country, I think. It's a nice place to live. It has its problems.
(What do you mean, free? What is free about it?)
Supply, you know. The people are not starving. Even though mostly around the world people are being laid off. But it is pretty well organized I would say. How can I put it. We're not prying into other countries.
(We're not what?)
You know, like asking the other countries for anything. Like I said, I think we're pretty organized here – as far as sticking our noses in other people's business. That's my opinion.
(Anything else you would tell this person about the United States?)
(Shakes head to signal nothing more to say.)

Lynne's inability to go beyond observed and remembered sequences to a causal analysis of present forces is reflected in her performance on the chemicals task. When asked to determine which single liquid or combination of liquids created yellow, Lynne responded by trying each single liquid in order. When she discovered no single liquid produced the yellow, she abandoned the task and said, 'It cannot be done.' When asked if there was anything else she would like to do, Lynne looked puzzled and said 'No'. According to standard procedure, the experimenter then suggested to Lynne that she try two liquids together. She tried one combination of two liquids and repeated her claim that it (the creation of yellow) could not be done.

A linear thinker: Elaine is thirty-nine years old, black, went to college for two years and is a personnel officer. She expresses a strong interest in politics and follows the news closely. She has a relatively sophisticated conception of political affairs. When considering a specific sequence of events, Elaine automatically moves beyond the information given to consider possible causal factors (underlying motives and prior actions). She also evaluates whether or not the action taken conforms to a standard of correct action. Elaine understands international relations in terms of dyadic exchanges. Such an exchange between two countries is understood to reflect the attempts of each country to satisfy its own needs. Elaine also has a clear understanding of the roles of the individuals involved in these exchanges. The individuals are understood to be leaders, the top of a governmental hierarchy. These leaders are never confused with the nations they lead. Despite the sophistication, there are clear limits to Elaine's understanding. She only understands countries as simple hierarchies with control emanating from above. She does not recognize that international exchange occurs within contexts, both of the internal politics of the nations involved and of the larger world order. Finally, she regards the rules and norms which given these exchanges between countries (and those which govern political activity within a country) to be specific prescriptions for appropriate action, not general or ideal principles of exchange. In addition, these prescriptions are not themselves an object of consideration. Rather, they are givens – the basis, not the object, of analysis.

The following are excerpts from the interview with Elaine.

(In response to a question regarding the nature of American involvement in Iran.)

. . . I feel that there must be a money factor involved; not to mention whatever kind of influence we get from there. I feel that they're using the hostages because the United States really wants them released and if they could negotiate enough to get them released, I feel what they want is they wish to obtain whatever – either the import thing or the money factor . . .

(Elaine suggested that the US could obtain the release of the hostages if they wanted it. When asked why they have delayed in doing so, she offered the following reply.)

Yeah, the reason I say that is because I read something in the paper pertaining to the United States closing down billions of dollars worth of Iran's assets or something. Something to that effect, and so they will not release the hostages until they get something, or whatever, and I feel that negotiations are taking place amongst the officials and that they're reaching some kind of conclusion amongst themselves. I don't feel that it's a public thing.

(Elaine was asked to explain a comment that American–Iranian relations were political and they should not be.)

When I say that, you know, countries are sort of intermingled. By that I mean we have the money or whatever, and you have the oil, and I'll give you some money and you give me some oil. I make this kind of thing in my country and you make this and that in your country so we can share. I feel that that is extremely important and in order for the countries to run that they must intermingle, but I don't feel that it should be done at the expense of our lives. That's what I mean by political junk.

(In response to the request to describe the Soviet Union to someone who knows nothing about the country.)

I'd say Russia is an extremely powerful country. I think Russia is a very well run country . . . I don't say everybody over there is happy, but I'd say that they've adjusted, the majority, because this is what they've known all their lives . . . I feel their country is run

so that their rules and regulations are enforced. I feel that they know what to expect and what not to expect. I don't feel that they have these tremendous surprises every six months.
(Why do you think their country has turned out the way that it has?)
Leadership.
(Leadership? Could you explain?)
Well, the people they put in and I feel they are strong people. I feel that they know about their government. They know about their particular country. They know about their customs. They know what to do with these people. They've done this all over and over, and I feel . . . I don't always agree with what they do, or how they do it, but I feel that their country is more stabilized I think, than ours.

Elaine's ability (a) to consider groups (combinations of individual actors), (b) to infer causes when no apparent cause has been observed and (c) to consider the combined effect of several forces is reflected in her performance on the chemicals task. When asked to produce yellow, she tried one liquid at a time and then concluded that more than one must be necessary to produce the effect. She then began to work her way through the possible combinations of liquids (albeit in a somewhat haphazard manner). When she discovered the correct combination, she was asked whether the effect was produced primarily by one or the other chemical or whether both were necessary. She replied, 'You need both mixed together to make the yellow liquid. That was easy, what is the next thing we are going to do?' She was surprised to learn that there was more to the task and seemed to regard the request to investigate 'what the other two liquids do' as superfluous. She tried the other two in combination, saw no yellow was produced and stopped and said, 'Liquids two and four don't do anything.' When asked if she would like to try any other combinations, she said, 'No'.

A systematic thinker: Carol is twenty-eight years old, white, has had one year of graduate education and is an editor. She follows politics, but expresses only a moderate interest. None the less, her ability to integrate information and understand political events is quite sophisticated. When making sense of political events, she immediately considers the international and domestic context in which those events take place. She views both the international order and the nation state as systems and considers the meaning of specific events in terms of their place in those systems. For Carol, individual political leaders are not the directing forces of political life. Instead, abstract collective influences – culture and economics – are understood to structure the course of international and national political events.

The following are excerpts from the interview with Carol.

(In response to a question regarding the nature of American involvement in Iran.)

Okay. I think it's . . . what's been happening in Iran in the last twenty years is an instance of America's general policy toward Third World and developing nations. And I think that basically what our policy is towards any country like that is to get anything we can from them and to use them for our ends in whatever way is possible. And I think in Iran, we've always been interested in the oil and sort of stabilizing the Middle East with a democracy modeled after a western democracy . . . Getting friends in power so that we don't have to worry about the Soviet Union having friends in power.

(Following her comment that American policy reflects a congruence of interests between government and big business.)

I mean it's not as simple as the bureaucrats and people who are running the country, running the machinery of government, are in the same economic class as the people who are running business. It's not that simple a thing, but there is a structural congruency between the interests of the state and the interests, economic interests, of the others . . . the state having to be interested in stability, having to be interested in economic growth and prosperity, and therefore, having to provide exactly the kinds of things that the actual economic interests want.

The systematic quality of Carol's thought was clearly evidenced by her performance on the chemicals task. When asked to make yellow, Carol first tried the liquids one at a time and then began to test combinations of liquids. When she discovered the correct combination, she said, 'Three and one interact to produce yellow. I don't know if any other combination will work. Am I supposed to try to find out?' When asked to determine the effect of the other two, Carol began first by trying them together. When this failed, she then tried each together with the combination which had already worked. On this basis, she concluded that one of the remaining liquids 'neutralized the interaction' and the other 'had no impact on the interaction of one and three.'

Discussion The theoretical view and supporting evidence presented here run counter to the social learning theory adopted in much of the research on public opinion. According to social learning theory, thinking consists of a rather piecemeal process of becoming aware of phenomena and then learning how they relate to one another. Differences in thinking are conceived in substantive terms (in terms of the content and range of the information integrated) and are explained with reference to the nature of individuals' exposure to the issue at hand (included here are objective factors such as the amount and substance of the information available and subjective factors such as the degree to which the individual is motivated to attend to that information). Allowing that the nature of an individual's exposure will vary from one domain of experience to the next, two conclusions may be drawn. First, a person will probably think differently about different events or issues. This is likely to be the case when different political issues are addressed (particularly when one is a domestic issue and the other is a foreign issue) and is almost certain to be the case when political and nonpolitical questions are considered. Second, differences in the way people think about a particular issue will reflect differences in exposure and interest rather than differences in the underlying structure of their thought.

Clearly the foregoing conclusions are contradicted by the evidence of structure and individual differences presented here. With an eye to the concerns of social learning theories of public opinion, it is worth considering what alternative explanations might be offered to account for these results. The most likely candidate would be one which focuses on exposure to information. Such an explanation would suggest that the commonalities and differences in subjects' thinking were not the product of underlying cognitive structures, but rather a reflection of similarities and differences in the exposure subjects had to the relevant information.

I believe the findings cannot be explained in these terms for the following two reasons. First, and most fundamental, questions of information pertain to *what* a person knows, not *how* he knows. Although the issue of exposure to specific information is certainly relevant to considerations of the substance of a person's thinking (its content and range), it is not relevant to the analysis of its structure. In my research, subjects' responses to the interviews were scored on the basis of their *structure*, not their *substance*, and all conclusions regarding any individual's thinking or differences between individuals pertain only to questions of structure. Consequently, considerations of exposure to information may be deemed irrelevant on theoretical and definitional grounds.

My research experience supports this theoretical distinction. I found that structure both exists and can be assessed independently of content. I encountered subjects who were aware of a number of relevant details about an issue or event but could not integrate or use that information at more than the sequential level. Similarly, I examined subjects who knew almost nothing about a particular situation but could use what little information they had to analyze or explore that situation in a clearly systematic fashion. Crude examples of the independence of structure and content are readily available in the reader's own experience. Consider the essays written by mediocre (but attentive) students and those written by very bright students. Although essays by both types of students may indicate a roughly equivalent awareness of the relevant facts, the way in which those facts are understood and used is clearly different in the two cases. The difference may reflect structural differences in how students of both types reason.

Second, the evidence of how subjects performed on the four tasks is difficult to account for in terms of their exposure to relevant information. To begin with, the evidence indicates that different subjects performed differently even in response to tasks (the chemicals and physics problems) where identical and complete information was presented to all subjects. Even more difficult, the evidence indicates that the same subject performed four quite different tasks which draw on at least two, if not four, very different domains of experience in exactly the same way. Although one might reasonably expect individuals' exposure and interest in these various domains to vary considerably, they none the less responded to them all in the same way. To account for this, an explanation of thinking based on exposure to information must stretch to account for differences where the necessary relevant information is held constant; it must also stretch to account for identities where levels of exposure and subjective interest almost certainly vary. Of course, in both instances, such explanation ignores our earlier point that the similarities and differences observed are those of structure, not substance.

The second question which can be asked from a social learning perspective is whether the results merely reflect differences in general training individuals receive to deal with tasks of the kind presented in the study. The argument here focuses on the impact of education. It suggests that, by virtue of what goes on in the classroom, better-educated subjects are more familiar with and better trained to deal with the tasks which require either experimentation or oral argument. To address this argument, an additional forty subjects were tested. All were second-year students in the same university and were majoring in the natural sciences. All subjects were administered the chemicals problem. Despite the fact that all of them were familiar with, and had roughly comparable experience of, scientific experimentation, they did not perform the task in the same way. Only 40 per cent performed the task at the systematic level. The remaining 60 per cent performed the task at the linear level. These results clearly suggest that structural differences in performance cannot be explained in terms of differing familiarity with the test materials nor can these differences be readily explained in terms of differences in educational background.[2]

STUDY TWO:
UNDERSTANDING OF AMERICAN POLITICS[3]

This second study adopts a somewhat narrower focus. The aim here is to explore the structure of individuals' political thinking as it is relevant to their understanding of domestic American politics. Subjects were asked questions concerning the structure of government, the dynamics of political activity, the requirements of citizenship and the factors influencing legislators' issue positions. The hypothesis tested was that an individual's understandings of these various political issues would reflect a common structure, one captured by our threefold typology of sequential, linear or systematic thought.

Subjects

The primary subject population consisted of forty adults. As in the first study, subjects were chosen so that a broad range of people (with presumably rather different understandings of politics) would be included in the study. Subjects ranged in age from eighteeen to seventy-five. Half the subjects were male. Approximately 70 per cent of the subjects were white, 20 per cent were black and 10 per cent were Asian. The incomes ranged from what is received on welfare to considerable wealth. One-third of the subjects had received high school education or less, one-third had some college education and one-third had two or more years of postgraduate education. For a limited purpose, an additional forty subjects participated in one of the research tasks. These subjects were third and fourth-year students at the University of California, Irvine.

Procedure

Subjects were told they were participating in a study of people's social and political attitudes. Each was interviewed individually about certain aspects of American politics and then asked to solve a political reasoning task. The interview and task took an average of one hour and twenty minutes to complete. The interview was tape-recorded and transcribed. Performance on the reasoning task was recorded in writing by the experimenter as the task was administered.

The in-depth interview and the reasoning task required the subject to make a large number of related assertions and, therefore, allow a determination of the structure of the subject's thought. Using the definition of the three types of political reasoning as a guide, the interview and the reasoning task were analyzed to determine how a subject of a given reasoning type would respond. In this manner, three categories of response – sequential, linear and systematic – were specified for each part of the interview and the reasoning task. The subject's responses were coded by two raters. Raters were blind to each other's ratings and to the subject's identity. Inter-rater reliability was 88 per cent. In case of disagreement, raters conferred and agreed upon proper coding.

The interview on American politics was conducted first. Each subject was asked to choose a issue in American politics which was of particular interest to him. This then provided the substantive focus for the questions which followed. In the first part of the interview, the focus was on the structure of American government. This part was the same as the American government interview used in Study One and was presented in a similar manner. Thus, the subject was asked questions such as who is responsible for the problem, what is government doing about the situation, who actually makes decisions, what roles do the Congress, the President, the Cabinet or the civil bureaucracy play, and how do these various aspects of government relate to one another in the decision-making process. When the meaning of a subject's response was unclear, the interviewer probed further with questions such as what do you mean by that, why do things work that way, etc. The coding scheme used to score responses was the same as that used in Study One.

In the second part of the interview, the focus shifted to a consideration of the dynamics of political action. Drawing on comments made in the first part of the interview, the subject's sense of what is happening, why it is happening and with what consequence, was explored. With reference to the issues they raised, subjects were first asked to describe the political activity they felt was occurring. Each action or sequence of events mentioned was followed up with questions attempting to lead the subjects to elaborate their description. For example, subjects were asked the following: you said 'x' is the case, what does this mean exactly; or, you said 'x' is occurring, what does this involve exactly? They were also asked to explain the activity they had described. Again their remarks were followed up by questions designed to have them elaborate and justify their explanations. Questions here included: why is 'x' happening in the way it is; you gave 'y' as a reason or cause, why is 'y' effective in the way that it is? Responses to these questions were coded as follows:

Sequential: Political activity is observed rather than analyzed. Thus, the sequential thinker offers descriptions rather than explanations. The focus is on events as they transpire. The vision is particularistic – it is limited to specific events which involve particular actors doing specific things. According to this understanding, there is a sense of things happening, but no sense of why they do or how they fit together. There is little sense of history and even less of the future. Whereas there is a recognition of the order in which events occur, there is no sense of causality – of necessary preconditions and outcomes. Instead, there is a sense of a passing present.

Linear: Political activity is analyzed in causal linear terms. It is understood as emerging from a past and leading to a future. Each action is considered as either an effect and thus the product of a causal agent or as a cause and thus leading to a future outcome. Linear political reasoning leads to a search for causes or effects even when none may be immediately apparent. This search is guided by prior learning, either as provided by direct experience or as provided by the political culture. The search generally ends with the discovery of a single appropriate cause (or effect in the case of prediction). There is little consideration of multiple causes. When multiple causal agents must be considered, there is a tendency to regard them as acting in unison. (For example, in the American context, the branches of government are understood to act cooperatively rather than as competitive entities which act as checks and balances on one another.) There is no consideration of interaction processes or systemic causes.

Systematic: Political action is interpreted and explained in the light of systematic causes. This analysis may proceed at two levels. At a more abstract level, the focus will be on a general cause, one which is an expression of the organizing force of the political system itself. Discussion here focuses on the impact that political cultures and institutions have on political exchange. At a less abstract level, the focus is on the multiple particular forces in a political system that converge to produce political outcomes. In this context, the multiple and interactive effects of various political actors are considered. Like causes, political outcomes are considered at two levels. They can be considered at the level of the whole system. Here, discussion will focus on system stability and transformation. Outcomes can also be discussed at the level of particulars and thus with regard to the multiple and related outcomes political action can produce.

In the final part of the interview, a different dimension of American politics was addressed – that of the relationship between citizen and country. The focus here was on the subjects' concept of 'good citizenship'. Subjects were asked to discuss what it means to be a good citizen. As in the earlier parts of the interview, any points they made in response were probed to determine their meaning. Responses were coded as follows:

Sequential: Citizenship is defined in terms of doing something concrete and specific for the country. A good citizen does something which is helpful – he or she does the country a favor – much as one person would do for another. Usually only one or occasionally two such acts are mentioned. They are generally suggested by the immediate context (i.e., the particular concerns recently covered in the interview). There is not any clear sense of the link between citizen duties and the values and requirements of the nation.

Linear: Citizenship is defined in terms of the specific set of duties that social convention requires that the citizen perform. These duties consist of a learned list of specific practices, a set of political rituals. There is an understanding that the citizen exists in a larger structured group, one which affects individual citizens. In this context, there is little sense of the ways in which either the political environment shapes the basic nature of individuals or the individual is a creative participant in political life.

Systematic: Citizenship is conceived in the light of its function in a political system. To persist, a political system requires the compliance of its citizens. They must think and interact in a manner which is consistent with the norms and values of the polity. At the same time, the political system must be responsive to the basic needs of its citizens. To do so, it must foster creative citizen participation in the establishing of communal goals. Specific citizen duties (e.g. obedience to the law, respect for authority, voting, etc.) are understood in the light of their association with the realization of one or both of these systemic requirements (compliance and participation).

Following the interview, subjects were asked to participate in a political reasoning task. They were tested one at a time. Each subject was presented with a stack of sixteen 3 × 5 index cards. Each card represented a Senator. The head of each card was labeled with the name of a fictitious Senator (e.g., Senator John Thompson). The cards were either blue or white, indicating the Senator's vote on a bill to provide government aid to poor women who wish abortions. On each card, there was a brief statement of the Senator's political party affiliation and his voting record on four types of issues: (1) welfare, (2) abortion, (3) tax relief for those with less than average income, and (4) government spending. The cards were prepared so that only one factor, voting record on government spending, was related to the Senator's vote on the issue of government aid for abortion.

Subjects were told that their task was to determine what single factor or combination of factors influenced the Senators' vote on the bill. They were told to keep in mind two facts: (1) that all the information needed to complete the task was on the cards, and (2) that the same reason or combination of reasons influenced all the Senators. They were then instructed to lay out the cards in front of them and arrange or group the cards in whatever way they found helpful. Subjects were asked to think aloud, or express whatever conclusions they were drawing. Questions were posed when the experimenter could not determine what the subject was doing or understand the conclusions the subject was drawing.

On completing the first task, the subject was instructed to complete a second. A new set of cards was introduced. Again the name of a fictitious Senator was printed at the head of each. The color of the card indicated the Senator's position on public prayer in schools, blue cards indicating support and white cards indicating opposition. On each card, four pieces of background information (age, education, religion and income) on the Senator were given. The cards were prepared so that two factors interacted to produce a supporting view (if you were older and had above average income, you would support prayer in the schools). Subjects were asked to determine what kind of Senator opposed school prayer. Instructions for performance of this second part of the task were similar to those given for the first part. Performance on the two parts of the task was coded as follows:

Sequential: Sequential thinkers find the task a difficult and confusing one. The request for an analysis of causation presents a demand not well understood within the sequential thinker's framework. Moreover, the search for a common single or categorical cause is also unusual. In response to the task, there is a tendency to address each card singly and invent a reason for each Senator's choice. If successfully directed to deal with all the cards at once, sequential thinkers begin by grouping the cards according to a single criterion.

They have difficulty maintaining the focus on this single factor and tend to shift from one factor to the next without fully investigating any one. Sequential thinkers also tend to read off the data incorrectly, drawing mistaken conclusions from the cards currently receiving attention. Finally, having generally failed to discover the correct solution to the problem quickly, they give up before investigating all the factors.

Linear: Linear thinkers find the task of searching for a cause a natural one. Whereas some may initially attempt to explain each Senator's vote individually, they easily make the transition to searching for a single explanation for all the Senators' votes when directed to do so. When attempting to solve the problem, they systematically search for a correspondence between one factor and the vote. Thus, they can satisfactorily solve the first part of the task. The second part of the task is, however, more problematic. It requires a recognition that factors may combine to produce interactive effects. Linear thinkers find the data matrix complex. They 'solve' the problem either by focusing in on one or another causal factor and suggesting that it operates most of the time or they may argue that one set of factors influences those in favor of school prayer and another set influences those against.

Systematic: Subjects readily comprehend the task of searching for an underlying common cause. Recognizing that the task involves considering a number of possibly interrelated causes, they search for multiple and interactive causes, as well as single causes. They do so not only by searching for causal factors directly, but also by attempting to exclude those factors which clearly do not have an impact. Thus, they are able to solve both parts of the task correctly.

Results

Two key structural developmental hypotheses regarding subjects' reasoning about American politics were examined. The first was that different individuals will reason about the same political phenomenon in the fundamentally different ways suggested by our threefold typology of sequential, linear and systematic political reasoning. To test this hypothesis, the attempts of different subjects to analyze the same political issue were compared. The one substantive issue which all our subjects addressed was citizenship. The structure of each subject's remarks was analyzed. *Our content analysis indicates that eight subjects reasoned at the sequential level, twenty reasoned at the linear level and twelve reasoned at the systematic level. This result provides clear support for the hypothesis of individual differences in political reasoning.*

Like the first study, the present one was designed to address questions of information and training which might be raised regarding this result. The question of information concerns the extent to which differences in subjects' understandings simply reflect differences in the amount of information subjects had at their disposal, rather than differences in the inherent quality of their political reasoning. To address this, subjects' responses to the Senators' task were examined. Given the hypothetical nature of the task, the amount of information available to subjects was strictly controlled. All subjects received exactly the same information. Consequently, differences in their performance could not be accounted for in terms of differences in the level of available information. The results indicate that nine of the subjects performed at the sequential level, twenty performed at the linear level and eleven performed at the systematic level. These results suggest that differences in performance are a function of differences in the inherent qualities of subjects' political reasoning rather than differences in the amount of information at their disposal.

The question of training raises the further concern that our results are simply an experimental artifact – a product of differences in subjects' familiarity with the general kinds of tasks they were asked to perform, rather than of differences in the inherent quality of their political reasoning. For example, it might be argued that highly educated subjects perform better than uneducated ones because of their greater familiarity with analytical questions and problem-solving tasks. To consider this question, additional research was conducted, holding education constant. The Senators' task was administered to forty third and fourth-year university students in an advanced political science course. All the students had considerable and roughly comparable exposure to the discipline of political science and to problem-solving tasks similar to the Senators' task. None the less, only half performed the task in a systematic fashion. This result suggests that the differences in individuals' performances cannot be explained simply in terms of differences in their familiarity with the test materials.

The second hypothesis was that an individual's political thought reflects a single underlying structure. To test this hypothesis, each subject's responses to the three parts of the interview (the organization of government, the dynamic of political action and the nature of citizenship) and the Senators' task were examined. *Thirty-four of the forty subjects reasoned at the same level across all three parts of the interview and the Senators' task*. Six reasoned consistently at the sequential level, eighteen reasoned consistently at the linear level and ten reasoned consistently at the systematic level. Of the remaining subjects, two reasoned at both linear and systematic levels and four reasoned at both linear and sequential levels. Of these six subjects, three scored at the same level on three of the four tests. These results indicate that an individual's political thought is structured in the ways suggested by our threefold typology of sequential, linear and systematic and is, in this sense, coherent.

To conclude, the analysis of the data provides strong support for both hypotheses. First, the results clearly indicate that different people reason about politics in fundamentally different ways and that these differences are adequately captured by our three types of political reasoning. It should be noted that these differences are not simply an artifact of either the amount of information available to the subject, the particular political question addressed or the manner in which the data were gathered. Comparable results were achieved when addressing two different topics (the nature of citizenship and Senators' voting behavior) and when using two different research designs (in-depth interview and clinical experiment). Second, the results show that a person reasons about different issues in the same structurally determined way. In the vast majority of cases, a given subject's understanding of how government is organized, what causes political events, what it means to be a good citizen and what affects US Senators' voting behavior reflects a single underlying structure. It should be noted that this structural consistency was maintained across two different assessment instruments, an interview and a clinical experiment, as well as across topics.

To provide a flavor of the data, some brief excerpts of subjects' comments on the structure of governmental decision-making are included. The first is drawn from an interview which was scored as sequential. Note that the comments made reflect an understanding of government which is largely undifferentiated. Government is thought of either in terms of Reagan or an undifferentiated 'they'. When some differentiation is forced, it is apparent there is no clear sense of a division of power or hierarchical order. Instead, there is a return to the view that 'they' decide, and do so as a single actor.

(You mentioned the role of government and talked about 'they' who make all the decisions. What exactly is going on here? How exactly is American defense strategy decided?)

I'm not sure exactly.

(Well, who do you think decides what we are going to do?)

Well, it's got to be Reagan . . . but maybe the Senate or the Congress behind him.
(Why does the Congress have to be behind him?)
Well, they have to have more than one person's vote, don't they? To pass any . . .
(How does that work exactly?)
I don't know exactly, I just know they all vote on something and then they give it to him and he could veto it or not, but he has the last say in it, doesn't he?
(Okay. So what happens if they wanted something and he didn't want it?)
If the Congress did and he didn't?
(Yeah. Do you think it would go through?)
Probably.
(How about if he wanted something to happen and they didn't?)
I don't think it would happen.
(Do you think basically that Congress is more powerful than the President or is the President more powerful than Congress?)
I don't know. I just think they all vote together . . . and whatever one says, the other says.
(Okay, all the stuff about missiles and planes is pretty complex. How do the President and the Congress know what is the best thing for the US?)
They just know, I mean that' s what they're paid for, it's their job.

The following excerpt is drawn from a discussion of government decision-making which was scored as linear. Here, there is a suggestion of a more elaborated (although substantively incorrect) understanding of the structure of government. Government is regarded as a differentiated entity, including actors and institutions that perform their own specialized roles. These various agents are integrated into a simple hierarchical structure. Power emanates from the top (in this case, Congress). There is no sense of cross-cutting influences among those of equal power or of the independence of those actors who are located further down the hierarchical ladder.

(How are decisions made regarding government spending?)
Well, I think it is the Congress. I think it's . . . let me think now. You have got the Congress, the House of Representatives, okay. I think we have these government experts who go all over the country. I think they bring information back and tell them such and such a place is in terrible condition . . .
(Who actually makes the decision?)
I think it goes through the President and then he brings it before

the cabinet and I think they vote on it and decide who gets what.
(How do you think Congress plays into it?)
  I think it plays into it. I think they have the . . . they're the
decision-making . . .
(How do they get into it?)
  Well, I think they . . . I'm just trying to think, I could go back to
school now . . . I'm trying to think.
(Okay. Why is it that the President gets to decide?)
  He doesn't actually get to decide, I don't think. He agrees or
disagrees and it is then passed to . . . the cabinet and then its
passed to the Congress. You see, I used to know all this stuff, what
the levels were.
(This is stuff you forget.)
  It's then passed to the House of Representatives. Anyway it is
passed to somebody. They make a decision and they accept it or
they say no. If they say no, then the President . . . they have to tell
him why blah, blah, blah. But he doesn't actually make the decision. I mean he says it and it comes out that the President
decided such and such a thing, but he didn't in essence decide
anything. He just threw it out on the floor and they decided.
(What if the President doesn't agree with the Congress?)
  They decide and he has to do what they pass.
(Okay, Congress decides to do something – it passes a law – then
what happens?)
  That's it . . . then everybody has to do what the law demands all
the way down the line.
(All the way down the line?)
  Yeah. From the President down to the lowest clerk.

The next excerpt is drawn from a discussion of government decision-
making which was scored as systematic. It is apparent here that
government is conceived as a complex entity. There are many levels of
power and each one includes a number of independent agents with
differing goals. Policy is produced at any one level through a process
of competition and negotiation. In addition, agents at lower levels in
the hierarchy are somewhat independent. Consequently, they have
their own impact on the development and realization of governmental decisions.

(Who decides what kind of government assistance will be available?)
  Well, that sounds like a simple question that deserves a simple
answer, but it isn't. Things are really pretty complicated. First of
all, you have all those people . . . Health and Welfare people,
White House aides, university experts and lobbyists . . . all these

different groups trying to influence the President's priorities and the two houses of Congress. They are presenting all kinds of contradictory suggestions, but they direct the government's attention to particular problems. Then, there is a hashing out between the various parties involved. Liberals are bargaining with conservatives, Republicans with Democrats . . . you know. And then there is negotiating between the House and Senate and then with the President. It's really complex when you think about it. It's amazing that anything gets done at all.

(And then what happens?)

Well, laws may be passed, but that's not the end of the story. No sir. There are all those thousands of petty bureaucrats, the local guys who are actually sitting in the local offices and facing the people. They in the end decide what is given when.

(What about the laws passed?)

Well . . . they have some effect. They provide some direction . . . limits. But they are interpreted by lower level officials and that gives those guys a lot of power. You could even end up with the opposite of what Congress intended. That probably happens a lot.

STUDY THREE:
UNDERSTANDING INTERNATIONAL RELATIONS[4]

This third study explores people's understanding of international relations. The focus is on their understanding of the structure, dynamic and resolution of conflict. This is examined in the context of people's response to one particular conflict, that which blossomed between the United States and Libya during the spring and early summer of 1986. As in the two previous studies, the aim here is to explore the structure of individuals' thinking and the differences which exist between individuals.

Subjects

Thirty-six subjects were studied. Apart from their southern California residence, the subjects were a varied group. They ranged in age from twenty to sixty-eight and were employed in a variety of occupations. About 75 per cent of the subjects were white, the remainder were Asian. All were American citizens. One-third received a high school education or less, one-third had some college education and one-third had some postgraduate education.

Procedure

The study was conducted in the summer of 1986. By chance, it was set to be administered just after the conflict between the United States and Libya peaked with the American bombing of Tripoli. Filled with the excitement and intrigue of terrorism, threat and counterthreat and the final bombing of Tripoli, the conflict was featured in the popular media and captured the imagination of the general public. It was therefore assumed that it was a situation about which all our subjects would be aware and in which they would all be interested. The conflict also had both very simple and concrete aspects (e.g., Gaddafi's threats or the bombing) and very complex and abstract ones (e.g., America's relations with its NATO allies and the general nature of the relationship between 'First World' and 'Third World' countries). Consequently, it was assumed that all our subjects would be able to understand it at one level or another. Having decided that the conflict provided an appropriate context in which to examine subjects' reasoning about international affairs, the decision was made to take advantage of the situation and restructure the stimulus materials accordingly.

Subjects were told they were participating in a study of people's responses to the American bombing of Libya. Each subject was interviewed individually and then asked to solve a problem. Depending on the subject, the interview lasted between thirty and ninety minutes. It was tape-recorded and later transcribed. The problem required approximately twenty minutes to administer and subjects' performances were recorded in writing. Using our definition of sequential, linear and systematic thought as a guide, the interview and problem were analyzed to determine how thinkers of each type would respond. Thus, three categories of response were specified for each part of the interview and the reasoning task. Subjects' responses were coded by two raters. Raters were unaware of the subject's identity or each other's ratings. Inter-rater reliability was 89 per cent. In all cases of disagreement, raters conferred and a score was assigned.

The interview was conducted first. It began with an exploration of the subject's understanding of the general structure of the conflict. Thus, the subject was asked to identify which people or groups were involved and to explain how they were related to one another. In the latter regard, the subject's sense of the existence and nature of the opposition and the alliances among participants was explored. Throughout, the subject's responses were probed in order to clarify his definition of the participants and his conceptions of their interrelationship. The subject's responses were coded as follows:

Sequential: The focus is on the here and now of a particular event or sequence of events. This consists of an awareness of a particular leader/country trying to act and being blocked by another leader/country. In this context, there is little sense of the aims of the blocking country in relation to those of the first country. (With instruction, the sequential thinker may be led to consider the aims of the blocking country, but in so doing, he will lose sight of those of the first. He may oscillate between perspectives but cannot consider them relative to one another.) Bound to a particular situation, there is little sense of the enduring or general qualities of a conflict. Others countries are considered only as they are observed to participate in the events. They are then viewed in terms of their specific action rather than with reference to their membership in any ongoing alliances or their place in the international community. Thus, loyalties and hatreds are transient.

Linear: International conflict is understood as an opposition between sides pursuing incompatible aims. Thus, the perspectives of the participants are viewed relative to one another. Unless the circumstance clearly dictates otherwise, conflict is understood in bipolar terms, as an opposition of two sides. Each side may consist of a nation or an alliance of nations. In either case, the side is hierarchically structured and acts as a unit with a basic homogeneity of purpose. In this context, the definition of the parties to a conflict emphasizes the differences between opponents and the similarities among allies. The conflict is also understood to exist beyond the specific situation considered. As a result, oppositions and alliances are assumed to be general and enduring.

Systematic: International conflict is understood in the broad context of international relations. At a general level, the conflict is understood as an expression of more general conditions of international exchange and is interpreted accordingly. At a more specific level, the conflict is viewed as a multisided affair. Each side may consist of an alliance of nations, a single nation and/or interest groups within a nation. Each side is itself a complex entity, characterized by several possibly conflicting interests. Conflicts are not regarded as necessarily total or general. They may emerge along one dimension of exchange (e.g., ideology, trade, etc.) and not exist at all in another. Thus, sides may be opposed on one important issue and yet act as allies on others.

The second part of the interview focused on the dynamics of conflict. Here, questions centered on why the conflict between the United States and Libya had emerged and why the participants were acting as they were. Subjects were asked to describe what had transpired. This was followed by questions in which subjects were asked to elaborate their description and to explain why it was events occurred as they did. Responses were coded as follows:

Sequential: International events are not considered in terms of their causes and consequences. Instead, there is a simple observation of events as reported on television (or by others) and a collection of fragments of information of who said and did what. These are linked in a sequence. One event simply follows on the next. Lacking a sense of causation, there is little projection into the future or the distant past. There is also little consideration of alternative courses of action. For the sequential thinker, the dynamic of international conflict is little more than a particular situation of one leader/country wanting something and not getting it.

Linear: There is a clear sense of the cause of international conflict. It is the result of one or each of the sides involved pursuing its own ends without regard for those of the other. Conflict is produced by individual sides and they are attributed responsibility for it. Unless the information available clearly dictates otherwise, there will be a tendency to view only one of the sides as an offender (initiating the conflict) and the other as a victim. Thus, one side's action will be explained in terms of its inherent nature (its drive for such ends as territorial expansion or wealth) and the other's action will be explained as a response.

Systematic: Conflict is understood in one of two contexts. On the one hand, it may be understood as an expression of perturbation of an international system which is normally integrated and internally harmonious. In this context, the conflict is viewed as an accident, the result of a peculiar set of particular conditions. There is a faith that the system will right itself and the conflict will dissipate. If conflict persists, it constitutes a basis for denying the existence of an international order and assuming a randomness to exchange at that level. On the other hand, conflict may be understood as the result of the exchange between national systems. In this context, each nation's action will be viewed *both* as an initiative toward or a response to the other and as an expression of its own internal affairs. The latter may refer to its characteristic forms of domestic interaction or the conditions of its internal governance. Often there will be a tendency to explain openly conflictual overtures as an international response to a national malaise (e.g. political instability, economic decline, etc.).

In the final part of the interview, the subject was asked to consider the possibilities for the resolution of the American-Libyan conflict. Questions centered on what a resolution of the conflict would consist of and how it might be best achieved. As in the other parts of the interview, the meaning of subjects' claims were probed and they were asked to justify the explanations they offered. Responses were coded as follows:

Sequential: Does not think of conflict resolution *per se*. Instead, focuses on a particular activity or event. In this context, resolution consists merely of what finally transpires – the initiating country gets to do what it wants or it does not. There is little sense of what strategic action might be taken by either participant or third parties. To the degree to which this is discussed, the need to achieve the initial desires of one of the parties will be reasserted.

Linear: Does think about the conflict between opposing sides. It may be resolved when both sides are satisfied. Given the conception of the conflict as an exchange between generally opposed sides with incompatible aims, this joint satisification solution will generally be regarded as unlikely. More often, the resolution of conflict is understood to depend on the final domination (and subsequent incorporation) of one party by the other. The linear thinker can think about how to resolve a conflict. Because the sides are seen as causal, attempts to resolve their conflict focuses on placing pressure or distributing resources so as to affect the relative power (and hence final chances of winning) of one or the other side.

Systematic: Conflict resolution consists of establishing a cooperative and orderly exchange between the conflicting parties. This is achieved by altering the conditions of exchange and/or by establishing mutual understanding of aims and methods. The former is achieved by imposing new regulation (e.g., international law) and the latter by education. In this context, mutual accommodation is seen as offering the only lasting solution to conflict. Resolution by domination is likely to be regarded as illegitimate by the victim and therefore tends to be inherently unstable.

After the interview, the subject was asked to participate in a problem-solving task involving arms reduction negotiation. The subject was assigned the role of negotiating on behalf of the United States while the experimenter played the role of the Soviet negotiator. The subject was given four cards. Each had a label, either long range missiles, short range missiles, sea-based missiles or research on space-based missiles. He was then told that his superiors in Washington had instructed him to come to a preliminary agreement with the Soviet negotiator for a joint reduction of arms. To do so, he could offer to reduce American arms of any single type or any combination of the four types. He was told that his goal was not to worry about what he traded, but rather to achieve an arms reduction agreement. He made his offers by handing over one or more of the armament cards to the Soviet negotiator/experimenter. Depending on the offer, the Soviet negotiator responded with an accept or reject card. Only offers which included both sea-based and long range missiles were accepted. Offers which included short range missiles were always rejected.

At various points, standard prompts were introduced by the experimenter. If the subject stopped after having offered only one armament card at a time, the experimenter prompted by suggesting that he could also try combinations of armaments. If the subject discovered the combination which was accepted, the experimenter asked two questions. First, he asked what was the relative impact of each of the two parts of the package (the offer to reduce sea-based missiles and the offer to reduce long range missiles). The subject was then asked to justify his response. Second, the experimenter asked the subject to discuss the impact of the offer of reducing other types of armaments (e.g., the research on space-based missiles or short range missiles) on the Soviet response. At this point, he was asked to justify his response and strongly encouraged to explore further by making additional offers. Whenever a subject wished to do no further negotiating, he was always encouraged to continue by one additional prompt (e.g., 'Are you sure there are no other offers you would like to try?'). Subjects' responses were coded as follows:

Sequential: The sequential thinker does not view the circumstances in causal terms nor does he think of the consequences of alternative strategies on their interaction with the Soviet negotiator. His action is guided by the instruction to make proposals. Thus, he tends to offer to reduce each single type of armament. Many sequential thinkers will stop at this point and simply state they cannot reach an agreement. When prodded to continue, they will arbitrarily choose one or perhaps two combinations and then give up the task. If they happen to hit the proper combination, they will explain Soviet acceptance primarily as the result of one or the other component of the offer.

Linear: The linear thinker naturally considers effects in terms of their causes and can therefore readily explore the consequences of different offers. Thus, he will tend to test both single offers and combinations of offers until he arrives at a combination which works. He will also understand that it is the combination rather than either one in particular which achieves the desired effect. However, when asked to explore the impact of the other possible offers, the linear thinker will have more difficulty. He does not think in terms of a system of interrelated cause and effect nor does he tend to define acts by virtue of their relationship. Searching for the act which produces a desired reaction, he does not understand the sense of further inquiry and will tend to give up and conclude that reductions of research on space-based missiles or in the number of short range missiles simply do nothing.

Systematic: The systematic thinker views the situation in systemic terms and thus sees a set of possible and multiple interrelationships among causes and effects. Furthermore, he defines causes and effects not in terms of the particular content of the acts themselves, but rather with regard to the quality of the relationships which exist between them. Consequently, he will view a given outcome in the light of a system of possible contributing causes and consider these in terms of their interactive relations (e.g., positive, negative and neutral). Thus, the systematic thinker will readily discover that an offer to reduce both sea and long range missiles produces agreement, the offer to reduce research on space based missiles is neutral (it is not sufficient to produce agreement but is acceptable), and that the offer to reduce short range missiles is negative (even when offered in conjunction with sea and long range missiles, it leads to rejection).

Results

The analysis of subjects' reasoning about international relations constitutes a further check on the structural developmental conception of political reasoning. As in the study of reasoning about American politics, the results indicate that subjects think about international relations in very different ways. This was reflected in their understanding of the conflict between the United States and Libya. For example, when asked to discuss the dynamics underlying the emergence of that conflict, five of the subjects reasoned at the sequential level, twenty reasoned at the linear level and eleven reasoned at the systematic level. This result is paralleled by the one achieved under the more controlled condition of the negotiation task. Although all subjects were given identical information, six subjects performed at the sequential level, twenty-one performed at the linear level and nine performed at the systematic level. Together, these results provide strong support for the claim that different people will make sense of international events in fundamentally different ways.

The data also allow a test of the second claim that an individual's understanding of the various aspects of international relations reflects a single underlying structure. To this end, each subject's responses to the three parts of the interview (the structure, dynamic and resolution of the American–Libyan conflict) and the negotiation task were examined. *Thirty-one of the thirty-six subjects reasoned at the same level on all three parts of the interview and on the negotiation task.* Five reasoned consistently at the sequential level, eighteen reasoned consistently at the linear level and eight reasoned consistently at the systematic level. This result suggests that people's reasoning about international relations is structured in the ways suggested by our typology of sequential, linear and systematic thought.

In sum, the analysis of the data provides strong support for the structural developmental conception of the way in which people think about international affairs. Given the focus on the structure rather than the content of subjects' responses and a design which included discussion of a real event and a laboratory exercise, this result cannot readily be attributed to such potentially confounding factors as the amount of information available to subjects or the demand characteristics of the particular method used.

To conclude, excerpts from the interviews are presented. The first interview was scored as sequential. It reflects a clear difficulty in understanding the nature of the opposition of the two countries. Indeed, the interviewee seems to confuse references to countries with references to individuals. At the same time, while events are noted there is little sense of why they occurred or where they will lead.

(There has been a lot of trouble between the United States and Libya in the last couple of weeks. What do you think is going on here?)

You mean the bombing and all that? (Yes, what was that about?) I don't know . . . we bombed them and killed some of what's his name? (Gaddafi?) Yeah, we killed some of his kids and there is going to be trouble.

(Why did we bomb Libya?)

He was causing a lot of trouble . . . you know, the shoot-ups in the airports and we had to punish him to make him stop.

(Why did we have to bomb him?)

Somebody had to do it. (Why?) Who else?

(Why was he causing so much trouble?)

I don't know.

(Do you think bombing him will work, that it will stop the terrorism?)

Yes. (Why?) I don't know, may be he'll go on anyway. (Why will he keep going on?) I don't know, he'll go on . . . do you think what's his name is crazy? (Gaddafi, why do you say that?) Well everybody says he's crazy, but he doesn't look weird to me. I don't know, maybe he is crazy.
(Aside from the present problem with Gaddafi, do you think we have other problems with Libya?)
Libya? (Yes.) I don't know . . . I think we get along with him OK.

The second set of excerpts which follows was drawn from an interview that was scored as linear. It provides a classic example of casting the conflict as a bipolar opposition of two groups. The interviewee is knowledgeable and his view more elaborate. Therefore, he mentions a number of nations, but these relate to one another as members of one of two opposed alliances, each of which has a simple hierarchical structure. The interview also provides a good example of linear explanation. Whereas the perspectives of the parties involved are clearly distinguished, they vary only in terms of their evaluation of events as good or bad.

(What exactly is going on here?)
I don't know, it is sort of in the background now. (Well, what do you remember of what was happening then?) With what, the terrorism or when Reagan attacked Libya? Who was involved? Well, it was the US and Libya. They terrorized our citizens and we bombed them.
(How do you think the US got involved?)
We are always involved with the Arabs one way or another. (How is that?) Well, basically it has to do with Israel. We have an alliance with them and the Arabs hate Israel and so they hate us. That's why all the terrorism. Although Gaddafi can't be very significant. (Why is that?) Well, they didn't do anything to help him. They just left him in the cold. (Why is that important?) Well if you have a friendship that you care about, you help out, don't you? They didn't.
(Why exactly did Libya get involved in all this terrorism?)
Gaddafi is a lunatic, but its more than that. He is trying to get into the whole act. He is insignificant and he is trying to be a big shot and help out Syria. (Syria?) Yeah, Syria . . . they're the ones who lead the Arab countries. (How is it that they are able to do that?) Russia. They are like Russia's lieutenants in the Middle East. (Why do they serve Russia?) Well, Russia's right on their border and they better do what they're told or else.

(Do you think the bombing will stop terrorism?)

No. The only way you'll stop the terrorism is to jail all the terrorists and bring down the governments who are directing them. (Anything else?) I don't know. Give them Israel I guess. But that we can't do that, you can't give in to somebody just because they push you around.

The last excerpts are drawn from an interview that is scored systematic. It includes references to multiple causes of events and also tries to consider the interrelationships among them. This is particularly evident in the discussion of the intensity of Arab dislike of the United States. In a way that is also typical of systematic analysis, it includes a consideration of the various meanings of actions and how this affects the exchange between those involved in conflict.

(What exactly do you think is going on here?)

It's related to the Arab-Israeli conflict. The United States has shown support for Israel and the Palestinian terrorism is one response.

(Why exactly is Libya involved?)

There are a number of reasons. First, all the attention serves Gaddafi well. To his own people, he appears more than he is and it maintains his position at a time when the oil prices have to be affecting the domestic economy. It also helps at the international level. It makes him appear as a wild, uncontrollable force. This has to give him an additional edge whenever he negotiates with other countries over anything, aid to Israel, the price of oil, the cost of imported French perfume, anything. (Why is that?) It makes him appear less predictable, as though he could shut down relations or talks at any moment. Other countries pay an additional price just to appease him to the point where he will then negotiate as others would. I think he is very clever really.

(How about the United States, why is it involved?)

I am not sure really. Part of it is obvious, we are the brunt of terrorist attack, but that just puts the whole question back a step. Our relationship to the Arabs is a complicated one. We regard them as important business partners and wish to foster good relations and yet regard them as undemocratic, lesser beings who are hostile to an important strategic ally, Israel. Both dimensions operate in our relationship with the Arab states and intensify our conflict with them. Because of the business interest, we have a strong presence there and draw a lot of attention and concern, indeed expectation. Because of our political position and racism, the expectations are frustrated. This creates more animosity than

just being opposed on certain issues. I think this is particularly true in Arab culture, but I don't really know, I can't say.
(Do you think the bombing will stop the terrorism?)
No, I expect it will simply exacerbate the situation. If the support of terrorism is critical to Gaddafi's political position, he will continue to support it unless he is convinced Reagan might respond with a full scale invasion. Even then, he may continue his support, if somewhat more discreetly. In any case, the terrorism will go on without Gaddafi. (Why is that?) There is a real impasse here. There is a conflict over terrority, over Israel and the American position on that issue. I don't think we understand their view of the problem well at all. And we will have to if any meaningful rapprochement is to take place.

CONCLUDING REMARKS

The three studies were designed to explore the structure of people's understanding of politics. The first addressed the question of the generality of this structure. It examined people's reasoning about two very different political issues (one domestic and one international) and how this related to their reasoning about nonpolitical phenomena (a chemistry problem and a physics problem). The second study focused on people's understanding of American politics. It explored people's understanding of the structure of government, the nature of political action and the relationship between the citizen and the state. The final study considered people's understanding of international relations. The focus here was on people's understanding of American –Libyan relations and the study examined their sense of the structure of that conflict, the dynamics of its emergence and the possibility and nature of its resolution.

The results of the three studies provide strong support for the claims regarding the structural qualities of political reasoning and the nature of individual differences. Considered together, the studies clearly indicate that there is a general structure to people's political reasoning. In the first study, not only did forty-two of fifty subjects reason in the same way about both a domestic political issue and international one, they also attempted to solve two natural science experiments in the same manner. In the second study, thirty-four of forty subjects reasoned about various aspects of American politics in the same structurally delimited way. Finally, in the third study, thirty-one of thirty-six subjects reasoned about several dimensions of the conflict between the US and Libya in the same way. Overall, strong evidence of structure was found in 107 of 126 cases. In all cases this was true even though both the topics of discussion and the nature of the tasks varied considerably. The three studies also provide ample evidence of differences between individuals in the structure of their reasoning. Combining these results, twenty subjects reasoned consistently at the sequential level, fifty-six reasoned consistently at the linear level, and thirty-one reasoned consistently at the systematic level.

These results are supported by other research on adult reasoning. Unfortunately, little of this research focuses on political reasoning. One interesting exception is a study conducted by Dana Ward (1982). Using distinctions which follow on Piaget's early work on egocentrism, Ward discovered differences in adults' understanding of such political concepts as freedom and democracy that were roughly comparable to those reported here.[5] Despite the relative lack of direct research on adult political reasoning, there is a considerable amount of research on the nonpolitical reasoning of adults which is suggestive. First, there is the work on the closely related topic of moral reasoning. Led by the work of Lawrence Kohlberg (1969, 1971, 1981, 1984), this research has demonstrated that adults reason about moral issues in structurally different ways.[6] Second, there is research conducted in the United States which casts doubt on the Piagetian claim that all adults reach the same final stage of cognitive development. This research indicates that while some individuals do achieve the stage of formal operations, many do not (e.g., Sinnott, 1975; Kuhn et al., 1977; Hardy-Brown, 1979; Commons et al., 1982). Third, there is research that has discovered cross-cultural differences in levels of cognitive development. This research indicates that individuals exposed to less complex social environments will not achieve formal operational thought (e.g., Peluffo, 1967; Prince, 1968; Luria, 1976; Dasen, 1977). Taken together, the results of these strands of research parallel those reported here. They suggest that there is a structure to adult reasoning which may vary across individuals.[7]

As argued earlier, both the theoretical perspective and the empirical results presented here contradict the social learning theory adopted in much of the research on public opinion. Whereas that theory focuses on the content of thought and the effect of exposure to information, mine focuses on structure and, in the first instance, the effect of the individual's own way of thinking. From its different perspective, social learning theory leads to the twin conclusions that (1) the same individual is likely to have different exposures to different domains of experience and therefore is likely to exhibit different levels of sophistication when thinking about different issues, and (2) given comparable exposure and training, different individuals will think about the same issues in a similar fashion. Clearly, the results of the three studies here contradict these two conclusions. All three provide evidence that individuals will think about very different subject matters in the same way. This was most dramatically illustrated in the first study where subjects approached topics as different as the structure of American government, the hostage crisis in Iran, the cause of a chemical reaction and the force propelling a swinging pendulum in the same way. The research also provides evidence of the independence of cognitive structure and exposure to specific information. The chemicals and pendulum task presented in the first study, the Senators task presented in the second study and the negotiation task presented in the third study all provided subjects with identical and complete information. None the less, in each case, different subjects performed those tasks in qualitatively different ways.

The research also contradicts a key assumption underlying rational actor models of political reasoning. Rational actor theorists assume there is a structure or logic to people's thought. In their terms, thought is rational. While different theorists may describe this rationality differently, they agree that in either its full or limited/bounded form, it is a characteristic of all individuals' thought.[8] If this is to suggest no more than that all individuals pursue goals, the claim is acceptable although somewhat uniformative. However, if this extends to some conceptualization of what individuals can think about and how, this claim is denied by the evidence. All three studies indicate that there are fundamental differences in how people reason and consequently in how they analyze and understand political events. The evidence suggests that rather than a single rationality, there are at least three distinguishable forms of rationality.

When evaluating the results of the research reported here, it is important not only to consider issues of theory confirmation, but also the quality of the descriptions of political thinking generated. In chapter 2, the descriptions offered by the belief systems research were criticized for (1) focusing on preferences and therefore only indirectly characterizing or assessing reasoning and understanding, (2) imposing a definition of politics and meaning rather than being sensitive to people's own subjective definitions, and (3) offering only negative or minimal descriptions of the sub-rational or sub-ideological ways in which most people's political reasoning appears to deviate from that imposed standard. Considered in this light, the descriptions offered here compare quite favorably. They directly address questions of how people reason about and finally understand politics. In so doing, they also assume that individuals define the nature and boundaries of politics in their own terms and that these terms may vary in fundamental ways from person to person. So oriented, our descriptive typology provides the basis for a rich description of the various ways in which people make sense of politics. This extends to a characterization of how people conceive of the space and time of political events, how they understand the dynamic which motors those events, and how they define the nature of the action and the actors who are involved. Three important points should be noted. First, the typology offers an equally rich and positive description of both sophisticated and unsophisticated forms of political reasoning. Second, the richness and breadth of these descriptions are not achieved with a loss of coherence. The features of the individual's political understanding are all understood to derive from the basic structure of his thought and the form of reasoning which produces it. Third, and following from the second, these descriptions have power. Relying on an abstract and structural conception of individuals' thinking, they are defined independently of any particular observation and are therefore quite general.

It is important to note that these gains in description are not simply a function of focusing on understanding rather than opinion and using in-depth interviews rather than surveys. Rather, they are the result of self-consciously abandoning the liberal and enlightenment conception of thinking underlying the belief systems research in favor of the structural developmental conception developed in chapters 3 and 4. It is this alternative epistemological base that provides the direction needed to construct a descriptive typology of the requisite orientation, breadth and power.

To illustrate the importance of epistemology to research on ideology, let us consider Robert Lane's study of ideology (1962, 1973). It provides the most prominent alternative to the belief systems research. Rather than examining individuals' specific political beliefs or preferences, Lane focuses on the understanding of political ideas and institutions. In so doing, he assumes that political reasoning and ideology may take not one, but several forms. He is therefore sensitive to the fact that the domain of issues which are relevant to the analysis of an individual's political ideology may vary and include ostensibly nonpolitical concerns. He explains the differences in individuals' political reasoning in terms of both the inherent qualities of the individuals themselves and the nature of the demands placed upon them by their environment. In this light, he regards the analysis of personality and culture (particularly that of the workplace) as central to the conceptualization of ideology (see also Lane 1978a, b; 1983).

Taking this direction, Lane addresses many of the substantive concerns adopted in my own research. Indeed, my interest in ideology was first stimulated by a reading of his 1962 study. None the less, there are important differences. Most basically, Lane does not adequately address the epistemological issues I regard as fundamental. I believe that his research suffers accordingly. Lane's study of ideology is weak in two significant respects. First, he describes ideologies in a fragmentary and piecemeal fashion. *Political Ideology* begins with a description of the ideologies of a small number of the men of 'Eastport'. This description consists of an unwieldy analysis of how each man responded to each subtopic of each of the several issues raised in the course of the lengthy interview. No overarching or integrative statement is offered regarding any individual's or the group's understanding of the political concerns investigated. Instead, there is a myriad of illuminating, but disconnected, commentaries on the particular topics the men discussed. Second, Lane's depiction of the men's political ideologies lacks generality. For the most part, it emerges from the data themselves. Consequently, it may be that the description is only relevant to Lane's fifteen residents of Eastport at the time of interviews. There is no basis for inferring that it would generalize to a different group of people or that it would hold even for the same group interviewed at a different time.

The problems with Lane's study are at root epistemological. They reflect his implicit attempt to straddle the divide between structural developmental and liberal conceptions of thinking. The substantive aims of Lane's research, the interpretative study of the qualities of individuals' political reasoning and the analysis of the differences among individuals, reflect the influence of structuralist and developmental writings. However, his conceptualization and analysis are ultimately guided by liberal definitions. For example, let us consider his concept of structure. In a typically liberal fashion, Lane does not view structures as forces which are generative and defining, but as purposive and organizing systems. Thus, he defines a structure (ideology) to be the product of a goal-oriented unit (the person as agent) which organizes its objectively defined elements (knowledges, beliefs and actions) according to the functional requirements (both internal and external) of self-maintenance (Lane, 1973). Structures are identified in terms of their specific purposes and constituent elements which are, in turn, identified in terms of their content.[9]

Based on this epistemological definition of cognitive structure,

Lane's theoretical concepts and his interpretation of interviews lack the abstraction, integration and generality of structural developmental theorizing. His analyses of ideology are necessarily anchored in a discussion of the specific content of people's understandings and the idiosyncratic configurations these understandings combine to create. Lacking a sufficiently abstract concept of ideology to define political thought across content domains, Lane is forced to address each new political question or issue on its own terms. Consequently, his descriptions of ideology are necessarily piecemeal. For the same reason, Lane is also unable to offer a general description of ideology that is independent of and can then be applied to (and tested by) the interviews he conducted. Instead, he is limited to constructing a description of ideology which derives from an examination of those interviews and therefore necessarily reflects the particular characteristics of his subjects at the time they were interviewed. In sum, because Lane adopts some of the substantive foci of structural development research, his work on ideology yields an unusually rich characterization of individuals' political thinking. However, because he fails to adopt the formal requirements of structural developmental theorizing, that characterization lacks sufficient coherence and conceptual power.

To conclude, the studies presented here constitute only a first step in the exploration of the structural developmental theory of ideology. More empirical research is needed before the typology of forms of political reasoning can be accepted with confidence. Different kinds of political issues must be addressed (e.g., the concept of law, the relation between religion and politics, the nature of power) and additional experiments on political analysis must be devised. In the latter regard, it would be particularly interesting to investigate the consequences of differences in reasoning for decision-making. In addition to empirical validation, the typology requires further theoretical elaboration. For example, it would be interesting and important to explore the relationship between understanding and evaluation in this context. Insofar as the quality of the objects of thought and the kind of relations forged between objects vary across types, it seems likely that the nature of what people want and how they place those wants relative to one another, to other people and to themselves will also vary. Similarly, it seems likely that people would differ in the way in which they evaluated those things that they might potentially value or want. For example, it may be that linear thinkers tend to evaluate in ways suggested by cognitive balance theories (e.g., Festinger, 1957; Heider, 1958) whereas sequential and systematic thinkers will not. In addition to broadening the current definitions of the types, it would also be useful to consider the possibility of a fourth type of thinking, one more developed than systematic thought. The existence of such a fourth type is suggested by some fascinating recent research in developmental psychology (e.g., Riegel, 1973; Commons et al., 1982; Edelstein and Noam, 1982).

A critical area not yet explored is that of the process of the development of political reasoning. Several sets of issues arise here. First is the need to address questions regarding the sequence of the developmental progress. The theory suggests that the order of this development should be invariant. This claim may be readily tested by examining the development of political reasoning in children. This may be done using either longitudinal or cross-sectional designs.[10] Second is the need to address questions regarding the relationships between environments and individuals. A precondition for inquiry in this area is a theoretical basis for distinguishing among environments. As suggested by the theoretical statement in chapter 4, environments must be defined in terms of their structures and in a way which is relevant to the qualities of individuals' political reasoning. Once a satisfactory definition is available, empirical research can then proceed to explore both the static and dynamic qualities of the relationship between individuals and environments. To begin with, it may focus on evidence of correspondence between the structure of an environment and the level of development achieved by individuals in that environment. Ultimately, however, research will have to focus on the dynamic of development itself and examine both how changes in the structure of situations lead to a transformation in the reasoning of individuals and how changes in the reasoning of individuals lead to a restructuring of the environment in which they live.

6
Summary and Epilogue: Toward a Social Psychology of Politics

The aim of this book has been to provide a new approach to the study of political thought and ideology. This approach was introduced as a response to the difficulties plaguing the current empirical research in this area. Although its initial findings were intriguing, this research was found to offer a view of people's ideologies that is largely unrevealing, conceptually weak and of little heuristic value to the general study of politics. These failings were attributed to the adoption of a theoretical framework and underlying epistemology which do not allow for an adequate exploration of the subjective meaning of the political attitudes people express.

In response, a new approach, a structural developmental one, was presented. Growing out of the epistemological tradition of Hegel and Marx, it reflects a critical view of the enlightenment/liberal view of thought which underlies the concepts and methods of the current research on ideology. Both the nature of ideology and its relationship to reason are subject to fundamental reconsideration. As a result, reason and ideology are redefined as isomorphic, the joint products of the constructing individual and the determining social environment, and the focus of research is redirected from the study of political attitudes to the analysis of political reasoning. As developed in the book, this structural developmental approach builds on the psychology of Jean Piaget. This was then modified in light of a more careful consideration of the social bases of reasoning. This led to a reconceptualization of both the dynamic of development and the stages through which it progresses.

As presented here, structural developmental analysis is distinguished both by its theoretical premises and its empirical methods. Theorizing is based on four fundamental claims. First, political thinking is a constructive activity, it yields a definition of political phenomena and the relations which exist among them. In this sense, it has an underlying structure and is, in its own terms, coherent. Second, political thinking is pragmatic, it is realized in the concrete reality of individuals' attempts to interact with one another in a purposive and socially delimited manner. Third and following from the first two, political thinking develops. Insofar as the structure of the individual's thinking is incommensurate with that of his social environment, his thinking will be transformed. The old structure will be objectified and a new one constructed. Finally, not all political thinking will share the same basic structure. Because different people may be socialized into differently structured environments, they may achieve different levels of cognitive development and therefore will think about politics in fundamentally different ways.

Given this theoretical orientation, the aim of structural developmental research is to provide a model of how individuals think and then to make sense of differences between individuals with reference to a theoretically defined hierarchy of developmental structures. This requires an interpretative investigation of the meaning of what people say and do. Empirical research is designed accordingly. The focus is on single individuals and how they perform across a variety of tasks. The tasks themselves are designed so that both the individuals' understandings of the task and the meaning of their responses may be fully explored. This requires methods of data collection other than those normally employed in research on political ideology. Isolated opinions are not considered a sufficient indication of an individual's political understanding. Instead, the process whereby these opinions are formulated and related to one another (that is, reasoning and judgment) is considered the critical phenomenon to be observed. Consequently, large scale surveys are replaced by in-depth interviews and clinical experimentation as the primary means of gathering data.

In the book, three forms of political thinking, sequential, linear and systematic, are defined. Relying on this typology, it was hypothesized that the political thinking of adults has an underlying structure and that this may differ in very fundamental ways from one individual to the next. To test this hypothesis, the thinking of 166 adults was explored in the course of three studies. The first study examined the general structure of their thinking as it was manifest both in the solution of physical problems and in the consideration of political ones. The second focused on people's understanding of domestic American politics. Here, their conceptions of the structure of the federal government, the causes of political action and the nature of citizenship were considered. The third study examined people's understanding of international politics. People's under-standings of international conflict and its resolution were tested in the context of their response to questions regarding American relations with Libya. All three studies provided strong empirical support for the theoretical claims. Over three-quarters of our subjects gave evidence of an underlying structure of their thinking, one which was well captured by the threefold typology of sequential, linear and systematic thought.

In this final chapter, the implications of this structural develop-ment theory for political studies are discussed. This starts with a consideration of its relevance to the research on political behavior. Included here is some commentary on recent research which adopts a schema theory approach. The discussion concludes with a consider-ation of the implications of the work presented here for social and political theory. Throughout, the remarks are brief and speculative. The intention is to open debate and point to areas for further inquiry.

POLITICAL BEHAVIOR RESEARCH AND SCHEMAS

A key contribution the theoretical arguments and empirical research presented here make to the understanding of political behavior is to highlight the need for a more careful consideration of the way in which individuals' responses to political events, social conditions and the overtures of government are subjectively mediated. In chapter 4, I have described the forms which this mediation takes and the conse-quences it has for the political understandings the individual con-structs. In my view, the fact and variety of this subjective mediation must be taken into account in both the design of political research and the crafting of public policy.

Consider the example of a central concern to students of political behavior, the effect of political party affiliation on voting behavior. Typically, researchers exploring this question begin with the assump-tion that all people understand political parties and their relationship to them in the same way. Consequently, there is little interest in the meaning of party identification. Instead, this is assumed to be trans-parent and attention centers on observed variations in the strength of that identification. Historical and demographic factors are examined in order to explain this variation and then party identification itself is used to help explain vote choices. This model underlies much of the basic research on party identification from the seminal work on the American voter by Angus Campbell and his colleagues in the 1950s (Campbell et al., 1960) to the recent work of Wattenberg (1984).

My own research suggests this approach is misdirected in several important respects. Most fundamentally, the assumption of a common understanding of political parties and party identification is incorrect. It is virtually certain that the members of a large stratified voting population will have reached different stages of development and therefore will understand the nature of political parties and their relationship to them in very different ways. The first step in research must therefore be to explore and illuminate the nature of these various understandings. As suggested in chapter 3, this requires open-ended interviewing and experimentation in order to insure that the subject will clearly reveal the quality of his conception of political parties and the meaning of his identification with them. In my view, the causes and consequences of fluctuations in the strength of party identification are mediated by this subjectively constructed understanding. Therefore, only on the basis of prior research on people's political reasoning can the researcher hope to explain party identification or predict its impact adequately.

To illustrate the point, let us take the example of the different ways in which sequential, linear and systematic thinkers understand political parties and consider the impact of these different modes of understanding on the causes and consequences of the party identifications of thinkers of each type. In each case, we must determine how the person conceives of both political parties and his own identity. The comments here are necessarily brief. For a full account of the nature of thinking of each type, the reader is referred back to chapter 4.

The sequential thinker has little sense of the domain of politics and the natural objects of his thought are specific individuals rather than a group of any kind. Consequently, political parties have little meaning for him. They are by nature too abstract and the arena in which they act is too remote. In addition, he does not reflect on himself or on his ties with others. Thus, issues of self-identification and affiliation mean little to him. The sequential thinker understands and is motivated by what is immediate and physically rewarding. Consequently, he will be moved to act on behalf of others only insofar as it suits his own needs or whims. In the eyes of other types of thinkers, his attachments will appear unpredictable, unreliable and short-sighted. Given the nature of his understanding, it does not make sense to raise the issue of party identification when analyzing the behavior of the sequential thinker. It is not part of the vision of the world he constructs and therefore does not exist either to be influenced by external events or to shape his response to them. At most, the sequential thinker may appear to act in a party-affiliated manner when he is moved to do so by immediate and tangible rewards.

The case of the linear thinker is quite different. He does have a sense of politics. He sees it as a hierarchically structured arena in which individuals and groups struggle for power. He views groups as internally homogeneous and defines individuals by their group membership. The linear thinker is also able to take himself as object. Thus, the question of self-identification arises. In the linear thinker's terms, this is really a question of self-placement, a matter of the groups with which one is associated. Because the linear thinker is able to conceptualize groups and defines himself in relation to them, it may be appropriate to consider his political party identification. As suggested in chapter 4, the categories which the linear thinker utilizes and the objects upon which he focuses are powerfully determined by the focus of those around him. This suggests that when party membership is made salient by virtue of culture or historical circumstance (e.g., an election), the linear thinker will define himself and others in these terms. Because his very self is at stake, once created, this affiliation will run deep and its effect will be strong. It will provide a lens through which the linear thinker will view and evaluate the candidates and the issues of the day.

Like the linear thinker, the systematic person also thinks in terms of groups and his relationship to them. However, he does so in a very different fashion. He sees politics as a system of regulation which is crafted in order to achieve certain overarching goals or principles. Particular political forces, preferences and policy decisions are evaluated in this light. This then provides a context for his conceptualization of political groups. They are viewed as internally differentiated collectivities which serve as vehicles for the realization of general ends. In the mind of the systematic thinker, these ends transcend the particular aims of given individuals or groups. As a result, he does not choose ends with reference to any particular group, but instead evaluates groups with regard to their role in facilitating or obstructing the achievement of the ends he has already defined. When conceptualizing himself, the systematic thinker considers the integrated whole of his attitudes, actions and background. In this sense, he identifies himself more in personal terms and less with regard to external social affiliations. Consequently, under most circumstances, he will be less committed to political parties than his linear counterpart. This is not to suggest no commitment. In the context of his systematic vision of politics, he recognizes the role of parties as vehicles for electing candidates and promoting specific policies. Therefore, when there are particular social goals he wishes to realize, he will choose the most appropriate party and may support it vigorously. Unlike the linear thinker, however, the systematic thinker's affiliation is strictly instrumental. Insofar as a party or its candidates stray from his basic social objectives, he will vote against them.

In sum, because people may reach different levels of political development, they will understand political parties and their relationship to them in different ways. Some people (e.g., those who think sequentially) may never properly identify with a political party. Others who do identify may do so in very different ways. Consequently, their party identifications may emerge and be strengthened by different kinds of factors and exercise very different sorts of effects. The description and explanation not only of party identification, but of any aspect of the political activity must be crafted accordingly.

The issues raised here are not only relevant to the research on political behavior. They are also of obvious importance to those responsible for the crafting and execution of public policy. The aim of any public policy is to direct citizens' behavior in a way which realizes collective goals and values. To be effective, it must be crafted with an eye to how the information and rewards provided will be understood by the target population. Failure to do so will lead to situations where the people in question are responding either in unexpected ways or not at all. Policymakers are regularly confronted with unexpected outcomes and apparently inexplicable disappointments. In my view, this can be explained, in part, by their inability to recognize the nature of the differences which may exist between themselves and their target population, differences which extend beyond questions of expressed preference to more fundamental ones of reasoning and understanding. An example of this was presented in chapter 1, where the inability of community organizers either to achieve changes which endure after their departure or to understand the reasons for their failure was discussed. In concert with the present argument, it was suggested that this may have been caused by the basic difference between the understanding of persons, action and government constructed by the organizer and by his target population.

Before concluding, I would like to briefly comment on some recent work on public opinion that has been guided by what is loosely referred to as 'schema theory'. This work is of interest not only because of its current popularity, but also because it focuses on the cognitive and subjective dimensions of political thinking. However, despite certain manifest similarities, this schema approach differs from my own in several important respects.

Although now used by political scientists, the concept of schema originated in the work of cognitive psychologists. It was first developed in a variety of somewhat different ways in the early part of this century and is now frequently used in the analysis of memory and inference.[1] According to most definitions, a schema consists of a set of elements (representations of objects or actions) which are placed in relation to one another along some temporal, spatial or categorical dimension. For example, one might have a schema for a social greeting which includes the sequence of steps involved in first approach (e.g., making eye contact, smiling, moving toward the other) and initial verbal exchange (e.g., saying, 'hello', waiting for a response, asking about the other's health). Alternatively, one might have a schema for the Democratic Party which includes a number of social groups (e.g., the poor, the blacks, the Jews) and policy positions (e.g., protect the environment, favor welfare programs).

Although schemas are often defined in these static terms, they are understood with reference to the role they play in the processing of information. A person's schemas structure how he initially perceives information and retrieves it from memory. New information is assimilated into preexisting schemas and attempts to recall old information are oriented by those same schemas. For example, we may have a schema that Ronald Reagan is a master of public relations. We then observe an instance where Reagan is confronted with a potentially embarrassing political situation which does not adversely affect his public image. Our schema of Reagan orients our interpretation of the event and we understand the outcome observed to be the result of Reagan's purposive handling of the press and the public. Later, when thinking about Reagan and his activities, our memory search will be oriented by our schema that Reagan is a master of public relations and we will remember most easily those occasions when he succeeded in maintaining a favorable image.

As suggested by the preceding example, schemas function as aids in the organization and use of the vast array of information to which the individual is exposed. In so doing, they enable him to draw inferences and thereby 'go beyond the information given.' Whereas a schema consists of a set of interrelated elements, often the observation of just a single element is enough to evoke the entire schema. For example, we may have a schema of personal competence which includes the ability to solve a variety of difficult problems. We then observe George solving one such problem. This may activate our schema of competence and cue the other information incorporated in it. As a result, we may infer that George is a competent person, capable of effectively solving a whole range of problems. In this manner, schemas provide considerable conceptual leverage – minimal information may yield quite general conclusions. At the same time, this schema-mediated inference may lead to distortion and misunderstanding. For example, in George's case, it is possible that his ability to solve the problem was a result of luck or specific training and not of George's general abilities. In this case, the evocation of the 'competence' schema is inappropriate and will lead to subsequent errors in predicting and understanding future behavior.

As demonstrated by these examples, the cognitive psychologist's concept of schema may be readily applied to the analysis of social cognition. Indeed, the concept of schema has been recurringly popular among social psychologists. Used to advantage in the 1950s and early 1960s (e.g., De Soto, 1960; Singer, 1968) and reintroduced in the late 1970s, most influentially by Abelson (1976b), the concept has been applied to a number of areas of concern to social psychologists including the perception of oneself (e.g., Markus, 1977), other people (e.g. Cantor and Mischel, 1979) and social events (e.g., Langer, 1975).[2] Generally speaking, the social psychologists have followed the direction set by the cognitive psychologists. They regard schemas as forms of cognitive organization and examine their effect on the individual's processing of socially relevant information. There is, however, a difference in emphasis. Much of the cognitive psychological research focuses on the structure of schemas and assumes this reflects qualities of mind.[3] Adopting a different orientation, social psychologists have tended to consider schemas in terms of their content and view them as a product of the environment to which the individual is exposed.

Following the lead of the social psychologists, political scientists have adapted the notion of schema to the study of public opinion. Although first suggested by Robert Axelrod (1973), this approach was only applied later by Kinder and Abelson in their study of the perception of political candidates (1981). This was followed by Conover and Feldman's (1984) research on the organization of political attitudes and Doris Graber's (1984) fascinating in-depth study of how people process the news. In separate studies, Richard Lau (1986) and Milton Lodge and Dorothy Hamil (1986) have extended this work to the study of a variety of political schemas (e.g., issue schemas, group schemas, party schemas, candidate schemas). This research has produced a number of interesting findings on the schematic quality of people's political information processing.

As suggested by this brief review, there are some clear similarities between the schema approach and my own structural developmental one. Given a shared focus on the cognitive, subjective and active qualities of political thinking, the approaches share many theoretical aims and methodological sensitivities. There are, however, significant differences. First, the schema research tends to focus on the content of reasoning – the specific prototypes or scripts people use to make sense of particular types of people, issues or events. Structural developmental research focuses more on the formal structural qualities of reasoning.[4] As such it complements the schema researchers' more substantive analyses of the particular paths political reasoning follows with a more formal and holistic analysis. Second, the structural developmental approach places a stronger emphasis on the subjective mediation of environmental influences. In schema theory, great attention is paid to the manner in which a person's political schemas shape his perception and understanding of political phenomena. However, schemas themselves are generally regarded as cultural products which are simply learned by individuals. While sympathetic to this analysis of the content of political schemas, the structural developmental approach suggests that the relationship between subjectivity and culture is more complex when the *structure* of schema use or reasoning is considered. Cultural influence remains important, but it is understood in the larger context of the *mutually* determining relationship which exists between collective and individual constructions of social life.

In sum, the structural development approach addresses some of the same concerns as the schema approach, but does so at a different level. In so doing, it complements and extends the research on political schemas. In the language of that research, it provides a theory and method for the formal and holistic analysis of schema use. The theory leads to an awareness that political thinking has a more profoundly subjective component than is generally recognized in the schema research. This in turn leads to a number of methodological caveats. Variation in the structure of thinking suggests that the schema researcher, like the belief systems researcher, must resist the temptation to rely only on survey data. Furthermore, whatever the data gathering method employed, the researcher must be very cautious both in his interpretation of an individual's responses and in his aggregation of responses across individuals.

PIAGET, HABERMAS AND SOCIAL THEORY: SOME PRELIMINARY REMARKS

The primary concern thus far has been the analysis of the political thought and action of individuals. Despite this manifestly psychological focus, my investigations have always been structured by a social psychological point of view. Throughout, I have assumed that the construction of meaning, the essential structuring component of social life, reflects the interplay of individual and collective forces. As yet, this perspective has not been developed into a fully elaborated social theory. My current aim is to build on the theoretical arguments and empirical research presented in the preceding chapters in an attempt to do so. Here, I conclude by sketching the direction in which this effort now leads.

In one sense, my work may be regarded as an attempt to reconstruct Piaget's theory of cognitive development by introducing expressly sociological considerations. This has led to a reconceptualization of reasoning in more social psychological terms and a commensurate redefinition of both the individual and society. Following this path, I am moving in a direction already taken in a very interesting way in the recent work of Jürgen Habermas. Both to clarify my own theoretical trajectory and to illustrate the variety of promising theoretical avenues which a reconstruction of Piagetian theory can open up, I present my own programmatic ideas in the context of those already sketched by Habermas.

Although importantly influenced by Piaget, Habermas' efforts emerge in response to the problems and goals of social theory. His aim is to construct a critical theory, that is, a theory which can provide the analytical and ethical foundation needed to uncover the structure underlying social practices and to reveal the possible distortion of social life embodied in them. His project is to develop both the philosophical underpinnings and the social theoretical framework such a critical theory requires. The project is an enormous one and I only offer a skeletal outline here.

Turning first to the question of method, Habermas argues that a well grounded critical theory requires a mode of inquiry which is appropriate to its object. Reviewing the strengths and weaknesses of a range of hermeneutic and positivist approaches, he concludes that critical social inquiry must be both interpretative and causal analytical. An interpretative method is required because the object of inquiry, social interaction, is embedded in and regulated by a weave of cultural definitions. The task therefore becomes one of discovering the meaning of the activity observed. At the same time, critical inquiry must be causal analytical. This is necessary because cultural meanings do not constitute the totality of social life. They are linked to economic and political conditions which are somewhat independent of them. Consequently, inquiry must go beyond a hermeneutic interpretation of society as a cultural text and analyze both the genesis of that text and the political and economic processes upon which it depends. Most important to Habermas, such a causal analysis provides a basis not only for the explanation of cultural phenomena, but also for the normative critique of culture as ideology (in the pejorative Marxist sense of the term).[5]

The sense of this interpretative and causal analytic method depends on the construction of an appropriate philosophical foundation. In Habermas' view, this must be guided by a recognition of both the relativity of meaning and the power of reflection. The historical character of meaning and social causality must be acknowledged, but within a universal frame of reference. The acknowledgement of historical relativity is necessitated by the evidence of differences in the forms of cultural integration and economic organization produced by societies at different periods in their historical development. As we shall see, the superimposition of a universal frame of reference is needed to resolve the methodological problems that acknowledgement creates.

The assumption of the historical relativity of meaning raises problems for interpretation. The assumption is that all attempts to construct meaning are limited by the cultural context in which they take place. In this context, interpretation becomes an act of translation, a matter of encoding the language or meaning of the culture being observed into that of the observer. The methodological problem here is that such translation consists of little more than a historically specific construction of the meanings of one culture through their assimilation to those of another. According to Habermas, the problem is resolved by the construction of a universal theory of language or meaning-making. A reflection on language, such a theory would provide a 'metahermeneutic' standard which would overcome the historical constraints inherent in ordinary language.

The assumption of the historical relativity of social causality creates a problem of a different kind. Here, the difficulty is one of explaining the transformation of the causal dynamics of social life from one historical period to the next. The problem is solved by the construction of a 'metacausal' theory of social development. An abstraction developed with reference to systematic empirical research, such a theory would provide a framework both for the explication of the causal relations operative at any given moment in history and for the analysis of the processes which lead to their transformation.

Recognizing the historical relativity of forms of meaning and social organization within a universal frame of reference, Habermas constructs a philosophy which is truly a 'philosophy of history with a practical intent'. With the definition of universal criteria for the interpretation of meaning and the assumption of development, analysis is inextricably linked to evaluation. Not only is a standard for interpreting social formations defined, but so is one for evaluating their adequacy. The result is a view of history which not only leads to the analysis of the past, but also to an evaluation which anticipates the future. Theoretical aims become intertwined with emancipatory ones. In the end, theory and theorist enter into the 'self-formative process of the species'.[6]

With these reflections, Habermas outlines the methodological and critical requirements which must be met by a critical social theory. To begin with, it must be grounded in the analysis of concrete historical situations, perhaps most importantly the contemporary one. At the same time, this empirically oriented analysis must be structured by a prior definition of an ideal of interpretation and social interaction. This ideal must itself be conceived as implicit in the real, both as a theoretical anticipation and a historical potential. Consequently, the definition of this ideal must be linked both to a theory of the development of understanding and to a theory of the development of society. Finally, the relationship between these two lines of development, theoretical and the practical, must be explicated.

Given the intellectual tradition to which he responds, Habermas views the task of constructing such a critical social theory as one involving the reconstruction of historical materialism. However, it is also clear why he might state that 'the stimulus that encouraged me to bring normative structures into a developmental–logical problematic came from the genetic structuralism of Jean Piaget as well . . .'[7] In fact, Piaget's theory both achieves most of the methodological and conceptual goals Habermas defines in his philosophical discussions and provides a model for social theorizing which meets most of the requirements just outlined.

Consider first the philosophical issues. Piaget's work is premised on the assumption that action is subjectively mediated and hence intrinsically meaningful, and that this subjectively constructed meaning may vary between individuals. In this regard, his work is guided by the psychological equivalent of a social theorist's assumption of the historical relativity of meaning. At the same time, Piaget's attempt to build a general theory of subjectively constructed meaning and its development reflects the presumption that a sensitivity to the relativity of meaning can be incorporated in a general theory which transcends the ordinary theorizing of the thinking individuals he analyzes. In this regard, he establishes what is essentially a universal frame of reference. In so doing, Piaget also links analysis to evaluation. His stage theory not only provides a characterization of different modes of thinking. It also entails an evaluation of the relative adequacy of each of those modes with reference to the standard set by the final stage of development he postulates.[8] Piaget's methods reflect this philosophical orientation. His empirical analyses both focus on the interpretation of the essential structure of the meaning an individual constructs and are oriented toward understanding the extra-subjective conditions which trigger a transformation in that structure at any given stage of development. At the same time, these analyses have a strong evaluative dimension and yield clear direction for concrete educational interventions. In this sense, Piaget's approach clearly reflects an underlying 'philosophy of (psychological) history with an emancipatory intent'.

Building on this foundation, Piaget's psychological theory provides an excellent model for a critical social theory. On the one hand, Piaget's theory of cognition is grounded in systematic empirical research, but is structured by a prior definition of its ideal form. This ideal is defined in terms of the internal coordination and flexibility inherent in formal operational thought. Happily, Piaget also defines the practical as well as the theoretical dimensions of this ideal and places them in correspondent relation. Thus, the intellectual coordination achieved by the formal operational thinker is related to the interpersonal coordination achieved in cooperative social exchange. On the other hand, the ideal thus defined is linked to a theory of development. Moreover, this theory of development integrates epistemological claims regarding the ontogenesis of knowledge and psychological claims regarding individuals' cognitive development.

In sum, Piaget's genetic epistemology and developmental psychology provide just the direction Habermas requires in his attempt to build a critical social theory through a reconstruction of historical materialism. Of critical importance, however, there is one deficit in Piaget's approach which Habermas seeks to correct; that is the assumption that meaning-making is an essentially subjective activity. Counter to this, Habermas argues that meaning is fundamentally an intersubjective entity and that Piaget's conception of both the nature of meaning and the process of its development must be recast in this light. In this context, Habermas' theoretical aims may be characterized as follows: (1) to define the intersubjective quality of the construction of meaning and explicate both its real and ideal nature, (2) in response to the mainstream of Marxist theory, to establish that this intersubjectivity, rather than modes of production, stands at the center of both societal formations and the dynamic of their development, (3) to define stages in the development of this intersubjectivity as they correspond to the stages of subjective development defined by Piaget, (4) to build a theory of the dynamics of development which goes beyond a consideration of individuals to that of the symbolic environments into which they are socialized. In this regard, Habermas' theoretical effort has a point of departure and a general direction quite similar to my own. As we shall see, however, the path I intend to follow is rather different from his.

The centerpiece of Habermas' social theory is his conception of communicative action. Building on Wittgenstein's (1953) *Philosophical Investigations*, he begins with a view of meaning as embodied in use. The claim here is that the meaning of words and statements is not a thing unto itself or a construction of the individual subject, but rather is constituted by the ways in which words and statements are used by individuals in language games. The categories individuals use to understand and represent their experience are thus products of language. Language games themselves are rule-governed, the range of permissible moves and their consequences are prescribed. Together, the collection of language games played in a group defines its form of life. In defining communicative action, Habermas expands this position in two important respects. First, communicative action is defined to include any action, nonlinguistic as well as linguistic, oriented toward a cooperative achievement of mutual understanding. Second, structuralist considerations are introduced. In this regard, Habermas suggests that the rules that govern communicative activity not only be conceived with reference to their manifestation in concrete, particular social exchanges or languages, but also as expressions of an abstract structure of interpersonal coordination which may underlie the entire set of exchanges of the social group in question.[9]

In further developing his conception of communicative action, Habermas offers a functional analysis of the requirements of successful communication. Following the pragmatic analyses of John Searle (1971), he suggests that to be successful, a communicative act must: (1) be comprehensible and thus conform to the structural requirements of language, (2) be true and thus accurately refer to some objective circumstance, (3) be sincere and thus truthfully reflect the intentions of the speaker and (4) be appropriate and thus conform to the social norms governing the exchange between speaker and hearer. Habermas then builds on this base to construct a universal pragmatics. He begins by suggesting that a central problem which must be addressed is one of understanding why it is any rational person would accept a communicative overture. In pragmatic terms, the question is why would a reasonable listener assume that a speaker is addressing him in a way which is comprehensible, true, sincere and appropriate. The answer lies in the fact that each of these aspects of a communicative act may be subject to test. In Habermas' terms, associated with each is a validity claim and thus all are subject to rational examination.[10] Continuing in this vein, he argues that communicative activity implicitly presupposes the opportunity to investigate freely the validity claims upon which all communication relies. He then explores what this entails. Focusing on issues of objective truth and social appropriateness, Habermas argues that the rational consideration of claims of either type depends on consensus achieved through a free discourse. Both truth and appropriateness can only be adjudicated through argument in which all social and psychological constraints are set aside. Participants must be able to argue the issue at hand not only by recourse to conventional norms, but also by reflection on the logic governing those norms. Furthermore, they must all be equal partners in the dialogue such that none can force their point of view on the others. Finally, to insure sincerity, each must be free of any psychopathology which might inhibit their ability to perceive or appropriately consider their own or another's situation. Together, these define the conditions of what, for Habermas, is the ideal speech situation.[11]

The notion of the ideal speech situation is critical to Habermas' universal pragmatics and to the social theory he wishes to construct. While acknowledging that this ideal may never be realized in any real exchange, Habermas argues that it is none the less implicit in the very logic of communication and thus is assumed or anticipated in any communicative overture. As such, the ideal speech situation constitutes a standard for the evaluation of the adequacy of real communication situations. Any which do not meet that standard must be regarded as inherently distorting and in need of rectification. Thus, his theory of communicative action meets his philosophical requirement that analysis have a practical intent. In communication, real and ideal are intertwined and analysis and critique become inseparable.

Having thus explicated the nature of communicative action, Habermas then places this activity at the center of social life. In his view, structures of communicative action define the essential nature of groups and individuals, and both must be reconceived in this light. With regard to groups, he argues that at the core of any society are the norms which govern the communicative exchange between its individual members. These norms have an underlying structure or logic. Abstract in nature, this structure constitutes the 'organizational principle' of society and delimits the range of possible institutional forms and practices which may arise. This focus on the structures of communicative exchange is central to Habermas' reconstruction of historical materialism. Modes of production remain a force to be considered, but their structural and historical effects are understood to be mediated by a logic of structure and development intrinsic to normative structures.[12] Habermas also conceives of individuals in communication theoretic terms, that is as participants in a communicative exchange. Thus, he defines the ego as the totality of the individual's capacity to act in a comprehensible, true, sincere and appropriate manner. On this basis, Habermas reconstructs the developmental psychology of Piaget and Kohlberg. Cognition and moral consciousness are redefined by derivation from more basic concepts of communication and its requisites, and development is reconceived as a process whereby individuals are socialized into the symbolic structure of their social environment.[13] As both are conceived in relation to communicative action, the normative structure of society and the ego structure of the individual are of course intimately interrelated. Normative structures are realized in the action of individuals toward one another and ego structures are manifest through participation in normatively governed social exchange. Each logically implies and actually depends on the other.[14]

Finally, Habermas develops his social theory with regard to this assumption of the historical relativity of meaning. In this context, his theory of communicative action necessarily becomes a theory of the development of normative structures. To begin with, he outlines the logic of this development. In so doing, he draws on Piaget's genetic epistemology and transposes the stages of the ontogenesis of knowledge into the domain of a communicatively constructed intersubjectivity.[15] The result is a description of the forms of reciprocity (mutual recognition and coordination) which emerge at each stage in the development of communicative exchange. Accompanying this is a description of the forms of individual cognition and moral reasoning associated with each of those stages. The progress of these stages is a logical one. Together they define a logical hierarchy and an invariant sequence.

At this point, Habermas introduces a clear caveat. His theory of the development of normative structures is not intended to provide a characterization of social history as a progress motored simply by the requisites of its own logic. Rather, it is an attempt to delineate the logical space in which that progress takes place. While limited by this logical space, change is affected by a host of particulars and externalities which render it contingent and allow for stagnation and reversals in the development of normative structures in a given society. Examples include military invasions, ecological crises or such singular events as the Black Death which swept feudal Europe.

To provide a theoretical frame of reference for explaining the evolution of society, Habermas builds a dynamic model in which system crises may, given appropriate circumstances, result in the development of normative structures. The steps in this process are as follows. At any moment in its development, a society is structured by a given organization principle. This delimits the possibilities for the regulation of the forces of production and social exchange. This abstract organization is concretely embodied in the institutional nuclei which function as the relations of production and determine the dominant form of social integration. Endogenously produced technical and practical knowledge or historical contingencies can produce changes in the relations and forces of production. In either case, this may yield system problems which overburden the structurally limited steering capacity of a society. The resolution of the ensuing crisis depends on the development of normative structures.

Structural development occurs through a process of 'social learning'. Although a societal phenomenon, this process depends first on the transposition of surplus individual learning. Individual members of a society may develop (both cognitively and morally) beyond the level required by their social environment. These individuals then create technical and practical knowledge which may be assimilated into the culture. Because the structural underpinnings of this knowledge are inconsistent with the basic organizational principle of society, it remains latent – that is, it does not yet have any practical social or economic application. With the development of the crisis at hand and given propitious conditions, social movements may arise which draw on this culturally available knowledge to transform the organizational basis of society. The normative structure which emerges then delimits both the form of any new social integration and the possibilities for the implementation of available productive forces or the development of new ones.[16]

As made clear in this brief outline, Habermas sketches a broad theoretical panorama. The result is clearly important and suggestive. There are, however, a number of significant problems and ambiguities. My work on political reasoning suggests two which are of particular significance. The first pertains to the descriptive adequacy of his concept of communicative exchange, the second to the theoretical adequacy of his explanation of social development. Together, they point to difficulties which lie at the very heart of his theory.

Consider first Habermas' concept of communication. Following the tradition of language analysis from Wittgenstein through Austin to Searle, Habermas assumes that, within the structural limitations of

any given stage of social development, a key feature of communication is its success. Purposes and intentions are derivative of the
language games in which people enter and thus can be communicated in that context. The rationale for his 'linguistic turn' and the
sense of his view of meaning as intersubjectively constituted follow
from this. In my view, this assumption of success captures one important dimension of communication, but, at the same time, it systematically excludes another – its failure.

A moment's reflection on one's own experience yields clear prima
facie evidence that the failure to achieve mutual understanding is as
endemic to communication as is its success. Apart from communicative exchanges which center on ritual courtesies or on specific
concrete action, how often does one end with a sense of not really
having understood the other person or of not having been fully understood by him? In another vein, how often does one sense thoughts
and feelings which are somehow significant, probably influence one's
action and yet cannot satisfactorily be communicated to another? *The
suggestion here is that there exist subjective meanings which are
not simply derivative of and reducible to intersubjective ones.*
Additionally, there is the suggestion of a relationship, albeit an
imperfect one, between these privately constructed and publicly
communicable meanings. The very terms of our frustration, a sense of
something missed in a communication, suggest that although they
have a quality of their own, private meanings are engaged by and
implicated in communicative exchange.

Apart from personal reflection, there is systematic research which
provides compelling evidence and subjective meanings which are
expressed in intersubjective discourse, but remain independent of it.
A good example is the developmental psychological research upon
which Habermas himself draws, such as Kohlberg's studies of moral
reasoning. Another example is provided by the studies of political
reasoning presented in chapter 5. In both cases, the empirical
research is guided by the premise that the apparent dialogical
meaning of the statements an individual makes may obscure another
private meaning. Consequently, the investigatory strategy adopted is
one involving the extensive probing of the individual's own sense of
the claims he makes. In the present context, the key result of this
research has been to demonstrate that underlying discursively constructed meanings is a substrate of related, but structurally different
and largely uncommunicated subjectively constructed ones. [17]

In my view, these observations require that Habermas' concept of
meaning and communicative action be supplemented. First, meaning

must not be viewed simply as a matter of a particular use. The significance of a communicative act depends on its place in a weave of related actions and reactions. Consequently, meaning must be analyzed with reference to its implicit structure or logic as well as its concrete instantiation. Second, it must not be assumed that a communicative exchange has a single nature. The meaning of a communicative act is constructed not in one context, but two – that of the subjective activity of the individual actor as well as that of the cultural and linguistic environment in which he participates. This suggests that communicative action and intersubjective meaning are always structured and defined at two levels. Finally, the complexity of the relationship between these two constructions must be recognized. They produce clearly incommensurate results and therefore the structure of one cannot be reduced to that of the other. None the less, subjective and cultural constructions both operate upon the same manifest terrain of specific concrete social interaction. Consequently, the structure of each reflects and is realized in the singular reality of intersubjective meanings and communicative exchange. Therefore, although different, the two levels of construction are necessarily interdependent. The nature of this complex relationship must be clarified and both subjectivity and culture must be redefined in this light. (This task is addressed in part by the analysis of individuals' political reasoning presented in chapter 4.)

Related to this first set of issues concerning the definition of communication is a second set regarding the explanation of social development. In his analysis, Habermas adopts a social psychological perspective. Thus, he sets the stage for his explanation by considering both sociological (the organizational principle of society which delimits possibilities for social exchange) and psychological (the cognitive structures which delimit the interactive competences of the individual) factors. Following his analysis of communication, these two factors are considered as two faces of the same essential phenomenon. Although instantiated in different ways, societal and individual organization depend upon the same structure of communicative exchange for their form. Consequently, they exist in a correspondent relationship, a society comprising a system of social interaction and a world view which reflect the constructions of its individual members, and an individual becoming a thinking independent agent through his socialization into the symbolic structure of society.

So defined, the relationship of individual to society suggests a natural tendency toward equilibrium. Habermas' analysis of development therefore focuses on an explanation of why this equilibrium is undermined and movement toward a new stage of normative and cognitive development is initiated. To this end, he invokes his notion of social learning. The focus here is on endogenously produced knowledge which has the potential to provide the basis for the transformation of either a society's mode of production or its norms of communicative exchange. Although transposed to a cultural level, this knowledge is the result of the development of the cognitive and social abilities of individuals beyond what is required by the structure of opportunity and constraint inherent in the contemporary organization of society.

One obvious question which arises here is how to explain this surplus learning, that is the development of individuals' abilities beyond what the social environment fosters or even allows. The point of this question becomes sharper when posed with reference to the recurring claim Habermas makes that individual development is a matter of being socialized into the structure of that environment. Put in different terms, the problem is one of explaining how subjective development can surpass the development of intersubjectivity when the former is presumed to be derivative of the latter.

Only two related lines of explanation appear available. The first is to suggest that historically contingent system problems arise which are recognized by individuals and somehow stimulate their further development. How this occurs and why it is possible ultimately depend on the second line of explanation. This involves a straightforward reliance on the developmental psychology of Piaget and Kohlberg. Following Piaget, one can argue that by interacting with a physical as well as social environment, individuals may develop formal operational thought. Continuing with Kohlberg, one can claim that this provides the requisite cognitive basis for the possible development of post-conventional moral reasoning. Hypothetical and transcendent in nature, formal operational thought and post-conventional moral reasoning can yield the reservoir of surplus learning which may then be exploited by the culture and drawn upon at time of societal steering crises. In my view, this explanation by recourse to a largely unreconstructed developmental psychology is unsatisfactory. It depends on psychological theory which ultimately frees subjectivity from intersubjectivity and individual development from history and therefore is subject to the criticisms of Piagetian theory offered at the beginning of chapter 4.

In the end, it seems that Habermas' equilibrium model of the social psychological constitution of communicative exchange renders any explanation of development external or inconsistent. To account for disruption, one must either go beyond the theory in search of historical contingencies or deny it through an overly psychological account. A more comprehensive and internally consistent explanation requires a reconceptualization of the relationship between individual and society. The assumption of the complementarity of these two faces of social exchange must be supplemented by one of their disjunction, and the equilibrium model must be replaced by one of a constructive tension. The suggestion here is that a consistent and comprehensive explication of the structure and the development of social exchange is best achieved by placing the dynamics of the latter at the heart of the theoretical enterprise.

These observations on the adequacy of Habermas' descriptive conception of communication and the critique of his explanatory conception of social development complement one another. The first requires a synchronic conception of social exchange which reflects the structural complexity and disharmony inherent in its nature. The latter requires a diachronic conception of that exchange which acknowledges the tension and consequent potential for development which is endemic to it. Together, they suggest the need for theorizing which builds upon and explicates the following set of assumptions: (1) the structure of social exchange is constituted at two levels, individual and societal; (2) although interdependent, these two sources of structure clearly differ from one another in essential ways; (3) constructed at both the level of the individual and the society, the structure of social exchange is inherently uncertain, and (4) associated with this uncertainty is a tension which is central to the process of social development. This sets a theoretical course which departs significantly from the path Habermas is now following.

Toward a theoretical social psychology of action

I conclude by briefly sketching the skeleton of a theory which can address the foregoing concerns. First, the nature of the individual and society are defined. The complex relationship between the two and the associated dynamic inherent in social life are then discussed. Finally, to illustrate the theory, it is applied to the question of legitimacy. It is important to note that my thinking here is preliminary. The remarks which follow are intended to be suggestive, not definitive.

To begin, let us consider the structure of individual and societal constructions of social exchange. A conception of the first has already been developed in the analysis of individuals' political reasoning presented in chapter 4. Reconstructing Piaget's theory of the structure and development of thinking, the key claim made there is that while the activity of thinking is subjectively determined, it is also shaped by social structural influences. With regard to the structure of thinking, it is argued that the coordination of meanings is not simply an internal matter, but is essentially dependent on an awareness and use, albeit an imperfect one, of cultural definitions and socially regulated patterns of exchange. Similarly, with regard to the development of thinking, the claim is made that the transforming activity of reflexive abstraction is not simply a subjective act prodded by the negations of social experience, but one which was dependent on the positive direction provided by the meanings and organization of the sociocultural environment.

In this context, questions regarding the nature of society have been raised, but only insofar as they affect individual development. Here, we turn to them directly. As suggested by the foregoing developmental psychology, a society structures and thereby defines and coordinates the interaction between individuals. As such, it reflects their influence. Individuals define themselves and their environment in a manner determined by the structure of their thought and they direct their action in the light of the resulting understanding. To be effective, the regulation of the exchange between these self-orienting individuals must build on their subjective construction of social action. Otherwise, it runs the risk of being ignored or systematically misconstrued. Therefore, the institutional arrangements which emerge in a collectivity, and the social structure which those arrangements constitute, must reflect the understandings and purposes of the individual members. As a result, the social structure of a group is itself structurally delimited by the capacities of its individual members.

At the same time, however, society is necessarily independent of its members and determines their nature. To coordinate the actions of individuals, a society provides rules and definitions to regulate their exchange. Forms of interaction are defined and relationships among them are established. These delimit the action possibilities available to individual members. Accommodation and conformity yield a satisfaction of purposes. Failure to recognize the interactive limitations and social definitions leads only to incomprehension, social sanction and personal frustration. In this manner, a society constrains how individuals can coordinate their own action and thus structures the nature of the understandings they can subjectively construct.

So defined, societies and individuals are similar in several respects. Both are forces which act to organize and define social action. In addition, both are dually constituted – by their own structuring influence and by that of an external force (the individual in the case of society and the society in the case of the individual). In the latter regard, both individuals and society are capable of reconstruction in response to structural pressures from without. The individual can reflect on pressures to coordinate his action placed on him from above and a society can evolve in response to pressures for coordination placed on it from below. Apart from these similarities, however, there are a number of important differences as well. One is critical here. Although they are related through the common ground upon which they operate, individual and societal coordinations are structurally different. While the former organizes and defines action in the context of other actions, the latter organizes and defines interactions in the context of other interactions. In this sense, the quality of the coordination achieved at the societal level is necessarily of a higher order than that produced at an individual level.

With these concepts of the individual and society in mind, we turn to the analysis of social exchange. Regulated by society and enacted by individuals, social exchange is complexly structured. It is both defined and directed at two levels. These two levels are profoundly related. Societies provide a form of organization which is consistent with the abilities and purposes of its individual members, and individuals construct meanings and values which are pragmatically appropriate. Indeed, neither can be conceived without reference to the other. Although they interpenetrate in this manner, these two levels of coordination are also necessarily different. The societal always superordinates the individual. Together, the mutual dependence and structural difference between individual and societal coordinations of action produce an inherent tension. Each creates pressures for the structural transformation of the other. The result is a tendency toward development at the very core of social life.

This developmental dynamic may be best considered by following a step in its progress. Let us begin with the consequence of the pressure which the socially structured environment imposes on the individual. The individual begins with a structured understanding of his social environment and a commensurate logic for his action. In the light of the socially structured realities of interpersonal exchange and the culture definitions to which he is exposed, the individual is forced to accommodate his thought and action to these collectively consti-tuted definitions and forms of interpersonal exchange. In psychologi-cal terms, he must develop and reconstruct the terms in which he reasons. At the very least, he must develop to the degree that he can act and react in a manner consistent with the forms of social regulation. In arriving at this point, he ensures that his under-standings are valid and communicable, and that his purposeful activity will be generally successful. At the same time, he contributes to the stability of the patterns of social exchange. At most, the individual may develop beyond this to the point where he is able to construct a self-directing structure of thought and action which mirrors the structure of his social environment.[18] The resulting awareness of the logic of interpersonal exchange allows the individual not only to respond appropriately to another's initiatives, but also to manipulate the conditions under which he and the other interact. It thereby confers considerable personal advantage. More importantly, this development also necessarily destabilizes collective life. Once the individual coordinates action in a manner parallel to the collective, the collective must reconstruct its mode of coordination to meet the challenges to regulation created by individuals with these advanced capacities. To manage effectively social exchange, the collective must generate cultural definitions and social regulations which may objectify, order, and thereby coordinate the understandings and actions of these more developed individuals. In other words, society itself must develop, which is to say, its meanings and organization must be reconstructed according to the requisites of a higher form of structuration. Once achieved, a new order is imposed on individuals and the progress continues.

In this context, it is clear that social life is inherently ambiguous and unstable. It does not exhibit the clarity, stability or simple predictability of a singly structured phenomenon. Determined neither by individuals nor by society itself, the manifest reality of social exchange is inherently uncertain. This is, however, a structured uncertainty – the possible form of a given exchange is always bounded by limits imposed from above by the cultural environment and from below by the individuals involved. Cast in more dynamic terms, social exchange always consists of self-transforming tensions. The definitional and organizational structure of action constructed at one level is always being reconstructed at the other level creating the conditions for possible development at the first. In this regard, social exchange is a destructuring totality with an inherent potential for development.

It should be noted that reference here is to the potential or possibility for development inherent in social exchange. There is no intention to suggest that development is simply a function of the internal machinations of an inexorable process. At every point, the maintenance of current achievements and the possibilities for future development depend on specific contingent historical realities such as the physical resources available, the degree of stress and insecurity prevalent in daily life, the nature of relationships with other societies, and the specific manner in which the structurally delimited possibilities of social and individual organization are realized in the society in question. Of course, what specific arrangement of these exogenous variables facilitates the maintenance, dissolution or reconstruction of the status quo, will depend on the structurally determined requirements defined at each stage of development.

In sum, I advocate a conception of social life which is at once deeply social psychological and dialectical. In my view, social life expresses the dynamic interplay between the constructing subject and the organizing collective. As sources of meaning and organization, each of these structuring forces is at once dependent upon and independent of the other. The social reality which results is always complex and potentially self-transforming. At any moment, it rests on an uncertain ground which shifts between subjective and cultural coordinations of action and discourse. Over time, it strains toward a development motored by tensions inherent in its very nature.

To illustrate the direction in which this points, let us consider an issue quite different from those addressed thus far, that of legitimacy. In so doing, we will examine the foregoing theory in the context of those commonly developed by liberal political theorists on the one hand and more conservative and/or sociologically oriented ones on the other. Again, the discussion here is preliminary. A more careful resolution of these matters is left for another time.

Liberal theorists offer what is an essentially naturalist account of legitimacy. They begin with the assumption that inherent in human nature are certain basic values. These either refer to specific purposes or conditions (e.g., Locke or Mill) or are broadly defined in terms of the requirements of self-actualization (e.g., the more contemporary work of Isaiah Berlin). In both cases, the focus is on the substance of what individuals want or need. Individuals know their wants and needs and define their values accordingly. Given the universality of human nature, these values are essentially the same. Specific conditions and cultures will affect the particular ways in which they are expressed, but the basic orienting considerations remain the same for all people.

Expressly political considerations are invoked when the problem arises of satisfying the needs of individuals competing for scarce resources. This problem may be considered as one requiring a general determination of the relative importance of various needs. For the most part, considerations are premised on the assumption that every individual is the best judge of this question. Cast in these terms, the problem becomes one of determining appropriate procedures for adjudicating competing claims and the chief concern becomes one of fairness or justice. Political legitimacy tends therefore to be cast in procedural terms. The focus is on particular outcomes (e.g., who shall govern, which policy alternative should be adopted, etc.), but their legitimacy is assessed with regard to the fairness of the procedures whereby they were decided.[19]

The sociological perspective offers a very different account of value formation and hence presents a very different notion of legitimacy. According to this perspective, human nature, and with it the wants and needs of individuals, is a cultural and historical product. Societies have their own self-constituting structures, and the understandings and wants of individuals are defined accordingly. In this view, personal values are nothing more than private rationalizations of collectively defined goods. As such, personal values are culturally and historically relative.

In this context, the question of legitimacy becomes more an analytical than a normative one. There are two focal concerns: first, the manner in which collective values are generated and then adopted by individuals; and second, the conditions under which the resulting consistency between social practices and individual values breaks down. Some have argued that this analytical enterprise itself has normative consequences. In Marxist parlance, the revelation of the cultural relativity of a set of values necessarily undermines the reification of those values and associated social practices. Whereas this may be correct, the normative question itself, what is legitimate practice, can be addressed directly. It is most readily regarded as a culturally relative issue. Thus, it is left to the members of each society to determine, according to that society's conventions, what is legitimate. Where residual liberal tendencies foster an ambition for a more universal basis for political critique, the socio-historically minded analyst flounders. The difficulty is that the critic, like those he criticizes, is necessarily caught in the web of society. Thus, his criticisms as well as the object of his criticism are culturally and historically bound.

The social psychological view advocated here yields a different analysis of the nature of values and thus leads to a distinctive conception of legitimacy. The analysis of value is based on two key assumptions. The first is that values and the activity of evaluation, like any defined object of thought and any form of reasoning, are structurally delimited. At both individual and collective levels, the activity of constructing meaning and coordinating action determines the quality of valued ends and the nature of the relationships that exist both among those ends and between them and individuals. The second assumption suggests that the evaluative activity defined at each of these levels imposes itself on the other. On the one hand, the social context imposes a logic of evaluative practice on individuals. It is expressed as a procedural and substantive morality and serves the purpose of integrating personal action within socially structured patterns of exchange. On the other hand, individuals impose their subjective definition of personal goals on their social exchange. They thereby delimit the kinds of social values which may be collectively defined and the kinds of practices which may be socially sanctioned. Together, these two assumptions, of structure and of the interpenetration of structures, suggest that values are forever bound in the psychological and social process of definition and redefinition. Individuals are always reconstructing their values in light of the social demands placed upon them and societies are always reconstructing their demands in light of the developing capacities of the individuals they coordinate.[20]

Building on this understanding of value, legitimacy must be conceived with regard to two analytical suppositions: (1) that value is a social psychological product, a construct which reflects the personal requirements of individuals acting in a social environment and the social requirements of a collective coordination of interpersonal exchange; and (2) that, by virtue of its internal dynamic, this value-creating process is potentially restructured and may therefore produce fundamentally different results at different times.

Legitimacy is thus defined in two ways, synchronically and diachronically. The synchronic definition yields a more analytical and descriptive concept of legitimacy and is less fundamental. In these terms, legitimacy is conceived as a product of a particular society of individuals at a given moment in time. As a social psychological product, it has a dualistic nature. It necessarily reflects individuals' conceptions of goals and is, therefore, best determined by individuals themselves. At the same time, legitimacy must reflect the socially structured regulations of cooperative interpersonal exchange and is therefore best defined in the light of collective rules, implicit as well as explicit. These two dimensions of synchronic legitimacy are both equally significant and distinct. As a result, the normative dimensions of social life will necessarily be ambiguous and uncertain. This ambiguity is structurally delimited and therefore will be different at each stage of social development.

The second conception of legitimacy is diachronic. It is more fundamental and prescriptive. Here legitimacy is conceived in the light of the exigencies of the process of social development. The dialectic of development is such that collective and individual definitions of values will be constantly destructuring and restructuring one another. Every present condition has already defined the terms of its own inadequacy and therefore the basis for its own delegitimation.

As collective moralities become personal values which necessitate the redefinition of collective moralities, both collective and individual values are undermined. Both bases of possible legitimation of social practice are always about to be modified or replaced. Hence the determination of legitimacy must ultimately be cast in terms of an overall historical progress and consequently from outside the present culture rather than from within it. The conclusions drawn, therefore, will necessarily constitute a critique both of current personal values and contemporary social morality.[21]

It should be clearly recognized that all such critiques of legitimate practice are themselves historically and culturally specific. As abstracted negations of present practices, they build on current social definitions and thus are anchored in them. In this sense, all attempts to transcend culture will necessarily be bound to a given historical moment. This is not to suggest, however, that such criticism is somehow incorrect or itself illegitimate. The use of the claim that knowledge is temporary in order to limit critique is meaningful only when anchored in a *non*developmental framework. Viewed from a developmental perspective, the momentary quality of knowledge is an essential fact of human existence. At the same time, it is a critical element in the process of the continuing elaboration of human values.[22]

An attempt has been made here to offer a better understanding of the nature of reason and ideology. In the process, important traditions of empirical research and social theory have been challenged. Suggesting new directions for both theory and research, the approach proposed here offers great promise. As demonstrated, it provides a revealing and conceptually powerful framework for the analysis of the nature and forms of political reasoning, one which provides a foundation for the study of the polity as well as the individual citizen. The approach needs to be developed further. Theoretical questions regarding the relationship between individual and social constructions of meaning must be addressed more carefully. In addition, research methods must be refined and new subject matter such as conceptions of law, notions of value and understandings of particular social policies must be studied. Throughout, theoretical inquiry and empirical research must be joined. Each must guide and be guided by the other. The goal must be no less than the transformation of both the 'theory' and 'science' of politics.

Notes

1 INTRODUCTION AND OVERVIEW

1 For more on the sociological nature of the political socialization research and its consequent inadequacies, see Rosenberg, 1985b.

2 Although the concept of 'attitude' often seems to be an inevitable way of thinking about people, it is only one of many. It enjoyed its greatest popularity in social psychology from the thirties through the fifties. For summary statements of this position, see Gordon Allport's review article for the *Handbook of Social Psychology* (1935) or the section on attitudes in the widely used psychology text of the 1950s authored by Krech and Crutchfield (1958). In the early texts on social psychology, such as the classic text of William McDougall (1908), the concept of an attitude does not exist. In the late 1960s, the concept of attitude was eclipsed as the preferred mode of conceptualization. In the last two decades, social psychologists have been increasingly interested in the process of thinking and concepts such as attribution, schema and heuristic have been adopted (e.g., Kelley, 1967; Abelson, 1976b; Tversky and Kahneman, 1982.)

3 While there are important similarities between Piaget's structuralism and the continental structuralism which grew out of Saussure's work on language, there are three important points of divergence. First, structuralism focused on the static qualities of thought, its basic binary oppositions. As suggested by his first assumption, Piaget focused on thought as an activity. In this context, he might view the oppositions addressed by structuralism as a subjectively constructed product. Second, structuralism was idealist. Thought was viewed simply as a quality of mind. Piaget's pragmatism attempted to bridge the gap between idealism and realism. Thus, for Piaget, thought was embedded in reality. This second difference underlies the third. The structuralists see thought as static, as a reflection of mind. Piaget sees the structure of thought in relation to reality and hence as a developmental phenomenon.

4 An example of the failure to appreciate this distinction can lead to unwarranted conclusions such as Runciman's equation of British and continental structuralisms (Runciman, 1966). For a seminal discussion of the concept of structure, see Merleau-Ponty (1963).

5 In this context, it is interesting to consider the attempt of the Swiss social psychologist Wilhelm Doise to investigate empirically the social psychological dynamics of cognitive development (Doise et al., 1975).

6 For examples of Piaget's consideration of the impact of social environments, see Piaget, 1965a, 1966.

7 For reviews of the literature, see Wicker, 1969. A response to the problem in the social psychological research was to suggest that attitudes were too broadly conceived and the complexity of the context in which behaviors were performed was not appreciated in the early research. In this vein, Fishbein and others have suggested formulations in which attitudes toward specific behaviors under particular conditions are assessed. This research does generate better attitude-behavior correlations, but at great cost to the generality of the descriptive concepts they used. For example, see Fishbein and Ajzen, 1975.

8 The two categories used here, liberal and sociological, are categories in a Wittgensteinian sense, they refer to two families of theories. In the liberal family, I include both Hobbes and Locke and later representatives like Berlin and Macpherson. I also include much of the current work which applies economics to the study of political phenomena in the tradition of Anthony Downs. In the sociological family, I include most Marxist political theory and both structuralist and functionalist schools of thought.

9 Theorists have certainly disagreed on what these are, but each theorist has a clear sense that certain basic values, e.g. survival, self-realization, respect for others, do exist. For examples, compare classical theorists like Hobbes, Locke and Mill or more modern theorists like C. B. Macpherson and Isaiah Berlin.

10 Here, much of Marxist political philosophy finds itself in very murky waters. This reflects the ambiguous and often contradictory status accorded the individual. While the individual's thought, values and action are understood as social products, there is often recourse to a certain transcultural or transhistorical vision of human nature. This vision provides criteria for the critical evaluation of any given sociohistorical formation, much as it does in liberal theory. The problem of course is both the individual and the theorist are seen as historical products and hence the ethical standards either holds must be considered as historically relative. Thus, the psychological ambivalence produces considerable theoretical confusion. For example, the critical theory of the Frankfurt School flounders on these grounds.

2   THE EMPIRICAL STUDY OF IDEOLOGY

1 My aim here is to develop a more adequate theory of individuals' political thinking. The sociologically inclined reader should not, however, despair. I am aware of sociological critiques of methodological individualism and consider them to be of some value. However, I also retain the notion that political thinking can be usefully considered from a psychological point of view. If it can be constructed, such a psychological theory raises a host of interesting questions not only for the sociological analysis of ideology, but for sociology itself as well.

2 For an early and very influential discussion of this movement and the research on attitudes, see Allport, 1935. It is noteworthy that in adopting this perspective, two important alternatives were ignored. First, there was that perspective in social psychology which focused on issues of meaning, symbolism and communication (e.g., Mead, 1924-5, 1934). Second, there were the more sociological perspectives which conceived of political thought with reference to the collectivity rather than the individual (e.g., Lukacs, 1971; Durkheim, 1938).

3 A third point which may be raised extends this second one. The concern here is the domain of issues properly considered in the study of belief systems. Voiced most influentially by Robert Lane, the criticism is that the belief systems research artificially limits the issues examined to those which are ostensibly political and

thereby ignores those issues which are of subjective political relevance to the interviewee. Given that these excluded issues are associated with political beliefs and contribute to the organization of the overall belief systems, the failure to study these issues necessarily undermines any study of political belief systems (Lane, 1973). This third criticism is more threatening to the Converse-style research than the preceding two. Unlike the others, it speaks to the theory behind the Converse conception as well as the method. Lane's point is that the psychological sources of constraint are important and are not a simple product of social influences. Consequently, people's beliefs must be seen as a subjective and possibly idiosyncratic product as well as a cultural one. Viewed in this light, the study of people's political thinking requires a method tailored to the exploration of individuals rather than aggregates. The methodological implication is that surveys would have to abandoned, at least in the first instance, in favor of more sensitive indepth interviews.

4 While to some, Converse's 'oversight' in imposing the liberal/conservative dimension may appear an inexplicable error in the midst of otherwise well conceived research, the decision is quite compatible with his view of belief systems as socially constrained. Assuming the liberal/conservative dimension structures elite belief systems (there is, however, no evidence to suggest it does and some of Converse's own evidence suggests it does not), then whatever integration the belief systems of mass publics do show should be organized around that dimension. Consequently, factor analysis and its often uninterpretable result may be justifiably avoided.

5 For a good analysis of the weakness of this line of criticism, see Kinder, 1982.

6 In the analysis of Nie and his colleagues, 30 per cent of the respondents were classified as ideological thinkers. This result is quite different from the ones obtained by Converse. This is most probably a consequence of the difference in methods used. Whereas Converse's results are based on human coders' content analyses of the sense of short answers, Nie's results are based on computer analysis of the word content of those responses. Less sensitive to the illogical or unexpected ways in which common words may be used, Nie's technique would tend to overestimate the level of subjects' political conceptualization.

7 The factor analytical studies of attitude structure offer us no more than the simple correlational analyses. Indeed, the difficulties may be greater. Unlike the correlational studies, the factor analytical studies are not based on a theoretical definition of the dimensions underlying political thinking. The researcher is therefore left trying to make some post facto sense of the factors which emerge. This is generally quite difficult. The problems involved are compounded by the fact that the configuration of factors will vary with the kind and number of attitude items used. One may reasonably question the meaningfulness and utility of an analysis which depends on the interpretative whim of the individual researcher and the specific combination of survey items used to build the factor model.

8 Perhaps the best example of the creative and structural aspect of psychoanalytic theorizing is Freud's analysis of the nature of dreams (1913). For interesting examples of the application of psychoanalytic theory to political thinking see Lasswell, 1960, Pye, 1962 and Wolfenstein, 1967.

9 For examples of sociological analyses of political ideology, see Marx, 1974, Lukacs, 1971, Mannheim, 1936 and Geertz, 1964.

3   THE STRUCTURAL DEVELOPMENTAL APPROACH

1 For examples of this view, see Wittgenstein, 1953; Searle, 1971; Bach and Harnish, 1979.

2 See Ryle's argument (1949). For a restatement with reference to Piaget, see Hamlyn, 1978, p. 49. To anticipate the later discussion, Piaget rejects this position in the light of his developmental analysis of the structure of thought. The basic thrust of his argument is that although any particular concept may be arrived at in a variety of ways, the underlying structure of that concept (and hence its essential logic or meaning) is arrived at in only one way - through the ontogenetic development of knowledge itself.

3 Reference here is to the impact of positivism on the social sciences. For a classic statement reflecting this view, see Robert Merton's, 1957. For a useful review of the general position, see chapter 1 of Berstein, 1979.

4 Piaget is a Hegelian in his emphasis on the dialectic exchange between subject and object and its consequences for the transformation of meaning. He differs from Hegel in that he places this dialectic in the context of the pragmatic exchange between the acting (as well as thinking) subject and an external reality. Piaget's view differs from Marx's in two critical respects. First, whereas the essential reality for Marx is socioeconomic, for Piaget it is physical. Second, whereas development for Marx is merely linear and mechanical, for Piaget it is truly logical. With Hegel, Piaget (1971c) argues that 'behind the development of reason is reason.'

5 Piaget, 1968, pp. 143-7. For an elaboration of this point, see Hamlyn, 1978, pp. 13-42.

6 See Piaget, 1952, esp. pp. 357-407; Piaget and Inhelder, 1969.

7 Piaget, 1971a, p. 9.

8 Piaget makes this argument repeatedly. The formulation varies with the nature of his audience but the essential theme remains the same. For an example, see Piaget, 1971a, pp. 7-14. I think the logic of the argument is best developed, however, in Lawrence Kohlberg's discussion of the role of ethics and psychology in the analysis of moral reasoning (1971).

9 In Piaget's terms, the view of the philosopher is not 'decentered'. See Piaget, 1971b.

10 For a relatively recent example of Piaget's analysis of the interdependence of philosophy and science, see his lectures on *Psychology and Epistemology* (1971b).

11 For example, see Piaget, 1971b, pp. 1-6.

12 Piaget, 1971a, p. 15.

13 Although his writing on the subject is sparse, there is a strong metaphysical realism to Piaget's thinking. He assumes there is an objective reality which has its own structure and laws. For example, he writes, '. . . there are physical structures which, though independent of us, correspond to our operational structures, especially in sharing the quasi-intellectual trait of covering the possible and locating the real within a system of virtuals.' (Piaget, 1970b, p. 43).

14 Piaget, 1973, pp. 20, 27.

15 Inhelder and Piaget, 1958, p. 342.

16 What Piaget offers here is a concept of the relation between a whole and its parts. Implicit in his argument is that the whole cannot be reduced to the parts as in the atomistic view nor can the parts be reduced to the whole as in the structural view. Rather a middle road must be taken such that the parts are in some sense self-determining and influence the whole (in this context we have the determinations of meaning on action or reality on action), and yet they are determined by the

whole (in this context we have both the reality and meaning of action defined and determined by the fact of their union such that both are structured as well as structuring). In Piaget's view these semi-independent aspects are held together in the context of the whole in that there is parallel or compatible structuration between the parts and the whole. This parallel structuration and independence is revealed in the coordination and tension of an equilibrium. In this context, Piaget's view is rather similar to that expressed by Louis Althusser in his formulation of the concept of overdetermination. See Althusser, 'On the Materialist Dialectic,' (1964) and Althusser and Balibar (1970). Piaget's view is different in two important respects. First, whereas Althusser focuses on the contradictions inherent in the whole and its parts, Piaget emphasizes their essential coordination and equilibrium. Second, whereas Althusser (like Marx) views development as a mechanical and linear process, Piaget views it as a reflexive and logical one.

17 Piaget postulates a form of structural causality in which the nature of the structure of reality imposes itself on the subjectively directed operations. For example, he writes: 'Causal explanation requires that the operations that "fit" the real "belong" to it, that reality itself be constituted of operators. Then and only then does it make sense to speak of "causal structures," for what this means is the objective system of operators in their effective interaction.' (Piaget, 1970b, p. 40.)

18 Piaget, 1971b, pp. 1–6.

19 See Piaget, 1952, p. 415.

20 The discussion here focuses on the development of a reversible relation. For Piaget's own definition of reversibility, see Inhelder and Piaget, 1958, pp. 272–3. In Piaget's view, each stage of intellectual development leads to its own characteristic form of reversibility. For a discussion of infant development see Piaget, 1952. For the transition from sensorimotor behavior and the genesis of representational thought, see Piaget, 1962.

21 Piaget, 1970b, pp. 40–3.

22 Reference here is to 'the internal mechanisms of all constructivism'. (Piaget and Inhelder, 1969, p. 157.)

23 For an overview of Piaget's four stages, see Piaget and Inhelder, 1969 or Flavell, 1963. Others following in his tradition posit an additional post-formal operational stage. For three very different examples of the attempt to define a fifth stage of development, see Riegel, 1973; Commons et al., 1982; Edelstein and Noam, 1982. In my work, I describe three stages, sequential, linear and systematic, and allude to the possibility of a fourth. Regardless of the number or specific definition of the stages, the point here is that all the aforementioned researchers agree that development is periodic rather than gradual.

24 Piaget, 1973, p. 151.

25 Piaget, 1973, p. 164–5.

26 Emphasizing the universal quality of social exchange, Piaget writes:

Whether we study children in Geneva, Paris, New York or Moscow, in Iranian mountains or in the heart of Africa or on a Pacific Island, everywhere we observe certain social conduct of exchange . . . which takes effect independent of the contents of educative transmissions . . . [to capture this aspect, he writes further] we must begin by opposing the 'general coordinations' of collective actions to the particular cultural transmissions which crystallize in a different manner in each society. (Piaget, 1971b, pp. 49–50)

27 Piaget, 1971c, p. 360.

28 Piaget, 1971c, p. 345.

29 For a discussion of 'language as a product of intelligence, rather than intelligence as a product of language' see Piatelli-Palmarini, 1980, pp. 166-7. For a discussion of mathematics as the product of the 'fecundity of the subject's thought processes' which depend on the 'internal resources of the organism,' see Piaget, 1971c, pp. 344-5.
30 For examples of Piaget's explanation of interactive outcomes with reference to the psychology of individuals, see Piaget, 1973, pp. 157-66.
31 For example, see Piaget, 1971c, pp. 83-4.
32 Of course, the problem of discovering the structure of meaning exists not only when the subject's reasoning differs from that of the investigator. The problem of abstracting the essential structure of thinking remains even when both think in the same way.
33 Piaget stopped with adolescence because his research indicated that formal operations, the stage of full equilibration of meaning and reality, was achieved between thirteen and fifteen years of age. In his final years, he was forced to acknowledge that there were some problems with his designation of this age as the time when development was completed. In some circumstances, it was clear that development continued until a later age. More important, it was also clear that not all people ever became fully formal operational even in adulthood. This fact and its implications for his theory were never adequately addressed by Piaget (see for example, the weak response offered in his 1972 article). In my own view, it raises basic questions regarding the trajectory of development and the role of social environments in the process.
34 Good examples of the use of interview techniques are provided by Kohlberg, 1969; Kegan, 1982.

4 IDEOLOGY AND THE FORMS OF POLITICAL REASONING

1 Consistent with his focus on physical reality as the primary objective stimulus to development, Piaget devotes little attention to the analysis of social environment. Of the little writing he had done on the matter, the most important is collected in his *Etudes Sociologiques* (1965a). For a good example of Piaget's analysis of the impact of social environments on cognitive development, see Piaget, 1966.
2 This hypothetical comparison of tribes with and without exposure to formal schooling and the consequences for cognitive development follows on actual research and analysis. In studies of groups with and without formal schooling, pscyhologists have observed differences in the cognitive development of individuals from each group. They have explained their results along the lines suggested by our example. For example, see Bruner et al., 1966 or Cole and Scribner, 1973.
3 This discussion of the relation between the social and psychological bases of meaning-making and its implications for political analysis is continued and extended in chapter 6.
4 A growing body of research offers evidence in support of this view. Both cross-cultural studies and research focusing on a single society indicate that adults do think in structurally dissimilar ways, dissimilarities which suggest arrest at different stages of development. For evidence of differences in developmental achievement across cultures, see Peluffo, 1967; Prince, 1968; Luria, 1976; Dasen, 1977. For evidence of differences among Americans, see Sinnott, 1975; Kuhn et al., 1977; Commons et al., 1982. Viewed from a classical Piagetian perspective, these results

are theoretically anomalous. Viewed from the perspective presented here, they are to be expected.

5 For a good review of perceptual and environmental effects on attention and the consequence of this for attributions of causality, see Taylor and Fiske, 1978. Note that while Taylor and Fiske imply the research pertains to all thinking, I suggest it is primarily relevant to the analysis of linear thought.

6 In this context, it should be noted that although the linear relations may be objects of self-conscious consideration, this is the case only insofar as they pertain to particular objective phenomena. The linear thinker is able to think about his thoughts, but only as they relate to things, not as they directly relate to one another.

7 For examples of the research on agenda setting, see Shaw and McCombs, 1977 and Graber, 1978. We suggest this effect will be greatest for linear thinkers. Systematic thinkers are more the authors of their own thought and sequential thinkers do not think in terms which will sustain the focus and evaluation needed to achieve the agenda setting effect.

8 The clusters referred to here are similar to those discussed in the social psychological literature on prototypes and schemas (e.g., Cantor and Mischel, 1979; Taylor and Crocker, 1981). In that language, the linear thinker's observation of an actor may evoke associations with a particular schema or prototype and he will be defined accordingly. Of course, given the qualities of linear thought, these prototypes will necessarily consist of learned sets of associated specific and concrete acts and attributes. Thus, he may use the general language of personality traits (as they are associated with prototypes), but they will be meaningful only as they relate to a set of specific acts. Regardless of the terms used or the extent to which definitions are extended schematically, the linear thinker can only conceive of an actor as a cluster of concrete and specific attributes.

9 Although not mentioned here, physical appearance is potentially relevant, but only insofar as it is associated with characteristic behaviors. Thus, when observing a politician's appearance, the linear thinker is linking physical features to certain actions with which they are regularly associated. Thus, he defines appearance in active terms and uses it to answer questions such as: does this politician look like someone who can lead, get the job done and be trusted? Much of the image politicians project and its effect on voters' perceptions can be understood in these terms. For an example of the research on the relationship between appearance and voting, see Rosenberg et al., 1986 and Rosenberg and McCafferty, 1987. Of course, the impact should be particularly great on voters who reason in a linear manner.

10 This tendency to ignore the particular qualities of individuals when thinking in terms of groups may result in unusual or extreme manifestations of affection and loyalty to ingroup members and commensurately exaggerated manifestations of disloyalty to outgroup members. This feature of linear thinking may shed some light on the cognitive bases of dehumanization of the enemy discussed in the social psychological literature (e.g., Lerner, 1970).

11 Two streams of social psychological research are relevant here: that on the 'actor-observer' hypothesis posited by Jones and Nisbett (1971) and that on relative availability of environmental stimuli by Taylor and Fiske (1978). The two lines of work are related. In fact, the Taylor and Fiske discussion of the 'top of the head phenomenon' constitutes a more general statement of what is suggested by Jones and Nisbett. The latter pair argue that actors tend to explain their own behavior more situationally and the behavior of others more dispositionally. One explanation of this is that environmental forces impinging on one own's action

can more readily be perceived, whereas one's view of another's action is dominated by the sight of the other. Arguing in more general terms, Taylor and Fiske suggest that causal explanation orients to whatever is more available to the individual doing the explaining. For example, drawing on research on perception, they argue that people will focus on more distinctive elements or persons in the environment and attribute more causal influence to them (for the relevant research, see Taylor and Fiske, 1975; McArthur and Post, 1977). In our view, this research importantly elaborates the logic of linear thought. It does not, however, provide an adequate basis for the description of the causal inferences of either sequential or systematic thinkers.

12 Our concept of rules and their use is very similar to that of the concept of schema used in recent cognitive social psychology. In both instances, schemas are defined as an ordering of associations among specific beliefs and actions which are learned, but then structure a person's view of subsequent events. For a seminal discussion of the concept of schema, see Bartlett (1932). For more recent use of the concept, see Abelson (1976b) or Taylor and Crocker (1981). For examples of political research which draw on this idea, see Kinder and Abelson (1981) or Conover and Feldman (1984). It is important to note that while I find this research revealing, I believe it applies primarily to linear thinkers.

13 The linear thinker may also come to learn that actions have different consequences in different settings. Unlike the linear thinker, the systematic thinker anticipates this and, not knowing the general context of an exchange, will withhold any judgement until further information is gathered.

14 Here I discuss what the systematic thinker can construct as part of his political considerations. Because of insufficient exposure or interest, this system may not be a well differentiated or elaborated one. However, even in its most skeletal form it retains the essential qualities (e.g. systematicity, objective and subjective dimensions, ideal as well as real aspects) of a systematic construction.

15 This is not to suggest that the systematic thinker's vision is not culturally determined. The logic of his reasoning and his mode of definition are linked to the structure of his environment and hence are culturally relative. However, this linkage is not at the level of particular concerns.

16 In this context, individuals are themselves abstractions. They have no significant identity unto themselves. Their action vis-à-vis one another and hence their political significance is a function of their place in the political system. In this sense, they are mere placeholders and, when considered in isolation, are interchangeable. In this sense also, individuals are inherently equal.

17 In the American context, sociology is often associated with liberalism. There is some truth in this if one considers the accommodation of classical liberalism to sociology advanced by John Dewey and those who followed in his footsteps. However, with their shared focus on the collective as the basic element of social life, the marriage between sociology and conservatism is easily achieved. For an interesting discussion along these lines, see Robert Nisbet's essay, 'Conservatism and Ideology' (1962).

18 Modern society as discussed here does not refer to societies which are only technologically sophisticated and structurally complex. They must also incorporate much of the liberal/enlightment ethos of the seventeenth and eighteenth centuries in their structure and culture. Given the individualistic dimension of systematic thought, this is obviously important.

19 It is my belief that the requisite conditions for further development are not generally available at this point. As a result, I presume that virtually all individuals examined will evidence sequential, linear or systematic thought. This

is not to suggest that a fourth stage of thinking may not be evidenced in a very few cases or more broadly at some time in the future.

5 THREE EMPIRICAL STUDIES

1 Parts of this research were first reported in a paper entitled 'The Structural Developmental Analysis of Political Thinking' presented at the 1981 Annual Meeting of the International Society of Political Psychology, Mannheim, West Germany, and later in a paper entitled 'The Structural Developmental Analysis of Political Thinking: An Alternative to the Belief Systems Approach' presented at the 1982 Annual Meeting of the American Political Science Association, Denver, Colorado.

2 It should be noted that none of the university students in either sample performed at the sequential level. This suggests there is some relationship between education and level of cognitive development. In my view, this is to be expected. The structure of an educational environment tends to force development beyond the sequential level. To have entered university, a student must do reasonably well in his high school environment. This success would depend on reaching at least the linear stage of development. However, this relationship between cognitive development and education clearly is an imperfect one. Structural differences between individuals emerge even when their education is virtually identical. This suggests that the level of education is too crude a measure of environment and more adequate analysis will depend on the development of a better measure.

3 A preliminary acccount of this research was given in a paper entitled 'Reason and Ideology: Interpreting People's Understanding of American Politics' presented at the 1985 Annual Meeting of the American Political Science Association, New Orleans, Louisiana.

4 This research was first reported in a paper entitled 'How Adults Understand International Conflict: A Neo-Piagetian Approach' presented at the 1986 Annual Conference of Applied Social Psychology, Santa Cruz, California.

5 While Ward's study adopts a similar orientation to my own, there are important differences. He is less concerned with the issue of structure across domains. This reflects his interest in Piaget's early research which explored the development of children's thinking along the various dimensions of *a priori* thought distinguished by Kant. My work is more influenced by Piaget's later research on logical operations and the general structure of thinking.

6 I regard the research of Kohlberg and his associates as a seminal effort which has provided important insight into the nature of moral reasoning. Indeed, my own work has been influenced by his. This said, there are significant differences. Most fundamental, is the concept of the types or stages of thinking themselves. First, my typology is different from Kohlberg's and no unambiguous relationship exists between his categories and my own. Second and related to the first, my typology depends on elaborate and abstract definitions of the different structures underlying the various forms of political understanding. Kohlberg's descriptions of stages of moral reasoning include less attention to the structural underpinnings of the distinctions made. As a result, there is some confusion of structure and content. This problem becomes particularly evident in his discussion of stages 4½ and 5. In this regard, we are sympathetic to some of the criticisms of his work that attack the ideological substance of his higher stages (e.g., Gilligan, 1982).

7 Piaget's theoretical writings on equilibrium suggest that both internal demands for coordination and external demands for accommodation ultimately force thinking

to the formal operational level. However, the early evidence on adults who do not think formal operationally forced him to retrench somewhat. Thus, he suggested that perhaps adults would only be formal operational in areas of greatest demand and interest (e.g., their occupational pursuits). The article is an unusually weak piece insofar as it does not consider the far-reaching theoretical implications of such a conclusion. His conception of logical operations, cognitive structure and self-object relations would have to be fundamentally amended. In part, my own theoretical effort moves in this direction.

8 For representative discussions of concepts of rationality, see Peters, 1974; Pole, 1975; Benn and Mortimore, 1976; Simon, 1986. For social psychological research on limited rationality, see Kelley, 1967, 1972; Abelson, 1976a; Taylor and Fiske, 1978; Nisbett and Ross, 1980; Fiske and Taylor, 1984. Although this research points out the nonrational or limited qualities of reasoning, it retains the assumption that all people think in basically the same way.

9 Lane's concept of structure is typical of those grounded in liberal philosophy. For the distinction between structuralist and liberal concepts of structure, see the earlier discussion in chapter 1, pp. 10-11. For another attempt to draw this distinction, see Giddens, 1979.

10 I do not believe that children should be studied in order to test hypotheses regarding the structure of thinking. There are a number of reasons for believing that children's thought should be less coherent than adults'. For example, unlike an adult, a child is going through a period of ongoing development and change. It is possible that progress is starting in some areas and has not yet generalized to others. Consequently, a child is more likely to evidence horizontal *decalage*.

6 SUMMARY AND EPILOGUE

1 For early examples, see Bartlett, 1932; Hebb, 1949; and Piaget, 1952. For examples of current use, see Minsky, 1975; Niesser, 1976; and Rosch, 1978.

2 For good reviews of this research, see Taylor and Crocker, 1981; and Fiske and Taylor, 1984. For a more recent and critical perspective, see Higgins and Bargh, 1987.

3 Good, albeit rather different, examples of this are provided by the work of Piaget (1952) and that of Eleanor Rosch (1978).

4 As noted earlier, the concept of structure is used in a variety of ways with resulting confusion. Like the systems theorist, the schema theorist often equates structures and systems. Consequently, differences in structure of a given schema are often equated with the number of relevant elements, that is, bits of information or opinion, included. Operational examples of this are provided in the recent studies of Lodge and Hamil (1986) and Lau (1986). In both cases, raw numbers are relied upon to differentiate schematics from aschematics and the sophisticated from the unsophisticated. Little attention is paid to the constructive or definitional properties of thinking or to the quality of the relationships among the elements of a schema. For a comparison of this use of the concept of structure with out my own, see my discussion in chapter 1, pp. 10-11.

5 For Habermas' comments on the hermeneutic position and his defense of critique, see Habermas, 1977, pp. 335-63.

6 For a good review of Habermas' position, see McCarthy, 1978, pp. 126-62. For his application, see Habermas, 1975b, p. 113.

7 Habermas, 1979, pp. 124-5.

 8 Developmentalists such as Piaget and Kohlberg analyze development in the light of a clearly defined final stage which provides an analytical and evaluative standard. However, this is not to suggest that a developmental analysis requires the postulation of a telos or that one is required for evaluation. For discussion relevant to this point, see the comments on development and legitimacy which follow the present discussion of Habermas.

 9 Viewed from a Piagetian frame of reference, Habermas' assumption of the linguistic bases of meaning may be regarded as a 'socializing' of Piaget's concept of subjectivity while retaining its other essential elements. The notion of 'meaning in use' is similar to Piaget's operational concept of meaning. Only the interactive context shifts from the pragmatic relation between subject and object to that between subject and subject. Moreover, Habermas' interest in the social structure underlying the concrete rules of particular games is quite consistent with Piaget's attempt to analyze the cognitive structure underlying an individual's particular problem-solving strategies.

10 For a discussion of this, see his discussion of the rational foundation of the illocutionary force of speech acts in 'What is a Universal Pragmatics?' (Habermas, 1979, pp. 59–65)

11 Habermas, 1979, pp. 59–65.

12 Habermas, 1979, pp. 146–8.

13 See his essay 'Moral Development and Ego Identity' (Habermas, 1979), especially pp. 82–90.

14 For a discussion of the interdependence of societal and individual constructions and development, see Habermas, 1979, pp. 98–9 and 154–5.

15 Piaget's description of the stages of cognitive development are critical to Habermas' analysis of stages of social development. Having discussed biological models of evolution, Habermas writes, 'In social evolution as well, we shall not be able to classify social formations according to the state of their development until we know the general structures and developmental logic of social learning processes. Corresponding to the central nervous system here are the basic cognitive structures in which technical and moral-practical knowledge are produced.' (1979, p. 174)

16 In this vein, Habermas writes: 'I would even defend the thesis that the development of these normative structures is the pacemaker of social evolution, for new principles of social organization mean new forms of social integration; and the latter, in turn, first make it possible to implement available productive forces or to generate new ones, as well as making possible a heightening of social complexity.' (Habermas, 1979, p. 120. For discussions of social learning, see pp. 121–3, 144–5.)

17 This is not to suggest a simple introspectionist position or to argue that individuals are Liebnitzian monads. As argued in chapters 3 and 4, the structure of subjective activity is both realized through and reflects the individual's pragmatic exchange with the world, social as well as physical.

18 The point to which the individual will develop depends on the degree to which his social environment gives him the opportunity and responsibility to make decisions for himself and others.

19 For an important recent example of this, see Rawls, 1971.

20 Again the caveats regarding the role of exogenous or contingent factors noted as part of our general analysis are operative here. Consequently, there is no intent to suggest that the normative development of social life follows an inevitable path. Particular conditions may impede or reverse that process.

21 Given that all societies are subject to the same developmental progress, cross-cultural critique is both possible and legitimate. The standard invoked is that of the progress of human reason itself.
22 The position taken here is clearly different from that adopted by both Habermas and Piaget. I believe their claim to have defined a universal telos of social and psychological development to be based on an inappropriate underestimation of the extent to which culture and social structure penetrate the reflective activity of both the individual *and* the theorist. I also believe this claim to be unnecessary to structural developmental theorizing.

Appendix:
Summary Table of Types of Political Reasoning

DIMENSION OF THOUGHT	STRUCTURE OF IDEOLOGICAL THOUGHT		
	Sequential	Linear	Systematic
Mode of Reasoning	Tracking action on objects	Placing actions in relation to one another	Juxtaposing relations between actions
Time of Politics	Limited to the present and to the scattered memories the present evokes	Anchored in the present but through causal analysis can build to past cause and future effect	Begins with an extended frame of reference and then places the present in this context and interprets it accordingly
Space of Politics	Limited to what is immediate and observed	Anchored in the immediate, but can build out to remote causes and effects	Constructs an integrated map. Locates immediate concerns in this larger context and thereby defines them
Explanation of Action	Does not explain, just learns the order of specific observed sequences of action	Naturally searches for causes. This search generally satisfied by the discovery of a single cause	Explanation may be conducted at two levels. (1) Patterns of exchange explained in terms of underlying organizational rules. (2) Explanation of an effect in terms of interactive and multiple causes

Concept of Law	No real sense of rules of action and reaction. Learned sequences are readily reordered. No notion of standards or of necessity	Regular or conventional relationships betwen specific action and reaction regarded as both necessary and standard. Law is regarded as given and correct, and is ritualistically followed	Laws understood with respect to abstract principles or general group norm and seen to apply to a variety of interaction situations. Laws are viewed relative to one and as human artifacts which may be flawed and rejected
Concept of Groups	Groups thought of as concrete individuals. Qualities of the group confused with that of particular representative	Groups defined by shared features of the members. E.g., common appearance, territory or ritual	Groups defined by degree of integration of possibly very different people. Integration based on density of interaction and/or common understanding
Concept of Government Organization	Two-step, fluid hierarchy consisting of one person doing something to one or more others	Simple top-down (possibly multi-level) hierarchy. Within a single level of the hierarchy, common purpose and agreement assumed	Complex system performing a variety of interrelated functions. Power flows from bottom up as well as from top down. Also possible contradiction within one level of the hierarchy considered
Concept of International Relations	Aware of isolated acts of particular leaders. Little sense of the historical or geographic context of events. International affairs consist of relatively isolated incidents in which a citizen of one nation is saying or doing something to particular citizens of another	Views international activity in the context of a relationship of exchange between two nations. Nations are led by leaders and each nation acts in a singular, univocal way. The activity of each nation consists either of an attempt to realize specific goals or of a reaction to the initiatives of another nation	Sees a system of relations among a set of interacting nations. All bilateral relations are understood in this context. There are multiple dimensions to any international relationship. The action of any nation may be a response to its own domestic situation as well as to the international one

Bibliography

Abelson, R. P. (1976a). Social psychology's rational man. In G. Mortimore and S. I. Benn (eds) *The Concept of Rationality in the Social Sciences*. Oxford: Clarendon Press.

Abelson, R. P. (1976b). Script processing in attitude formation and decision making. In J. S. Carrol and J. W. Payne (eds) *Cognition and Social Behavior*. Hillsdale, N J: Lawrence Erlbaum.

Achen, C. (1975). Mass political attitudes and survey response. *American Political Science Review*, 69: 1218-31.

Adelson, J. and O'Neil, R. P. (1966). The growth of political ideas in adolescence: The sense of community. *Journal of Personality and Social Psychology*, 4: 295-306.

Allport, G. W. (1935). Attitudes. In C. C. Murchison (ed.) *A Handbook of Social Psychology*. Reading, Mass.: Addison-Wesley.

Althusser, L. (1964). *For Marx*. Baltimore: Penguin.

Althusser, L. (1971). Ideology and the ideological state apparatuses. In L. Althusser (ed.) *Lenin and Philosophy and Other Essays*. London: New Left Books.

Althusser, L. and Balibar, E. (1970). *Reading Capital*. London: New Left Books.

Axelrod, R. (1973). Schema theory: An information processing model of perception and cognition. *American Political Science Review*, 67: 1248-66.

Bach, K. and Harnish, R. M. (1979). *Linguistic Communication and Speech Acts*. Cambridge, Mass.: MIT Press.

Barlett, F. C. (1932). *Remembering*. Cambridge: Cambridge University Press.

Benn, S. I. and Mortimore, G. W. (eds) (1976). *Rationality and the Social Sciences*. London: Routledge and Kegan Paul.

Bennett, L. (1975). *The Political Mind and the Political Environment*. Lexington, Mass.: Heath.

Berlin, I. (1958). *Two Concepts of Liberty*. Oxford: Oxford University Press.

Bernstein, R. J. (1979). *The Restructuring of Social and Political Theory*. London: Methuen.

Bhaksar, R. (1979). *The Possibility of Naturalism: A Philosophical Critique of the Contemporary Human Sciences*. Brighton: Harvester.

Bishop, G. and Oldendick, R. W. (1978). Change in the structure of American political attitudes: The nagging question of question wording. *American Journal of Political Science*, 22: 250-69.

Bishop, G., Hamilton, D. L. and McConahay, J. B. (1980). Attitudes and non-attitudes in the belief systems of mass publics. *Journal of Social Psychology*, 110, 53-64.

Brown, S. R. (1970). Consistency and the persistence of ideology: Some experimental results. *Public Opinion Quarterly*, 34 (Spring): 60-8.

Bruner, J. S. (1959). A psychologist's viewpoint: Review of B. Inhelder and J. Piaget, *The Growth of Logical Thinking*. *British Journal of Psychology*, 50: 363-70.

Bruner, J. S., et al. (1966). *Studies in Cognitive Growth: A Collaboration at the Center for Cognitive Studies*. New York: Wiley.

Campbell, A., Converse, P. E., Miller, W. E. and Stokes, D. E. (1960). *The American Voter*. New York: Wiley.

Campbell, B. A. (1980). A theoretical approach to peer influence in adolescent socialization. *American Journal of Political Science*, 24: 324-44.

Cantor, N. and Mischel, W. (1979). Prototypes in person perception. In L. Berkowitz (ed.) *Advances in Experimental Social Psychology, Volume 12*. New York: Academic Press.

Cole, M. and Scribner, S. (1973). *Culture and Thought: A Psychological Introduction*. New York: Wiley.

Commons, B., Richards, A. and Kuhn, D. (1982). Systematic and metasystematic reasoning: A case for levels of reasoning beyond Piaget's stage of formal operations. *Child Development*, 53: 1058-69.

Connell, R. W. (1972). Political socialization in the American family. *Public Opinion Quarterly*, 36: 323-33.

Conover, P. and Feldman, S. (1984). How people organize the political world: A schematic model. *American Journal of Political Science*, 28: 95-126.

Converse, P. E. (1964). The nature of belief systems in mass publics. In D. Apter (ed.) *Ideology and Discontent*. New York: Free Press.

Converse, P. E. (1970). Attitudes and non-attitudes: Continuation of a dialogue. In E. R. Tufte (ed.) *The Quantitative Analysis of Social Problems*. Reading, Mass.: Addison-Wesley.

Converse, P. E. (1975). Public opinion and voting behavior. In F. I. Greenstein and N. W. Polsby (eds), *Handbook of Political Science, Vol. 4*. Reading, Mass.: Addison-Wesley.

Converse, P. E. (1980). Rejoinder to Judd and Milburn. *American Sociological Review*, 45: 644-6.

Crocker, J., Fiske, S. T. and Taylor, S. E. (1984). Schematic bases of belief change. In J. R. Eiser (ed.) *Attitudinal Judgment*. New York: Springer-Verlag.

Dasen, P. (1977). *Piagetian Psychology: Cross-Cultural Contributions*. New York: Gardner Press.

De Soto, C. B. (1960). Learning a social structure. *Journal of Abnormal and Social Psychology*, 60: 417–21.

Doise, W., Mugny, G. and Perret-Clermont, A. (1975). Social interaction and the development of cognitive operations. *European Journal of Social Psychology*, 5: 367–83.

Downs, A. (1957). *An Economic Theory of Democracy*. New York: Harper and Row.

Dowse, R. E. and Hughes, J. A. (1971). Girls, boys and politics. *British Journal of Sociology*, 22: 53–67.

Durkheim, E. (1938). *The Rules of Sociological Method*. Chicago: University of Chicago Press.

Durkheim, E. and Mauss, M. (1961). Social structure and the structure of thought. In T. Parsons, E. Shils, K. D. Naegele and J. R. Pitts (eds) *Theories of Society*. New York: Free Press.

Easton, D. and Dennis, J. (1969). *Children in the Political System: Origins of Political Legitimacy*. New York: McGraw-Hill.

Edelstein, W. and Noam, G. (1982). Regulatory structures of the self and 'postformal' stages in adulthood. *Human Development*, 25: 407–22.

Festinger, L. (1957). *A Theory of Cognitive Dissonance*. Stanford: Stanford University Press.

Field, J. O., and Anderson, R. (1969). Ideology in the public's conceptualization of the 1964 election. *Public Opinion Quarterly*, 33: 112–17.

Fishbein, M. and Ajzen, I. (1975). *Belief, Attitude, Intention and Behavior: An Introduction to Theory and Research*. Reading, Mass.: Addison-Wesley.

Fiske, S. and Taylor, S. (1984). *Social Cognition*. Reading, Mass.: Addison-Wesley.

Flavell, J. H. (1963). *The Developmental Psychology of Jean Piaget*. New York: Van Nostrand Reinhold.

Freud, S. (1913). *The Interpretation of Dreams*. London: Allen.

Freud, S. (1972). *Civilization and its Discontents*. London: Hogarth Press.

Fromm, E. (1960). *The Fear of Freedom*. London: Routledge and Kegan Paul.

Gallatin, J. and Adelson, J. (1970). Individual rights and the public good: Cross-national study of adolescents. *Comparative Political Studies*, 3: 226–42.

Geertz, C. (1964). Ideology as a cultural symbol system. In D. Apter (ed.) *Ideology and Discontent*. New York: Free Press.

Gerth, H. and Mills, C. W. (1954). *Character and Social Structure*. New York: Harcourt, Brace and World.

Gewirtz, J. L. (1969). Mechanisms of social learning. In D. A. Goslin (ed.) *Handbook of Socialization Theory and Research*. Chicago: Rand McNally.

Giddens, A. (1979). *Central Problems in Modern Social Theory*. Berkeley: University of California Press.

Gilligan, C. (1982). *In a Different Voice: Psychological Theory and Women's Development*. Cambridge: Harvard University Press.

Goldmann, L. (1964). *The Hidden God*. London: Routledge and Kegan Paul.

Graber, D. A. (1978). Agenda setting: Are there women's perspectives? In L. K. Epstein (ed.) *Women and the News*. New York: Hastings House.

Graber, D. A. (1982). 'Have I heard this before and is it worth knowing?' Variations in political information processing. Paper presented at the 1982 Annual Meeting of the American Political Science Association. Denver, Colorado.

Graber, D. A. (1984). *Processing the News: How People Tame the Information Tide*. New York: Longman.

Greenstein, F. I. (1965). *Children and Politics*. New Haven: Yale University Press.

Greenstein, F. I. (1975). Personality and politics. In F. I. Greenstein and N. W. Polsby (eds) *Handbook of Political Science (Vol. 2)*. Reading, Mass.: Addison-Wesley.

Haan, N., Smith, M. B. and Block, J. (1968). Moral reasoning of young adult: Political-social behavior, family background and personality correlates. *Journal of Personality and Social Psychology*, 10: 183-201.

Habermas, J. (1975a). Moral development and ego identity. *Telos*, 24: 41-56.

Habermas, J. (1975b). *Legitimation Crisis*. Boston: Beacon.

Habermas, J. (1977). A review of Gadamer's *Truth and Method*. In F. Dallmayr and T. McCarthy (eds) *Understanding and Social Inquiry*. Notre Dame: University of Notre Dame Press.

Habermas, J. (1979). *Communication and the Evolution of Society*. Boston: Beacon.

Habermas, J. (1984). *The Theory of Communicative Action. Reason and the Rationalization of Society*. Volume 1. London: Heinemann.

Hamlyn, D. W. (1971). Epistemology and conceptual development. In T. Mischel (ed.) *Cognitive Development and Epistemology*. New York: Academic Press.

Hamlyn, D. W. (1978). *Experience and The Growth of Understanding*. London: Routledge and Kegan Paul.

Hamlyn, D. W. (1982). What exactly is social about the origins of understanding? In G. Butterworth and P. Light (eds) *Social Cognition: Studies of the Development of Understanding*. Brighton: Harvester Press.

Hardy-Brown, K. (1979). Formal operations and the issue of generalizability: The analysis of poetry by college students. *Human Development*, 22: 127-36.

Hastorf, A. H. and Isen, A. M. (1982). *Cognitive Social Psychology*. New York: Elsevier.

Hebb, D. O. (1949). *The Organization of Behavior*. New York: Wiley.

Heider, F. (1958). *The Psychology of Interpersonal Relations*. New York: Wiley.

Higgins, E. T. and Bargh, J. A. (1987). Social cognition and social perception. *Annual Review of Psychology*, 38: 369-425.

Himmelweit, H. T., Humphreys, P., Jaeger, M. and Katz, M. (1981). *How Voters Decide: A longitudinal study of political attitudes and voting extending over 15 years*. London: Academic Press.

Inhelder, B. and Piaget, J. (1958). *The Growth of Logical Thinking: From Childhood to Adolescence*. New York: Basic Books.

Jackson, T. H. and Marcus, G. E. (1975). Political competence and ideological constraint. *Social Science Research*, 4: 93–111.

Jennings, M. K. and Niemi, R. G. (1968). The transmission of political values from parent to child. *American Political Science Review*, 62: 169–84.

Jones, E. E. and Nisbett, R. E. (1971). The actor and the observer: Divergent perceptions of the causes of behavior. In E. E. Jones, D. E. Kanouse, H. H. Kelley, R. E. Nisbett, S. Valins, and B. Weiner (eds) *Attribution: Perceiving the Causes of Behavior*. Morristown, NJ: General Learning Press.

Judd, C. M. and Milburn, M. A. (1980). The structure of attitude systems in the general public: Comparisons of a structural equation model. *American Sociological Review*, 45: 627–43.

Kegan, R. (1982). *The Evolving Self: Problems and Process in Human Development*. Cambridge, Mass.: Harvard University Press.

Kelley, H. H. (1967). Attribution theory in social psychology. In D. Levine (ed.) *Nebraska Symposium on Motivation*. Lincoln: University of Nebraska Press.

Kelley, H. H. (1972). Attribution in social interaction. In E. E. Jones et al. (eds) *Attribution: Perceiving the Causes of Behavior*. Morristown, NJ: General Learning Press.

Kinder, D. (1982). Enough already about ideology. Paper presented at the Annual Meeting of the American Political Science Association. Denver, Colorado.

Kinder, D. R. and Abelson, R. P. (1981). Appraising presidential candidates: Personality and affect in the 1980 campaign. Paper delivered at the 1981 Annual Meeting of the American Political Science Association, New York.

Klingemann, H. D. (1973). Dimensions of political belief systems: Levels of conceptualization as a variable. Some results for USA and FRG 1968/69. *Comparative Political Studies*, 5: 93–106.

Klingemann, H. D. (1979). Measuring ideological conceptualization. In S. Barnes et al., (eds) *Political Action: Mass Participation in Five Western Democracies*. Beverly Hills, Ca.: Sage.

Kohlberg, L. (1969). Stage and sequence: The cognitive developmental approach to socialization. In D. A. Goslin (ed.) *Handbook of Socialization Theory*. Chicago: Rand McNally.

Kohlberg, L. (1971). From is to ought: How to commit the naturalistic fallacy and get away with it. In T. Mischel (ed.) *Cognitive Development and Epistemology*. New York: Academic Press.

Kohlberg, L. (1981). *Essays on Moral Development, Volume One: The Philosophy of Moral Development*. New York: Harper and Row.

Kohlberg, L. (1984). *Essays on Moral Development, Volume Two: The Psychology of Moral Development.* New York: Harper and Row.

Krech, D. and Crutchfield, R. S. (1958). *Elements of Psychology.* New York: Knopf.

Kuhn, D., Langer, J., Kohlberg, L. and Haan, N. (1977). The development of formal operations in logical and moral development. *Genetic Psychology Monographs*, 95: 97-188.

Langer, E. J. (1975). The illusion of control. *Journal of Personality and Social Psychology*, 32: 311-28.

Lane, R. E. (1962). *Political Ideology: Why the American Common Man Believes What He Does.* Glencoe: Free Press.

Lane, R. E. (1973). Patterns of political belief. In J. Knutson (ed.) *Handbook of Political Psychology.* San Francisco: Jossey-Bass.

Lane, R. E. (1978a). Waiting for lefty. *Theory and Society*, 6: 1-28.

Lane, R. E. (1978b). Autonomy, felicity, futility: The effects of the market economy on political personality. *Journal of Politics*, 40: 2-24.

Lane, R. E. (1983). Political observers and market participants: The effects on cognition. *Political Psychology* 4: 445-82.

Langton, K. P. (1967). Peer group and school and the political socialization process. *American Political Science Review*, 61: 751-8.

Langton, K. P. and Karns, D. A. (1969). The relative influence of the family, peer group and school in the development of political efficacy. *Western Political Quarterly*, 22: 813-26.

Lasswell, H. D. (1960). *Psychopathology and Politics.* New York: Viking.

Lau, R. R. (1986). Political schemata, candidate evaluations and voting behavior. In R. R. Lau and D. O. Sears (eds) *Political Cognition.* Hillsdale, NJ: Lawrence Erlbaum.

Leibow, E. (1967). *Tally's Corner.* Boston: Little Brown.

Lerner, M. J. (1970). The desire for justice and reactions to victims. In J. Macauley and L. Berkowitz (eds) *Altruism and Helping Behavior.* New York: Academic Press.

Levi-Strauss, C. (1963). *Totemism.* Boston: Beacon.

Levi-Strauss, C. (1966). *The Savage Mind.* London: Weidenfeld and Nicolson.

Lodge, M. and Hamil, D. (1986). A partisan schema for political information processing. *American Political Science Review*, 80: 505-19.

Long, A., McCravy, K. and Ackerman, S. (1979). Adult cognition: Piagetian based research findings. *Adult Education*, 30: 171-93.

Lukacs, G. (1971). *History and Class Consciousness.* Boston: MIT Press.

Luria, A. R. (1976). *Cognitive Development: Its Cultural and Social Foundations.* Cambridge, Mass.: Harvard University Press.

Luttbeg, N. R. (1968). The structure of beliefs among leaders and the public. *Public Opinion Quarterly*, 32: 398-409.

MacPherson, C. B. (1962). *The Political Theory of Possessive Individualism: Hobbes to Locke.* Oxford: Clarendon Press.

Mannheim, K. (1936). *Ideology and Utopia.* New York: Harvest Press.

Marcuse, H. (1964). *One Dimensional Man: Studies in the Ideology of Advanced Industrial Society*. London: Routledge and Paul.

Markus, H. (1977). Self-schemata and processing information about the self. *Journal of Personality and Social Psychology*, 42: 38–50.

Markus, G. B. (1979). The political environment and the dynamics of public attitudes: A panel study. *American Journal of Political Science*, 23: 338–57.

Marx, K. (1973). *Grundrisse: Foundations of a Critique of Political Economy*. New York: Random House.

Marx, K. (1974). *The German Ideology*. London: Lawrence & Wishart.

McArthur, L. Z. and Post, D. L. (1977). Figural emphasis and person perception. *Journal of Experimental Social Psychology*, 13: 520–35.

McCarthy, T. (1978). *The Critical Theory of Jurgen Habermas*. Cambridge Mass.: MIT Press.

McCombs M. and Shaw, D.L. (1972). The agenda-setting function of the mass media. *Public Opinion Quarterly*, 36: 176–87.

McDougall, W. (1908). *An Introduction to Social Psychology*. London: Methuen.

Mead, G. H. (1924-5). The genesis of the self and social control. *International Journal of Ethics*, 35: 251–77.

Mead, G. H. (1934). *Mind, Self and Society*. Chicago: University of Chicago Press.

Merelman, R. M. (1969). The development of political ideology: A framework for the analysis of political socialization. *American Political Science Review*, 63: 750–67.

Merelman, R. M. (1971). The development of policy thinking in adolescence. *American Political Science Review*, 65: 1033–47.

Merleau-Ponty, M. (1963). *The Structure of Behavior*. Boston: Beacon Press.

Merton, R. K. (1957). *Social Theory and Social Structure*. New York: Free Press.

Miller, A., Wattenberg, M. and Malanchuk, O. (1982). Cognitive representations of candidate assessment. Paper delivered at the 1982 Annual Meeting of the American Political Science Association. Denver, Colorado.

Minsky, M. (1975). A framework for representing knowledge. In P. H. Winston (ed.) *The Psychology of Computer Vision*. New York: McGraw-Hill.

Mueller, J. E. (1973). *War, Presidents and Public Opinion*. New York: Wiley.

Nelson, J. (1977). The ideological connection or smuggling in the goods, Part I and Part II. *Theory and Society*, 4 (3), 421–48; (4), 573–90.

Neisser, U. (1976). *Cognition and Reality*. San Francisco: Freeman.

Neuman, W. R. (1981). Differentiation and integration: Two dimensions of political thinking. *American Journal of Sociology*, 86 (6), 1236–68.

Nie, N. H. and Andersen, K. (1974). Mass belief systems revisited: Political change and attitude structure. *Journal of Politics*, 36: 545–91.

Nie, N. H., Verba, S. and Petrocik, J. R. (1976). *The Changing American Voter*. Cambridge, Mass.: Harvard University Press.

Niemi, R. G. and Weisberg, H. F. (1976). *Controversies in American Voting Behavior*. San Francisco, CA: Freeman.

Niesser, U. (1976). *Cognition and Reality: Principles and implications of cognitive psychology*. San Francisco: Freeman.

Nisbet, R. A. (1962). Conservatism and ideology. In R. A. Nisbet, *Community and Power*. New York: Basic Books.

Nisbett, R. E. and Ross, L. (1980). *Human Inference: Strategies and Shortcomings of Social Judgment*. Englewood Cliffs, NJ: Prentice Hall.

Parsons, T. and Bales, R. F. (1956). *Family, Socialization and Interaction Process*. London: Routledge and Kegan Paul.

Peluffo, N. (1967). Culture and cognitive problems. *International Journal of Psychology*, 2: 187–98.

Peters, R. S. (1974). Reason and passion. In R. S. Peters, *Psychology and Ethical Development*. London: Allen and Unwin.

Piaget, J. (1952). *The Origins of Intelligence in Children*. New York: International Universities Press.

Piaget, J. (1962). *Play, and Dreams and Imitation in Childhood*. New York: Norton.

Piaget, J. (1965a). *Etudes Sociologiques*. Paris: Editions Droz.

Piaget, J. (1965b). *The Moral Judgment of the Child*. New York: Free Press.

Piaget, J. (1966). Need and significance of cross-cultural studies in genetic psychology. *International Journal of Psychology*, 1, 3–13.

Piaget, J. (1968). *Six Psychological Studies*. New York: Vintage.

Piaget, J. (1970a). Piaget's theory. In J. Mussen (ed.) *Carmichael's Manual of Child Psychology*. Chicago: University of Chicago Press.

Piaget, J. (1970b). *Structuralism*. London: Harper and Row.

Piaget, J. (1971a). *Genetic Epistemology*. New York: Norton and Co.

Piaget, J. (1971b). *Psychology and Epistemology: Towards a Theory of Knowledge*. New York: Viking Press.

Piaget, J. (1971c). *Biology and Knowledge: An Essay on the Relations between Organic Regulations and Cognitive Processes*. Chicago: University of Chicago.

Piaget, J. (1972). Intellectual evolution from adolescence to adulthood. *Human Development* 15: 1–12.

Piaget, J. (1973). *The Psychology of Intelligence*. Totowa, NJ: Littlefield, Adams.

Piaget, J. (1978). *The Development of Thought: Equilibration of Cognitive Structures*. London: Blackwell.

Piaget, J. and Inhelder, B. (1969). *The Psychology of the Child*. New York: Basic Books.

Piaget, J. and Weil, A. M. (1951). The development of the idea of homeland and of relations with other countries. *International Social Science Bulletin*, 3: 561–73.

Piatelli-Palmarini, M. (1980). *Language and Learning: The Debate between Jean Piaget and Noam Chomsky*. Cambridge, Mass.: Harvard University Press.

Pole, D. (1975). The concept of reason. In R. F. Dearden, P. H. Hirst and R. S. Peters (eds) *Education and the Development of Reason*. London: Routledge and Kegan Paul.

Prince, J. R. (1968). The effect of western education on science conceptualization in New Guinea. *British Journal of Educational Psychology*, 38: 64–74.

Pye, L. (1962). *Politics, Personality and Nation Building*. New Haven: Yale University Press.

Rawls, J. (1971). *A Theory of Justice*. Cambridge, Mass.: Harvard University Press.

Riegel, K. F. (1973). Dialectical operations: The final period of cognitive development. *Human Development*, 16: 346–70.

Riegel, K. F. and Rosenwald, G. C. (1975). *Structure and Transformation: Developmental and Historical Aspects*. New York: Wiley.

Rosch, E. (1978). Principles of categorization. In E. Rosch and B. B. Lloyd (eds), *Cognition and Categorization*. Hillsdale, NJ: Lawrence Erlbaum.

Rosenberg, S. W. (1982). The structural developmental analysis of political thinking: An alternative to the belief systems approach. Paper presented at the Annual Meeting of the American Political Science Association. Denver, Colorado.

Rosenberg, S. W. (1983). The empirical study of ideology: The validity, power and utility of the theories we construct. Paper presented at the Annual Meeting of the International Society of Political Psychology. Oxford, England.

Rosenberg, S. W. (1985a). Reason and ideology: Interpreting people's understanding of American politics. Paper presented at the Annual Meeting of the American Political Science Association. New Orleans.

Rosenberg, S. W. (1985b). Sociology, psychology and the study of political behavior: The case of the research on political socialization. *Journal of Politics*, 47: 715–31.

Rosenberg, S. W. and McCafferty, P. (1987). The image and the vote: Manipulating voters' preferences. *Public Opinion Quarterly*, 51: 31–47.

Rosenberg, S. W. and Wolfsfeld, G. (1977). International relations and the problem of attribution. *Journal of Conflict Resolution*, 21: 75–103.

Rosenberg, S. W., Bohan, L., McCafferty, P. and Harris, K. (1986). The image and the vote: The effect of candidate presentation on voters' preferences. *American Journal of Political Science* 30: 108–27.

Runciman, W. G. (1969). What is structuralism? *British Journal of Sociology*, 20: 253–65.

Ryle, G. (1949). *The Concept of Mind*. New York: Barnes and Noble.

Samuelson, P. (1938). A note on the pure theory of consumer's behavior. *Economica*, 7, 22–37.

de Saussure, F. (1977). *Course in General Linguistics*. London: Fontana.

Searle, J. R. (1971). *The Philosophy of Language*. New York: Oxford University Press.

Sebert, S. Z., Jennings, M. K. and Niemi, R. G. (1974). The political texture of peer groups. In M. K. Jennings and R. G. Niemi, *The Political*

Character of Adolescence: The Influence of Family and Schools. Princeton, NJ: Princeton University Press.

Selman, R. L. (1975). Taking another's perspective: Role-taking in early childhood. *Child Development*, 29: 379–88.

Selman, R. L. (1976). The development of socio-cognitive understanding: A guide to educational and clinical practice. In T. Lickona (ed.) *Moral Development and Behavior*. New York: Holt, Rinehart and Winston.

Shaw, D. L. and McCombs, M. (1977). *The Emergence of American Political Issues*. St Paul, Minn.: West.

Simon, H. (1986). Human nature in politics: The dialogue of psychology with political science. *American Political Science Review*, 79: 293–304.

Singer, J. E. (1968). Consistency as a stimulus processing mechanism. In R. P. Abelson, E. Aronson, W. J. McGuire, M. J. Rosenberg, P. H. Tannebaum (eds) *Theories of Cognitive Consistency: A Sourcebook*. Chicago: Rand McNally.

Sinnott, J. D. (1975). Everyday thinking and Piagetian operativity in adults. *Human Development*, 18: 430–43.

Smith, E. R. A. N. (1980). The levels of conceptualization: False measures of ideological sophistication. *American Political Science Review*, 74: 685–96.

Stimson, J A. (1975). Belief systems: Constraint, complexity and the 1972 election. *American Journal of Political Science*, 19: 393–418.

Sullivan, J. L., Pierson, J. E. and Marcus, G. E. (1978). Ideological constraint in the mass public: a methodological critique and some new findings. *American Journal of Political Science*, 22: 233–49.

Taylor, C. (1971). What is involved in genetic epistemology? In T. Mischel (ed.) *Cognitive Development and Epistemology*. New York: Academic Press.

Taylor, S. E. and Crocker, J. (1981). Schematic bases of social information processing. In E. T. Higgins, C. A. Herman and M. P. Zanna (eds) *The Ontario Symposium on Social Cognition*. Hillsdale, NJ: Lawrence Erlbaum.

Taylor S. E. and Fiske, S. T. (1975). Point of view and perceptions of causality. *Journal of Personality and Social Psychology*, 32: 439–45.

Taylor, S. E. and Fiske, S. T. (1978). Salience, attention and attribution: Top of the head phenomena. In L. Berkowitz (ed.) *Advances in Experimental Social Psychology, Volume II*. New York: Academic Press.

Tedin, K. L. (1980). Assessing peer and parental influence on political attitudes. *American Journal of Political Science*, 24: 136–54.

Tversky, A. and Kahneman, D. (1974). Judgment under uncertainty: Heuristic and biases. *Science*, 185: 1124–31.

Tversky, A. and Kahneman, D. (1982). *Judgment under Uncertainty: Heuristics and Biases*. New York: Cambridge University Press.

Ungar, R. M. (1975). *Knowledge and Politics*. New York: Free Press.

Vaillancourt, P. M. (1973). Stability of children's survey responses. *Public Opinion Quarterly*, 37: 373–87.

Vygotsky, L. S. (1962). *Thought and Language*. Cambridge, Mass.: MIT Press.

Vygotsky, L. S. (1978). *Mind in Society: The Development of Higher Psychological Processes*. Cambridge, Mass.: Harvard University Press.

Ward, D. (1982). Genetic epistemology and the structure of belief systems: An introduction to Piaget for political scientists. Paper presented at the American Political Science Association. Denver, Colorado.

Wattenberg, M. P. (1984). *The Decline of American Political Parties: 1952-1980*. Cambridge, Mass.: Harvard University Press.

Wicker, A. W. (1969). Attitudes vs. actions: The relationship of verbal and overt behavioral responses to attitude objects. *Journal of Social Issues* 41: 41-78.

Wittgenstein, L. (1953). *Philosophical Investigations*. Oxford: Blackwell.

Wolfenstein, E. V. (1967). *The Revolutionary Personality: Lenin, Trotsky, Gandhi*. Princeton, NJ: Princeton University Press.

Wray, J. H. (1979). Comment on interpretations of early research into belief systems. *Journal of Politics*, 41: 1173-81.

Youniss, J. (1978). Dialectical theory and Piaget on social knowledge. *Human Development*, 21: 234-47.

Index